CONSCIENCE AND HISTORY

Ken McNaught sketching on Garden Island off Kingston, Ontario

KENNETH McNAUGHT

Conscience and History: A Memoir

UNIVERSITY OF TORONTO PRESS
Toronto Buffalo London

© University of Toronto Press Incorporated 1999
Toronto Buffalo London

Printed in Canada

ISBN 0-8020-4425-5 (cloth)

Printed on acid-free paper

Canadian Cataloguing in Publication Data

McNaught, Kenneth, 1918–1997
   Conscience and history : a memoir

   Includes bibliographical references and index.
   ISBN 0-8020-4425-5

   1. McNaught, Kenneth, 1918–1997.   2. Historians – Canada –
   Biography.   3. College teachers – Canada – Biography.   I. Title.

   FC151.M32A3 1999   971'.007'202   C98-932593-8
   F1024.6.M32A3 1999

The photographs that appear in this book are from the collection of
Beverley McNaught.

University of Toronto Press acknowledges the financial assistance to
its publishing program of the Canada Council for the Arts and the
Ontario Arts Council.

Contents

Foreword

This memoir was incomplete when Kenneth McNaught died in 1997. He had been working on the story of his life for some time, but had only thirteen chapters completed and a fourteenth under way. The manuscript covered the years from his birth, in 1918, to the early 1970s. It was handwritten in pencil, difficult to transcribe, and full of abbreviations and short forms. Although elegantly written, it was clearly a first draft. Had he lived to complete his autobiography, Ken certainly would have made many alterations to the text.

Even so, the prose flows splendidly and acerbically, as McNaught tells the story of his life and times. There is much here on his youth, his family, the shaping of his fundamental beliefs, his teaching in Winnipeg and Toronto, and his work as a historian. His account of the celebrated 'Crowe affair' at United College in Winnipeg, a seminal event in shaping concepts of academic freedom in Canada, is of particular historical importance. It was also a traumatic, career-altering event in the lives of the McNaughts and many of their friends.

Ken's life spanned decades of remarkable transition in Canadian academic and political life. His chapters bear out a view many of us held that Ken was 'one of the old school.' He grew up and gloried in older patterns of Canadian university life – when everyone knew everyone else, when the members of the University of Toronto history department gathered at 4 o'clock in Flavelle House for tea, and when summers were idled away at Garden Island and teaching at Queen's University summer school. In politics he was an old social democrat – fundamentally a CCFer who was never wholly comfortable with the New Democratic Party, especially after it entered its strident years. In the later chapters of his memoir, Ken keeps the faith with remarkable flexibility into the age of the New Left of the 1960s, but he was clearly uncomfortable with the notion of student power, Black Panthers, and the collapse of the civility that had always leavened his politics of principle. He was also, it seems, becoming less comfortable with the growing impersonality of the University of Toronto and his department. He often regretted the role he had played as a faculty activist, minor but significant, in helping to give the Toronto megaversity its current governing structure.

From October 1970 to the end of his life, Ken took a deep interest in Quebec and constitutional matters. He supported the imposition of the War Measures Act, worried about Quebec's assault on the Constitution, and became a staunch supporter of Pierre Trudeau's defence of the 1982 Constitution against the architects of the Meech Lake and Charlottetown accords. As the co-editor of 'English Canada' Speaks Out (1991), he wanted the book to take a hard line, and his own essay raised the possibility of violence in the event of separation.

Ken's formal retirement from the University of Toronto in 1984, celebrated with a memorable dinner in his honour at Toronto's Arts and Letters Club, resulted in only a change in venue in his ongoing career as historian, social critic, gadfly, gracious host, and raconteur. Until the very end of his life, Ken had style.

His appointment as an Officer in the Order of Canada was announced by Rideau Hall in January 1997, when he was already very ill. On 16 April that year, he travelled to Ottawa to be invested. Sadly, his wife Beverley was in the hospital herself, so Allison, their daughter, accompanied Ken.

Very sallow, walking only with difficulty and with the assistance of a cane, Ken was remarkably cheerful in Ottawa and obviously exhilarated at receiving the honour. He sat in the Rideau Hall salon between k.d. lang and historian Desmond Morton, each receiving the OC, and seemed to enjoy talking with the singer at least as much as with his fellow social democrat. What pleased him even more was the citation, read out before the sparkling audience:

He has been called 'the conscience of the nation' for his courage and integrity in defending academic freedom, and for his contributions in moving the country's political discourse beyond the classroom into the public domain ... he has had a formative influence on several generations, as his students themselves have become teachers of the theory and practice of social democracy.

That was precisely correct. As readers of this memoir will see, Ken changed positions over time on some issues, but not on the most important ones. J.S. Woodsworth was 'a prophet in politics,' in McNaught's timeless phrase. Ken McNaught became the conscience of the nation not in any vainglorious way, but simply by standing up and speaking out for what he believed, clearly and vigorously. Too few Canadians do that. McNaught did, and he deserves to be honoured for his courage and integrity.

A few weeks after the ceremony in Ottawa, on 2 June 1997, Ken died in Toronto. It was election day and, characteristically, Ken had made sure to cast his vote at the advance poll.

We have left Ken McNaught's memoir very much as he wrote it, clarifying only a few details and correcting obvious slips. The typing of the handwritten manuscript, a herculean feat, was ably done by Graham Rawlinson and Catherine Salo. The costs were assumed by the Donner Foundation, which, with the H.N.R. Jackman Foundation, provided the publication subsidy that allowed the University of Toronto Press to publish this work. Good social democrat that he was, we are certain Ken would have been gratified by the donors who assisted publication. Further support was provided by the University of Toronto history department.

Ramsay Cook graciously allowed us to use the eulogy he delivered at Ken's funeral as a postscript.

Beverley McNaught read the manuscript and corrected errors we missed. She also provided the photographs that grace these pages. This book belongs to both her and Ken.

J.L. GRANATSTEIN AND MICHAEL BLISS

CONSCIENCE AND HISTORY

1

Fashion now dictates a somewhat supercilious assessment of Old Toronto, a provincial town suffused with Orange bigotry, racial intolerance, prudish moralism, and a colonial frame of mind; a place where you could fire a cannon up Yonge Street on Sunday and injure no one. All true, of course. Yet, like the notion that progress is inevitable, this myopic recollection needs much closer focusing, a more imaginative historical perspective.

For someone born in 1918, the 1920s and 1930s were full of colour and excitement. Toronto was the Queen City, second only to Montreal – that scandalous, corrupt home of a million or so French Canadians who had escaped the fate of Maria Chapdelaine. It was a city full of confidence. At least this was so for those who were not to sink into the despair of joblessness after 1929. Identity, the obsession of later years, was a problem only to interlocking circles of intellectuals who subscribed to the new *Canadian Forum* and fell under the spell of Group of Seven painters. Primary school textbooks, virtually free, carried the inscription 'One Flag, One Fleet, One Throne' below a bravely fluttering Union Jack. Sir Henry Newbolt and Rudyard Kipling spelled out unquestionable values in their pages. Valour, honour, and violent patriotism also spoke clearly in the 3-cent British weeklies *Chums, Boys Own Papers*, and *Triumph*. What Carl Berger was to call the 'sense of power' was alive and well, even as pride of membership in the empire wavered. For me, the flood of a more distinctly Canadian nationalism would completely obliterate the romantic imperial afterglow. By 1939 the *Boys Own Papers* view of things was anathema. That of Beverly Nichol's *Cry Havoc*, William Arthur Deacon's *My Vision of Canada*, and Frank Underhill's acerbic assaults on British imperialism provided a new framework. Unsuspected at the time, the new was no less absolute, no less ahistorical than 'what had been shunted aside.' Some anomalies, which I perceived but dimly at the time, seem more clear in my present rear-view mirror.

I suppose the major anomaly is that, from within a secure middle-class environment, I became a pronounced dissident. I now know that this is not as surprising as I once imagined it to be. What Canadians have come to call Red Toryism describes the unspoken assumptions of my parents – if you add a strong dash of British Fabianism. The Tory ingredient was more than evident.

My paternal grandfather, WK, made a good deal of money in the jewellery business and investments. He became president of the National Club, the Canadian National Exhibition, and the Canadian Manufacturers' Association. In a 1906 provincial by-election, as a Sir James Whitney Tory, he defeated the labour candidate, Jimmie Simpson. He remained on good terms with Simpson (who, in 1935, became Toronto's first socialist mayor), and, in the legislature, he promoted compulsory sterilization of milk and cheap public transportation through rural extension of electric 'radial' rail lines. The radials used power produced by the public hydroelectric system, in the evolution of which WK had been closely associated with Sir Adam Beck. And this 'gas-and-water socialist' could tilt at windmills. He was particularly proud of his failed private member's Anti-Treating Bill. An abstaining Baptist, WK proposed to advance the cause of temperance by prohibiting patrons from buying drinks for anyone but themselves.

WK's conservative affluence lingered long after he died. For me this meant a very sheltered life. With regular subsidies from my grandmother, questions of affordability seldom arose. Comfortable houses in north Toronto, a maid, a large cottage on Lake Simcoe, two cars, private schools, and junior membership in the Royal Canadian Yacht Club and the Cedarhurst Golf Club all seemed entirely natural – until I was about fifteen and the sombre facts of the Depression suddenly took on meaning.

Wishful thinking I must try to avoid, but I am persuaded that knowing the opportunities and comforts of comparative affluence can sharpen one's perception of social inequity. A catalyst is needed, of course, and such an agent was active in my house. It was planted by my other grandfather, Joseph Sanderson, and it provided a distinctly contrapuntal theme. Grandpa Sanderson was a trusting man who lost more money than he made. He retired early after being cheated by his partner in a small brush factory. He spent a good deal of time reading the Scottish socialist weekly, *The Clarion*, and the writings of such critical spirits as William Morris and Charles Kingsley. Two of his political heroes were Keir Hardie, founder of the British Independent Labour Party, and Toronto's socialist leader, Jimmie Simpson – an allegiance that could not have endeared him to my other grandfather. On long Sunday strolls in Sherwood Park, he and my father debated the political-social issues that obviously divided the family. Grandpa Sanderson won – but not only because he was well read and persuasive.

My father was given the name of the street on which he was born, Carlton. I've always thought this weary failure of imagination resulted from his being the youngest of five children. In any event, he was always treated as the baby – a status underlined by a childhood disease that left his hearing impaired. He early drifted away from the nexus of moneyed glamour shared by his older siblings. Before Carl entered Jarvis Collegiate, one of his brothers, Charles, had co-founded Reed, Shaw & McNaught, a prosperous insurance firm, and was well on his way to the top rungs of Canada's financial ladder. His sister, Edna, was married to Hilton Tudhope who was already on track to the presidency of A.E. Ames, the country's leading bond house. Another brother, Harvard, had found wealth as a doctor in San Francisco, where he became head of the department of ophthamology at Leland Stanford University.

My father found refuge in reading, close observation of wildlife, woodworking, writing, book-binding, and sailing. During long summers at 'Nitschevo,' WK's handsome house on Centre Island, he mastered his 14-foot gaff-rig dinghy well enough that when he visited Charles's rambling 'cottage' on Go Home Bay he could compete in the Minnecog regattas – while the rest of the family watched from a commodious yacht. In, but not of, this competitive community of material success, the youngest son was pointed in a quite different direction.

In 1911 Carl graduated in political science at the University of Toronto. His closest friends in that year would also influence me – as mentors and role models. Frank Underhill was, of course, the star. His brilliant, eclectic mind led him into social analysis and risky political activism, while his restless enthusiasms would keep him a teacher and critic rather than a scholar. Carleton Stanley and Charles Cochrane were scholar-teachers par excellence. They were our symbols of a highly idealized vision of the academic life. Cochrane was to write one of the half-dozen finest works of Canadian scholarship: *Christianity and Classical Culture*. Stanley became a distinguished professor of

English. He made the fatal mistake, however, of moving into administration. As president of Dalhousie University at the end of World War II, he ran afoul of the business-oriented Board of Governors. When he resisted the board's push to expand the university's more 'practical' offerings for the inrush of veterans, his defence of the humanities brought dismissal.* An old friend of Stanley, Principal W.C. Graham of United College in Winnipeg, offered him a position in the college's English department. Thus, when I arrived in Winnipeg in 1947, our first dinner invitation was to the Stanleys' gracious home on Grosvenor Avenue. For several years, until he retired, Carleton Stanley was a dignified centre of scholarly sophistication at United. I did not, at the time, perceive the warning signals of falling out with the administration.

These three men followed paths that my father admired and envied. But for his impaired hearing, he would probably have ventured a similar course. As it was, he settled for writing. At university, he had edited the student newspaper, *The Varsity* (1910–11). Upon graduation, he became a newspaper reporter in Calgary and indulged his romantic naturalism as a mountain-climbing guide in the Canadian Alpine Club. Returning to Toronto just before the outbreak of war, he got a reporting job with the *Toronto News* and met my mother. Eleanor Sanderson was one of the city's first female reporters. At the *Toronto Star* she was assigned 'women's interest' stories and the charitable beat – the Fresh Air Fund and the Santa Claus Fund. She also began writing poems and short stories – an interest that did not abate and was encouraged by Greg Clark at the *Star*. From the 1920s on her writing was published in the *Canadian Forum* and elsewhere. From the 1930s until her death she wrote regular book reviews for William A. Deacon, literary editor of the *Globe and Mail*. Deacon became a close and good friend of my parents.

The engagement of Eleanor and Carlton did not sit well with my father's family. Not only had the youngest declined offers to enter the family's business milieu but he had taken up with an independent, even feminist, young woman of somewhat lower social status: a person, clearly, who would encourage Carl in his drift towards an impractical lifestyle. That drift was only briefly halted when Carl joined the army at the end of 1914.

WK was pleased. He himself had begun an enduring interest in mili-

*Editors' Note: The account of Stanley's dismissal here should be compared with that in volume two of Peter Waite, *The Lives of Dalhousie University* (Montreal: McGill-Queen's University Press 1998), chapter 5.

tary affairs as a colour-sergeant in the Queen's Own Rifles in 1866 – just after the Fenian unpleasantness of that year. In 1914 he was attached to army headquarters in Ottawa as an honorary colonel and busied himself superintending the construction of armoured cars and raising a good deal of money for the forces. At the same time, his son Charles became a member of the War Trade Board while his son-in-law, Hilton, was helping A.E. Ames float war bonds. Although Carlton had refused assisted passage into the world of finance, he did not reject his father's hefty influence in obtaining a commission towards the end of 1914. Thus, shortly before his marriage in February 1915, he was appointed captain and adjutant of the 84th Battalion, Canadian Expeditionary Force. This military involvement received considerably more family approval than did the nuptials. At the quiet wedding ceremony neither his mother nor his siblings were present, and neither bride nor groom had attendants. The aroma of smelling salts was evident when the newlyweds paid a brief visit to the groom's mother, at 614 Huron Street, where the formidable matriarch was trying to remain calm.

Following a short honeymoon in Montreal, the twenty-seven-year-old captain returned to his battalion's training quarters at Brantford. Very shortly, the 84th set off for England and a further period of training at Aldershot: all too brief a spell for its adjutant. Carl's hearing deficiency again tripped him up. On the parade ground and during manoeuvres his commands were clear enough, but during the first big inspection he failed to hear commands from the regimental colonel. I never heard him recall the event in any detail, but the resulting confusion is not hard to imagine. No doubt the medical officer got a good going over. In any event, Carl was immediately 'invalided' back to Canada.

Some of this string of embarrassment was mollified by further applications of influence and money. After moving into a new house at 136 Sheldrake Boulevard, Carl entered the advertising firm of J.J. Gibbons as a copy-writer and account executive. He brought with him the advertising accounts of several businesses of which his father and his brother Charles were either directors or presidents. He would remain in advertising, moving in the mid-1930s to A. McKim Ltd. But the love of writing, as of reading, art, and music, continued to separate both my parents from Carl's relations.

WK died in February 1919, about three months after I was born. Thereafter only my father 'kept in touch.' Each Christmas he drove my sister, Lesley, and me to make perfunctory calls upon Uncle Charlie and Aunt Edna. Charles lived in a mansion at 29 Forest Hill Road to which we were admitted by a Chinese houseman. After half an hour's chit-chat we moved on to 'Grey Gables,' Aunt Edna's vast stuccoed house set on the brow of a cliff overlooking Hogg's Hollow on the northern fringe of the city. Its nine acres of beautifully tended gardens were guarded by two slavering Great Danes. I never got out of the car until I saw the front door opened by yet another Chinese houseman, and I never lost my fear of big dogs. We (again without mother) paid more regular Sunday afternoon visits to my widowed grandmother. Grandma McNaught did not live in reduced circumstances. She occupied a large apartment in the Alexandra Palace on University Avenue. Here she was well tended by a paid companion. A chauffeur kept a splendid Willis-Knight sedan at her beck and call. Occasionally this gleaming beauty would draw up in front of our Sheldrake house and my sister and I would be whisked away for a late spring weekend at Nitschevo. We reached Centre Island on one or another of the Royal Canadian Yacht Club vessels, usually the *Hiawatha*. We two youngsters then led the way over bridges across quiet lagoons – followed by Alice, the companion, and Phillips, the chauffeur, who pushed Grandma along in an elegant wicker wheelchair. In the house at 204 Lakeshore, after a long day on the beach with new sandpails, we heard the spooky moan of foghorns calling out from the eastern and western island 'gaps.' Privilege, but not at all unpleasant.

If the McNaught-Tudhope grouping regarded my parents as misguided, the feeling was more than reciprocated – at least by my mother. She felt patronized – as in a sense she was. But she also felt completely confident – in her own creative abilities (she was an accomplished pianist as well as writer), and in her support of Carl's decision to reject his family's values and to hew as closely as possible to an idealized conception of the intellectual and artistic life – as compensation for not actually entering academe. The mistrust of those who pursued money was, of course, transmitted in full measure to her two children – by a kind of osmosis but also by open deprecation. We learned early to despise the contemporary symbols of mammon – the Flavelles, the Pellatts, the Eatons, and, with slight shading, some of our own relatives.

The irony is apparent, but it was a long time before I fully appreciated it. In the meantime, I was to benefit greatly from mammon's trickle-down.

2

Next door to us on Sheldrake Boulevard in the 1920s, Dora Mavor Moore, by then a single parent, was bringing up her three sons. A bit further along the street lived Don Ritchie, who later published an evocative history of North Toronto. It was a quiet, secure community serviced by horse-drawn carts delivering everything from coal, ice, and bread to more interesting parcels from Eaton's and Simpson's. In winter, wheels gave way to sleigh-runners. Then we hauled toboggans and bob-sleds the block and a half to what seemed like mountain slopes in Sherwood Park.

In 1922 my parents built a cottage at Cedarhurst, near Beaverton, on Lake Simcoe. Long summers and indulgent parents made Cedarhurst something close to heaven. The clutch of cottagers' children had the run of Angus Grant's neighbouring farm, where we 'helped' with milking and other chores; most of the time we spent swimming, boating, or golfing. In Beaverton, 2 miles away by dusty gravel road, we came to know the storekeepers and even a distant relative who had grown up in Cannington. My mother, especially, cherished this bucolic retreat. She kept aloof from most of her neighbours, especially the stockbroker set. We made frequent picnic excursions to the villages and countryside of the Trent Canal system – never driving at more than 30 miles per hour. Most evenings, mother returned early to her upstairs room, where she read or wrote to the background sounds of wind and waves. All this was made possible because a maid looked after the cooking and housework while a gardener tended the lawns and flower beds.

Mother somehow felt close to the permanent residents of Beaverton. She certainly imparted to us a sense of 'differentness' from the other city folk who merely visited for the summer. Shortly before she died she completed a Beaverton-based mystery novel. Recently my sister (now Lesley Sirluck) arranged for its publication and drew some charming pen-and-ink illustrations for the volume, which carries the title *Blame It on Wilmot*. Publication had been postponed for some forty years because many of the people portrayed were too easily recognizable. The book is subtly suffused with the city-country tensions of 1950s Ontario.

Did 'different' mean 'superior'? Looking back I must concede that my parents left us in little doubt that our different values were better values. This unspoken perception did not translate into class consciousness for the obvious reason that the object of our disdain was the economic class above us. Possibly there was a mild sort of reverse snobbery here, but I find that too opaque to discern clearly. Real class distinction I did encounter early; but it took a few years before I understood the milieu into which I was plunged at the age of eleven – or the irony implicit in that plunge.

In 1929 we moved to a larger house at 103 Blythwood Road. At the same time, I entered the preparatory school of Upper Canada College. A good deal has been written by UCC 'old boys' about that bastion of the establishment – some of it much too adulatory and some merely scandalous. I don't think sufficient note has been taken, however, of its real virtues – at least as they became evident to me in the 1930s. Let me begin this brief 'revision' by conceding that it took me about four years to recognize the virtues – and a further thirty or so to digest them.

The 'Prep' and the first two upper-school years I prefer, as far as possible, to forget. They featured quite a few canings for such misdemeanours as muffing the Latin conjugation of *porto, portas*, and refusing, as a 'new boy,' to fag for a senior in the upper school. Averse to team sports, I managed to avoid most of them. Pressure to engage in them diminished after a poignant event on the football field. One dark, wet November afternoon I inadvertently caught the greasy ball and made for the goal. Opponents peeled away as I ran – across my own team's touchline.

In the upper school I was thoroughly intimidated by the hierarchical power structure and the 'in groups' who adapted readily to the oft-reiterated precept that you must learn to obey before you can lead. I didn't particularly want to do either. Sons of the huge homes in Forest Hill and Rosedale had an easy, assured camaraderie – which my sheltered otherness made me unable and unwilling to penetrate. As a new boy I looked with awe upon such as Robertson Davies, confidently positioned among the masters on the dais at morning prayers, resplendent in the gleaming white blazer of a 'steward.' No need for him to adapt; he was at home.

Soon some doors opened. The variety of the school, and especially of its decidedly individualistic masters, released me from morbid concern about the superficially hostile atmosphere. Our teachers had none of the rigidities implanted by teacher training. Well educated and urbane, they regarded the province's curricular demands with charming unconcern and vigorous amusement. Our French classes were conducted with erratic violence by Owen Clancy, who had been secretary to H.G. Wells. My first serious introduction to Canadian history was directed by a son of one of the tsar's last ministers, Nicholas Ignatieff. I'm sure that 'Nicky' kept about one chapter ahead of his class, but he imparted a wonderful sense of involvement in the world around us. He organized a UCC branch of the League of Nations Society. This small group met on Sunday evening in the house of the headmaster, W.L. 'Choppy' Grant, who was president of the League of Nations Society. My first experience of street demonstrating was when Ignatieff led his group downtown, each suffocating in a stinky Great War gas mask, to hand out League pamphlets alerting passing business people to the risk of another war. Ignatieff showed a nice sense of irony when he gave me, as a prize for an essay on the two-year-old Cooperative Commonwealth Federation, a copy of T.W.L. MacDermot's *Recovery by Control*. 'Terry' MacDermot had just succeeded Grant as headmaster (1935). Although an early member of the League for Social Reconstruction, MacDermot advocated a Rooseveltian New Deal for Canada as opposed to the CCF socialist program – which I had applauded in my essay.

Geoffrey Andrew, in English, had us read B.K. Sandwell's elegant editorials each week in *Saturday Night*. As a result of Andrew's contagious enthusiasm, I began to write for the college literary magazine. In his history class, James Biggar spent more time on the architecture of medieval cathedrals than on datelines. Johnny Davidson taught a splendidly eclectic course on religion and anthropology. Davidson and his wife, Sasha, guided a group of us on a six-week bus tour of the British Isles in 1935 – featured by minimum supervision. In Minehead, Devon, I was evicted from a pub because of some critical comments on Britain's attitude towards Mussolini's Abyssinian adventure. In a wonderfully equipped art room H.G. Kettle revealed the techniques of etching, dry point, and watercolour – which led me to illustrate my own magazine stories and to provide a cover illustration of the college tower. That tower, in its splendid grounds obstructing Avenue Road's impatient flow of traffic, became for me a vaguely apprehended ambiguous symbol: of visual beauty, of continuity, and of the problem of privilege.

By 1934 I could see that there was much more on offer than discipline, training for leadership, and the short post-matriculation trip to Bay Street and the family firm. There were many youngsters eager to comprehend and enter a non-business world. Some of these boys became my friends. In Ettore Mazzolini's music class Godfrey Ridout soaked up everything the future director of the University of Toronto's Conservatory of Music had to impart – especially on the mornings when 'Mazz' took us to Massey Hall to hear the Toronto Symphony rehearse. In the camera club rooms John Steele and Hugh Robertson mastered the techniques that would bring them many awards: Steele in portraiture, Robertson in architectural photography. Tom Daly was developing the cultural-observer talents that would make him a pioneer documentary producer at the National Film Board. William Goulding, a companion in the art room, became a distinguished architect.

The reading we were encouraged to do led three of us to a precocious, yet serious, rejection of a central symbol of the college ethos: the cadet battalion. For my first two years in the upper school I had rather enjoyed wearing the smart uniform, the rifle drill, and marching behind the bugle band – on a route that usually took us past the neighbouring girls' school, Bishop Strachan. Then came Beverly Nichol's book *Cry Havoc*. Its passionate argument for pacifism completely captured me – as it did Michael Shalom Gelber and George Grant. Our action in requesting exemption from the battalion, as conscientious objectors, must have been most difficult for George, as the headmaster's son. I have learned recently that Choppy Grant, who was badly wounded in the Great War, had come to question Canada's participation in that war. At the same time, however, he believed cadet training to be prudent in the light of European events and also as training in 'manliness.' After much thought, he exempted the three of us. The passage of time has strengthened my admiration of his decision. He demonstrated that a conservative confidence in the basic precepts of Canadian society need not be illiberal. Indeed, as I considered this question much later, I concluded that such confidence is a requisite for genuine tolerance of dissent.

Choppy Grant's action was the more notable because it was taken in the full knowledge that it was anathema to a majority of the college Board of Governors and of the well-organized Old Boys' Association. His successor, Terry MacDermot, was much less attuned to the establishment than was Grant. MacDermot commented privately that 'the Battalion ... is clearly one of the social and business aids which gives this school its justification in the eyes of the privileged class which uses it'; and of the Old Boys he said, 'What a cheap vulgar uncouth lot they are ... these commercially bastardized clothes' horses are tiresome.' Yet it was Choppy's widow, Maud Parkin Grant, who gave strongest support to MacDermot's appointment.

To encourage awareness of public affairs, MacDermot instigated a mock election – to coincide with the federal election of October 1935. George Grant, whose uncle, Vincent Massey, was president of the Liberal Party, led the college Liberals. I, as leader of the CCF group, had already made J.S. Woodsworth my political hero. In the course of the campaign, my group distributed a pamphlet documenting the concentration of wealth and power in Canada: *The Fifty Men Who Owned Canada*. Unfortunately a sharp-eyed Tory noticed that number forty-nine was C.B. McNaught, my uncle Charlie. The ribald comments were embarrassing, but the outcome was preordained: Conservatives – 267; Liberals – 53; Reconstruction – 32; CCF – 15. This in the year that saw the Liberals re-established as Canada's government party. I think that this knee-jerk support of R.B. Bennett's vision of Canada was what decided me to spend my final high school year at North Toronto Collegiate – possibly influenced, too, by Mike Gelber's earlier decision to make the same move. Despite the impressive display of Tory tolerance at UCC, and its panoply of fine teaching and cultural opportunities, the college stood too obviously for social inequity.

In the summers at Cedarhurst we would watch long freight trains lumbering their way to the West, each car roof covered with unemployed men. In their hopeless search for jobs, they never failed to wave to us pampered watchers. In the winters I went to the formal dances and house parties (usually white-tie) of friends from UCC and Bishop Strachan School: corsages for your date obligatory as you called for her in your father's car. I didn't know at the time that no Jews were permitted at the Saturday dances, the springtime parties at the RCYC or the Granite Club, or at Cedarhurst, where cottage purchases were informally 'restricted.' The terrible class contrasts and brutal social indifference, however, came into even sharper focus.

In sermons to a middle-class congregation in Winnipeg's Grace

Church, around 1904, J.S. Woodsworth spoke of the 'sin of indifference.' He probably didn't use those words during his several stays at our agnostic Blythwood home, but he did, with quiet conviction, convey their meaning. His visits (always in the course of endless speaking tours) gave me a sense of immediacy, of exciting personal involvement. I had struggled through the League for Social Reconstruction's flagship publication, *Social Planning for Canada* (1935), and other publications on the left. JS brought to life what Frank Underhill once called the 'ghostly ballet of economic categories.' Moreover, this hero-in-our-midst was wide open to presumptuous teenagers. Sitting before a living-room fire after the evening's speech in the Carpenters' Hall or wherever, he never excluded me from the conversation. On one such occasion, very memorable to me, he predicted: 'One day you will write the history of the CCF.' While that did not come about, and my close friend, Walter Young, would perform the task brilliantly in *The Anatomy of a Party: The National CCF*, I was able to justify part of the prediction by writing a biography of JS himself.

My soul-searching about Upper Canada was stimulated by the eclectic and increasingly 'activist' life of that Blythwood home. Mother's writing and vaguely feminist orientation drew her into the Heliconian Club, a lively centre on Hazelton Street for women of literary, musical, or artistic bent. She also subscribed to the Women's International League for Peace and Freedom – a major interest of JS's wife, Lucy, and member of parliament Agnes Macphail. By and large, however, she remained apart from political organizations, saying that she was an anti-social socialist. In 1932, about the same time that one of her *Canadian Forum* short stories was included in the American annual *O'Brien's Best Short Stories*, she arranged the publication of Nina Moore Jamieson's rural essays, *The Cattle in the Stall*.

My father's interest in drawing and painting led to some wonderful times in and around our home. Through his connection with the *Canadian Forum*, he had come to know Barker Fairley; at the Toronto Writers' Club, his closest friend was Bertram Brooker. Fairley found relaxation from his scholarly studies on Goethe in promoting the work of the Group of Seven in the *Forum*, of which he had been co-founder in 1921, and in becoming a painter himself. Brooker is, in my opinion, second only to Fred Varley as a draughtsman and portrait painter, but his chief fame in the 1920s was as the first Canadian to exhibit abstracts – which I have never been able to appreciate. Brooker was also a writer. In addition to regular review articles on literature and art, he initiated and edited two volumes of *The Yearbook of the Arts in Canada*, while one of his three novels, *Think of the Earth*, won the Governor General's Award in 1937. His little-known pen-and-ink drawings for the *Book of Elijah*, despite their cubist flavour, are a peak in Canadian illustrative art.

Like Woodsworth, these men – my father, Fairley, and Brooker – were warmly supportive of young people. When they got together for sketching sessions, we offspring were usually included – my sister and I, Vic Brooker, and Tom Fairley. Irregularly on Saturday evenings, a still-life was set up in the Blythwood living room and each of us would attack it. Approval or criticism of the beginners was received by us with a pretty good grace. On Sundays (for none of us went to church), we often assembled at the Fairleys' house at the eastern end of Glengowan Road. From there we would stroll about the thick woods that reached all the way to Bayview Avenue. At some appealing spot we set up our equipment and went to work. Brooker, a shortish, dapper man with rimless glasses, nearly always chose one tree – a beech or maple with smooth bark. In a manner reminiscent of Lionel LeMoine FitzGerald, whom he had known in Winnipeg, he produced many exquisite pencil drawings. Looking over my shoulder one day, he pointed out that where a tree limb joins the trunk, the upper curve is not one concave line but a series of convex ones. To this day I know when I've made *that* mistake! On chilly autumn days, or in winter, we returned to the Fairley house. There Fairley's wife, Margaret, slender yet formidable in horn-rim glasses, would have taken time out from her literary labours on behalf of the Communist Party to prepare sandwiches. 'Quizzical' is the word that comes to mind when I think of Barker's deeply grooved face smiling benignly the while.

As my friend Don Ritchie has made clear, North Toronto in the 1920s and 1930s had a pretty good mix of people and mores. It was still close to the country. Across the road from us another friend, Bill Stewart, lived in a fine old house that retained the character of its farm origin. At the rear were an orchard and a small stable. In the early 1930s we would hitch one of the Stewarts' ponies to a wicker 'governess cart,' pack a lunch and bathing suits, and drive out Blythwood (mostly, then, a narrow gravel road) and down into Kilgour Park. Past the site of the present pre-emptive array of Sunnybrook Hospital, we reached a deepish bend in the Don River. There, not far from where A.J. Casson had recently painted one of his brilliant watercolours, we swam and ate. A bit later, Vic Brooker organized overnight bicycle trips; we would venture as far as the Rouge River to set up our pup-tents. An accomplished pianist, Vic also put together a small dance orchestra. I played violin with the group until even I couldn't stand the sounds from my carefully muted fiddle. Although I was badly defeated by the violin, the struggle went on long enough to implant a reasonably discriminating appreciation of the instrument's masters.

Often we and the Brookers went together to Toronto Symphony concerts at Massey Hall and to the Grange art gallery. Bertram was sarcastic about composers who 'paused on the doorstep' of their concluding bars. At the gallery I spent most time scrutinizing the strong, single-wash purples of Peter Haworth – better, I thought, than Frank Carmichael's more complex, sometimes muddled landscapes, or Lawren Harris's theosophic absurdities. My fascination with water colours led me to think of more formal training. I shied away from the prospect partly from a nervous suspicion that I might not make the grade, but also because my father and the family friends demonstrated that one can make a pretty good stab at art without becoming, exclusively, an artist. Without intellectualizing the problem, I came to feel connections among various aspects of creative activity with interest. Again, with no clear definition of such things as truth, beauty, and justice, I felt a growing unease about the inequities that gave great advantages to me while denying them to so many others. Those 'others,' of course, were all around us: at the back door asking for work, clothes, or food, and even near our ravine campsites in tin and tar-paper shelters – the Bennett-villes of Toronto's ravines. We called them tramps and were wary of them.

Who knows the precise reasons for becoming 'socially aware'? I've suggested some that moved me simply from looking at the Depression's human devastation. Many of my friends seemed able to look away, to accept their parents' view that most of the unemployed could find work if they really wanted it: that, in any event, prosperity was 'just around the corner.' If my friends reflected their parents' perceptions, however, so did I. Those perceptions sharpened rapidly in the early 1930s.

Blythwood Road became an unlikely centre of much more than still-life painting. It became one of the main Toronto gathering places for the people who were devoting a great deal of their time to running the *Canadian Forum*, the League for Social Reconstruction, and the CCF. My father had been drawn into the LSR by Frank Underhill in 1932 – attracted both by its social purpose and its flavour of academe. His admiration of Underhill deepened as he saw his friend of university days take the lead, publicly and dangerously, in opposing the vicious police suppression of public meetings and demonstrations that intensified after 1929. I think it is important to remember that the growth of Canadian democratic socialism in the 1930s is to be explained at least as much by concern for individual liberties as by the pursuit of social justice. Obviously the two issues interlock. Yet what initially spurred the LSR-CCF founders into battle was the totalitarian actions of police and governments, supported by nearly every newspaper and university president in defence of a system that denied 'individual development' to most people. A close reading of the LSR's *Social Planning for Canada* leaves no doubt that the goal to be achieved by central planning, public ownership, and encoragement of cooperatives was the freeing of the individual – not only from the deprivation suffered by the great majority of Canadians but also from the ubiquitous threats to freedom of speech and assembly. Michiel Horn's judicious book *The League for Social Reconstruction* makes this quite clear.

Just entering my later teens in 1935, I recall more about the ambiance than the content of the convivial Blythwood meetings. I know a lot more now about the people who frequented them and about their achievement. Most, but not all, were professors. Whether the subject was the always precarious finances of the *Forum* and who should write editorials for the next issue; the pamphlets, radio broadcasts, and lectures of the LSR; or the relationships of the LSR to the CCF, the meetings always moved towards lively general discussion. The meetings in town were supplemented by others at Cedarhurst. Vignettes come slowly to mind: a towering Frank Scott, up for a weekend from Montreal, piercing with his one good eye a diminutive Underhill while delivering a barbed analysis of Duplessis and the problems facing the CCF in Quebec; the sparky redhead Eleanor Godfrey, for a while editor of the *Forum*, easily drawing out the owl-like Northrop Frye – with whom she had recently studied English; the labour unionists Morden Lazarus and his sharp-witted wife, Margaret Sedgewick, contributing pointed comments on the need for collective bargaining legislation; Graham Spry talking about articles on the CBC. Usually at the centre was the classicist George Grube, heavy set, glowering through thick lenses and exercising his chairman's role – for which he became famous in the CCF. These, and other even younger people like David Lewis, Andrew Brewin, Saul Rae, Eugene Forsey, Escott Reid, Douglas LePan, Joseph McCulley, Geoffrey Andrew (from UCC), and Harry Cassidy formed circles of excitement, where involvement with their country's crisis was overwhelmingly infectious.

As I see all this in my mind's eye, I think of general comparisons in the present. All these people put in their long hours of organizing, writing, and speaking without pay – except minuscule wages for a few of the youngest, such as David Lewis, whose personal sacrifices as first national secretary of the CCF were enormous. No one paid the successive editors or contributors at the *Forum*. There were no travel grants or research moneys for those who wrote *Social Planning*. Well-heeled 'think-tanks' did not – perhaps blessedly – exist. When Frank Scott went to Regina bearing the LSR's draft of the CCF's 1933 manifesto, he drove there at his own expense in an elderly Franklin. In the wide circle of commitment, travel accommodation was not in up-scale hotels; the homes of friends were always open.

Newspapers across the land, with the exception of Joe Atkinson's *Toronto Star*, labelled these men and women 'atheistic communists' and called relentlessly for their dismissal. Yet strong currents of religious conviction ran through the interlocking groups. The social gospel gave flesh and spirit to a nationalist belief in progress. Frank Scott, King Gordon, Eugene Forsey, Andy Brewin, and many others had come to their concern with social justice through R.H. Tawney's Christian socialism. They condemned the profit motive not just for its economic inefficiency: it ran counter to deep feelings about interdependence, cooperation, and brotherhood. Two ministers, C.H. Huestis and Salem Bland, wrote regular social gospel columns in the *Star*. Bland, when denied university platforms, spoke for the CCF in union halls. Woodsworth, for all his rejection of formal creeds, founded his pacifist-socialism on religious faith – and he remained *the* political hero. Several LSR members also belonged to the Fellowship for a Christian Social Order: King Gordon, Forsey, Eric Havelock, Brewin, and Gregory Vlastos among them. In a 1934 statement they wrote: 'Believing as we do that there are no distinctions of power and privilege in the Kingdom of God, we pledge ourselves in the service of God and the task of building a new society in which all exploitation of man by man and all barriers to the abundant life created by the private ownership of property shall be done away with.' Visionary, if you will. But I do not sneer at these idealists as I look about me now at the triumph of the New Right: at their uncontrolled power of transnational corporations, the jobless 'recovery,' and a permissive, faithless society. As Vaclav Havel, the president of the Czech Republic, has observed: 'We are going through a great departure from God which has *no* parallel in history. As far as I know, we are living in the first atheistic civilization.' I save my sneers for Lord Thomson of Fleet, Conrad Black, the family cared for by Edper – and their legion of lackies.

The democratic socialists of the 1930s were nationalists – a gravely imperilled breed in the 1990s. Nationalism permeated our home. Among my parents' closest friends were William Arthur Deacon and his ebullient, liberated wife, Sally. Literary editor of the *Mail and Empire* (and of the *Globe and Mail* after 1936), Deacon did more to encourage Canadian writers than any other critic of his day. With Irish passion, teeth clamped on a huge dark pipe, he plunged joyously into the leading nationalist organizations: the Canadian Authors Association, and the summer conferences of the Canadian Institute on Economics and Politics at Lake Couchiching. He supported the CCF quietly, from the sidelines. As with others of my father's friends at the Writers' Club – Brooker, J.V. MacAree, E.J. Pratt, Merrill Denison, Robert Farquharson – Deacon was not just anti-imperialist. He, and they, knew the worth of a national community and the danger of submerging it – even in the interest of 'solving' economic problems. When Deacon published his paean of praise, *My Vision of Canada* (1933), economist Harold Innis congratulated him: 'You have done a magnificent service in this. I notice that you have had to endure some abuses but apparently it is still a minor crime to be a Canadian.' My father wrote several long and laudatory reviews of the book; my own excitement was great when Deacon gave me an autographed copy.

In these years we took several extended sketching trips by car through northern Ontario and Quebec. I still have some slightly faded watercolours – of the decaying O'Brien silver mine at Cobalt, of St-Simeon on the north shore of the St Lawrence. My version of Laurentian villages was rather too reminiscent of Haworth's treatment of Ontario. At Peribonka on Lac St-Jean we stopped at a primitive set of tourist cabins. The camp was run by an Eva Bouchard, who served at dinner the simplest and best dessert I've ever eaten: *syrop d'érable et crême* in large bowls. During a long evening conversation, Mme Bouchard asserted that she was the model for Louis Hémon's *Maria Chapdelaine*. My father was captivated. Back in Toronto he wrote an article about Eva Bouchard which was published in *The Canadian Magazine*. The feeling that everything, sooner or later, must be written about or painted I never resisted.

My earliest apprehension of French Canada came from several visits to Blythwood by Jean-Charles Harvey and his young assistant, Réal Rousseau. Harvey was seeking Toronto contacts for the promotion of his Montreal newspaper, *Le Jour*. No socialist, he nevertheless risked much as he fought threats to individual freedom and to the evolution of a liberal French-Canadian society. Thus he took aim at Adrien Arcand's fascists and the foreign-controlled capitalism of Premiers Taschereau and Duplessis. His several novels were condemned by the Jansenist Catholic bishops. One of these prohibited stories, *Les demi-civilisés*, was translated and published in 1937 as *Sackcloth for Banner*. My mother wasn't particularly keen about it, but I read with much interest the copy Harvey gave me. He wrote frequent pieces in *Le Jour* critical of the leadership-oriented Quebec nationalism then being promoted by the admirers of Abbé Groulx. A forerunner of the Quiet Revolution (and perhaps of Québec Inc.), he showed us another, francophone version of the persecution being endured at the same time by Frank Scott.

One important contribution my father made to the survival of the *Forum* I knew nothing about at the time. In the spring of 1936 the journal came to the end of its financial tether. Dad donated $1000. On this basis the LSR took over management of the *Forum* and, in 1938, initiated a sustaining fund that prevented future bankruptcy while circulation grew slowly. How my father managed his LSR-CCF activities while working full time at McKim's I don't really know.

In the years 1938–40 my father also took on two research and writing tasks. The first was commissioned by McKim's – *The Story of Advertising in Canada: A Chronicle of Fifty Years*. I suspect it was one factor in his not running into serious trouble at the firm for his public identification with the left. Nominally co-authored by a retired McKim executive, the book was actually written by my father, who incorporated some of the senior's recollections in the text. The volume remained for a number of years the only substantial historical analysis of its kind. The second job was commissioned by the Canadian Institute of International Affairs. Its purpose was to alert Canadians to the way in which foreign news was gathered and presented to them. Published as *Canada Gets the News*, it was a thorough analysis of newsgathering processes and editorial thrusts. It remained for several decades the only comprehensive treatment of its subject. Both volumes were published in 1940 by Ryerson Press. Ryerson's editor, Lorne Pierce, was as avid a promoter of Canadian nationalism as Bill Deacon. Dad, Pierce, and Deacon remained close, mutually supportive friends for the rest of their lives.

So, a change of gears. My move to North Toronto Collegiate Institute in the autumn of 1936 was decisive. In Latin class the top student and most attractive girl was Beverley Argue. We began dating and, by mid-year, neither of us was interested in anyone else. I still wonder at my immense good fortune. I believe that Bev saw from the outset that much of my assertive righteousness overlay a rather conservative nature. In any event, as our mutual attraction became love, we explored shared interests, while also debating some of them vigorously.

And Toronto remained exciting. Reginald Stewart's prom-symphony evenings at Varsity Arena required a 25-cent admission charge; the art gallery was free. We saw socially conscious plays at the Theatre of Action – such as Clifford Odets's *Waiting for Lefty* (which we tried hard to enjoy) and Karel Capek's symbol-loaded *Insect Play*, in which Mike Gelber was one of the leads – a tall, gangling green grasshopper. The circles continued to interlock. We drove often through the rolling country north of the city – always, it seems, on golden autumn afternoons. Parking my mother's car at some secluded vantage point, we dallied for two or three hours: Bev stretched out on the car robe, reading, while I executed yet another imperishable watercolour. Many years later, in Winnipeg, I thought of these shimmering afternoons when a young student asked Bev a quite impertinent question. The student was Ramsay Cook and he was in our home attending a meeting of the United College History Club. Having examined some of my paintings, he turned to Bev and said: 'Mrs McNaught, did Professor McNaught ever ask you to come up and see his etchings?' Well, Ramsay, now I can answer your question: 'Yes – but it wasn't "up"; it was out in the country.'

Bev came often to Blythwood Road. She and my mother found instant rapport – as well as a few antagonisms, the most significant of which were mother's deeply entrenched anti-Americanism and a reluctance to find even a minor fault in either of her children. I think that Bev saw a few, but she marvellously overlooked them. A love of reading shared by Mother and Bev was a powerful cement. I made no mistake in going to North Toronto Collegiate.

3

The University of Toronto campus in the autumn of 1937 more than met my well-nourished expectations. The creeping leviathan of the 1950s and 1960s had not yet swallowed whole streets. For four years Bev and I went several times a week to the Lantern Tea Room – on Willcocks Street, where one of the ugliest of science buildings has now taken the place of old houses and lofty elms. Lunch could be had there for 25 or 30 cents.

I very nearly registered at Trinity College, in the company of other Upper Canada College chaps. Inside the Trinity quadrangle, however, I sensed too much *déjà vu*. The floor plan resembled that of Upper Canada, the dustbane smelled the same, and I was being invited to join a select fraternity. A kind of inverted snobbery – which I mistook for egalitarianism – overtook me. Across the campus I registered in University College – the 'godless college,' but also the one to which my father had been attached. Bev, because some of her closest friends enrolled there, chose Trinity. Much later, two of my children went to Trinity and never regretted it for a moment. Before long, my sarcasm about Bev's choice abated – for reasons which seem to have grown stronger with the passage of time and which are similar to those that greatly complicated my assessment of UCC. These reasons concerned the problem of individual liberty when Frank Underhill and George Grube faced growing clamour for their dismissal because of their criticism early in World War II of British imperialism and their advocacy of neutrality. Underhill was in the greater peril. Employed by the state university, whose Board of Governors was appointed by the government, he was vulnerable to hostile rhetoric in the legislature and the press. Grube, on the Trinity faculty, found a firmer defence from his provost and from Convocation. John Strachan's 'elitist' institution seemed the more willing to tolerate eccentricity.

From the array of first-year honours courses, I chose modern history. A foregone conclusion: history was Underhill's department. Before the day of the free choice multiversity, all the honours courses were highly structured. Unquestioned was the now exotic assumption that the faculty view of how to best construct a program of study was likely to prove superior to the view of an eighteen year old fresh out of high school. History was considered to be not unrelated to the passage of time. Since the subject was also believed to be of assistance in understanding the present, and the place of one's own community in the world, it should involve close attention to those societies that had formulated the institutions, ideas, and culture underlying the Canadian present. Together with the dozen or so other students in the course, it never occurred to me to question any of this reasoning. I now think that my present high regard for continuity was seeded in those years. Possibly the structure and ethos of the course simply appealed to my innate conservatism.

That we proceeded from Greece and Rome through the Middle Ages to Modern Britain, Europe, and North America seemed not unreasonable. Moreover, while a sequence of core courses was mandatory, the range of choice after the first year was remarkably broad: I chose English, French, philosophy, geography, economics, and political science – at various stages. English literature with the young and hesitant Douglas LePan tempted me briefly to switch academic allegiance. Philosophy came very much alive with the distinguished senior George Brett, who made syllogistic reasoning and the evolution of his subject a sheer joy. Greek and Roman history with Louis MacKay and Charles Cochrane came laced with contemporary relevance – which, in my essays, I usually elaborated with shameless arrogance. About economics the less said the better. Vincent Bladen failed to convince me that the theory of the pricing structure was of any real importance.

Unfortunately, the great Harold Innis went right over my head, literally. His lectures in Canadian economic history followed close upon the lunch hour. He delivered them in the mouldering McMaster building on Bloor Street – in a room whose tall windows let in soporific rays of sunlight. These seemed to be about the only rays that entered that room. His tall grey figure stooped over the lectern, Innis read from his documents: 'In 1537, twenty-six Basque fishing ships visited Newfoundland ...' The brilliance of his interpretation of Canadian history did not dawn upon me until I began framing my own lectures in 1946. In the same creaky old building, Brough Macpherson lectured on the history of political thought. Looking about twenty years old, he wasn't really much more than that. Slender to the vanishing point, with a prominent aquiline nose lending hauteur to his drawling delivery, Macpherson lost no one's attention.

The great majority of our lectures, in all fields, were occasions – a claim that may well be greeted with scepticism in an age in which the lecture enjoys not much approval. Beyond the first year, most lectures were given to fewer than forty students. With very few exceptions, we recognized that lectures had been meticulously constructed by people genuinely engaged with their subjects. Providing one had done at least some of the preparatory reading, the lecture ambiance usually produced personal rapport and beneficial stimulus. Questions were infrequent, but all the honours courses included a one-hour tutorial meeting each week. Oxford, and particularly Balliol College, provided the tutorial model. Intimidating at first, and rather formal, weekly tutorial groups usually included not more than eight students each. The tutorial professor (before the day of graduate teaching assistants) assigned each student one essay topic for each of the two terms. Each group meeting began with a student reading an essay of between 1500 and 2000 words. While formal, the system had the merit of focusing discussion quickly. It also gave the professor an opportunity to dissect one's work in unnerving detail. These tutorials gave a sharp goad to student endeavour. Their watering down from the 1960s on was an unmitigated loss.

Compared with the shabby decrepitude of the Bloor building occupied by political economy and geography, the history department enjoyed relatively opulent quarters on College Street: Baldwin House, at the corner of St George Street, built in 1860. Its spacious rooms and halls were finished with gleaming dark woods. The main-floor lecture rooms boasted French doors. On the warmest days of spring and fall these doors were left open, the traffic sounds distanced by broad lawns and trees. From her desk in the second-floor hall, Freya Hahn administered the entire department – for a nine-month salary of $1000. She did all the typing, kept the student and faculty records, sorted out room assignments, and presided over faculty tea each afternoon. As my friend John Cairns recalled: 'She was considerably more important than most members of the faculty ... knowing where everything was and what should be done, indispensable, the model of a confidential secretary to the Head ... She had the secret of being at once direct, impersonally friendly, and immensely dignified.' I think now that Ms Hahn's very presence kept many waves from breaking too discordantly around us.

My introduction to university-level Canadian history came from two dramatically opposed quarters: Chester Martin and Frank Underhill. Martin I saw, perhaps unjustly, as a fussy old maid. A rather crotchety, pedantic Maritimer, he had founded the history department at the University of Manitoba and was wedded to the records of the Colonial Office – from which he derived his very constitutional view of Canadian history. He alerted us, frequently, to the crucial fact that responsible government was achieved in Nova Scotia 'without the breaking of a pane of glass.' Accurate, of course, as was his important work on dominion lands policy in the West. Purveyed to us across a green baize table in his massive ground-floor office, it was even less stimulating than Innis's tabulation of visiting fishing ships.

Underhill, of course, I was predisposed to venerate. I was not alone, however, in relishing the sarcastic wit and penetrating intelligence he brought to his portrayal of our robber barons and their political henchmen. Even the students who tramped down from Trinity and were visibly upset by much of what Underhill had to say about their friends, and progenitors, were seduced. Diminutive, restless, one finger rubbing his nose, he often strayed from sparse notes into extended, almost private analysis. Years later, as I strolled with Donald Creighton across the Fort Garry campus in Winnipeg, he turned to me: 'Ken, you were Underhill's student: What was it that made him so popular with the undergraduates?' A poignant moment. I had no better answer than the man who was asked if he had stopped beating his wife. I believe, however, that I am one of a select few who managed to remain friends with both these gladiators.

I took no undergraduate lectures from Creighton, although I was in one of his tutorials in European history. These he conducted with the same verve he later brought to his writing and teaching in Canadian history. I was particularly caught up in his enthusiastic involvement in the French Revolution and made the mistake of presenting a hyperbolic essay on the Terror. He quite properly gave me the lowest grade I received in all four years. When I later enrolled in his graduate seminar on federal-provincial relations, he allowed me to do my major paper on 'a socialist assessment of the Rowell-Sirois Report' and gave it a distinctively first-class mark. As a teacher, Creighton was not only fair; he bent over backwards to be fair.

I think the same may be said of most of our dedicated, scandalously underpaid professors: in 1933–4 Underhill's salary was $4445; Creighton's, $2396; Richard Saunders's, $1985. In addition to heavy lecture loads, they all conducted tutorial groups – and should be forgiven some tetchiness when it came to marking the relentless flow of essays. We were fascinated by their variety. To make up for the impenetrable maundering of the kindly Ralph Flenley's tripartite division of the Frankish Kingdom, Dick Saunders *became* Martin Luther. We could *see* Luther nailing his ninety-five theses to the church door in Wittenburg – and students from across the campus packed the back rows. I loved Dick's tutorials because he cast a wide net beyond merely political history. We drew maps (to which I diligently applied watercolours) and we talked of the bum rap suffered by Niccolò Machiavelli in conventional stereotypes. When I daringly illustrated in watercolour an essay on Catherine the Great, Dick didn't bat an eyelid. He merely questioned how much of Walisewski's biography of Catherine (in French) I had actually read.

Two men stood out for the suave elegance of their lecture performances. Edgar McInnis and George P. de T. Glazebrook lectured mostly on international affairs, although each produced important books in Canadian history. Glazebrook – haughty, linen handkerchief tucked into his sleeve – provoked some derision. His lectures, however, were lucid and crammed with 'judicious' reflection; a bit too establishment for me. McInnis – tall and immaculate – peered at us from heavy-lidded eyes that were further shrouded by luxuriant brows. His lectures, delivered in a sardonic drawl, commanded unwavering attention. One would never have guessed that he was an early member of the League for Social Reconstruction; he wore his objectivity like a badge of honour.

By far the most dramatic of our professors was Donald McDougall. Blinded during World War I, McDougall had overcome immense obstacles to win a Rhodes scholarship and a first at Oxford. By the end of the 1930s he had made himself a leading student of British and Commonwealth history. Although he wrote perceptive annual review articles on these subjects for the *Canadian Historical Review*, his overriding interest and scholarship was in the English seventeenth century. In McDougall's tutorial, each student kept to an assigned chair; I only once saw him misremember a student during discussion. In addition to his blindness, McDougall was Roman Catholic, which further marked him off in a very Protestant secular department. His treatment of the Tudors and Stuarts, with constant reference to the documents, was beautiful *histoire par les textes* – and probably more balanced than that of some of his colleagues. We attended his groups with a mixture of fear and admiration. I remember all too well his dissection of an essay I read on Cromwell – based too much on the biography by the rationalist John Morley. McDougall provided additional trepidation by constantly relighting an aromatic pipe and dropping still flaming matches in a shallow tin ashtray. But he never missed. He refused to carry a white cane and I once saw him, on his way to lunch at Hart House, nearly roughed up by some engineering students as he stumbled into their midst poking about with his walking stick.

Bertie Wilkinson, already a leading authority on the English fourteenth century, arrived from Manchester in 1938. Short and lithe, he was tweedy both in thought and clothes. Passionate about his subject and his country, he kept our noses in the documents. He was also incensed by Underhill's voluble advocacy of Canadian neutrality. When war broke out, Wilkinson became a principal organizer of the university's Canadian Officers' Training Corps. Few on the history faculty shared Underhill's foreign policy views – especially when he suggested at Lake Couchiching in 1940 that Canada's future lay within the American rather than the British imperial orbit. Yet, when demands in the legislature and the press for Underhill's dismissal reached fever pitch in 1940, the history department, from Martin through to Wilkinson, rallied behind his right to free speech. A petition was signed by deans and faculty throughout the university, and another by students. My father wrote a piece in the *Canadian Forum*, and I organized the student petition. Pressure was also brought to bear on the university president, Canon H.J. Cody, by Mackenzie King Liberals who had no love for Ontario's Liberal premier Mitchell Hepburn. A right-wing populist demagogue, Hepburn was thumping the war drums, calling on King to impose conscription and threatening the university's funds. Eventually, appearing every inch the Vicar of Bray, Cody stood his ground – after Underhill agreed to withhold further fire. The breaking of a man's spirit is never an edifying event. Not until much later did I begin to appreciate what went on in Underhill's mind in the years following 1940.

For four undergraduate years I soaked up a fair amount of what was on offer – and pushed my luck a good deal. Apart from regular swimming and squash at Hart House and the prescribed academic routines, I moved back and forth from propriety to marked impropriety. The

Historical Club was the extreme of propriety. Founded in 1904 by the history department's first head, George Wrong, it was quite openly elitist. Its twenty-five members, all male, usually in the fourth year, were nominated by professors and came from any of the Arts and Science departments. Its purpose was to establish closer, informal relations among professors, 'promising' students, and members of the Toronto establishment. Chester Martin carried on Wrong's tradition of enlisting prominent Torontonians as hosts for the club's monthly meetings: Sir Joseph Flavelle, E.B. Osler, Sir Edmund Walker, Vincent Massey, Newton Rowell, J.S. McLean, J.M. Macdonnell were among them. Two students read papers at each meeting – usually on contemporary issues in international affairs. Even my arrogance towards the elegant ambiance of these occasions didn't calm my nerves when my turn came, in 1941. Most of the history professors attended; one couldn't help a feeling of being 'on show' and of facing very stiff competition. I remember, too, my surprise at refreshment time, watching Frank Underhill chatting most amicably with our host, J.S. McLean. He was president of Canada Packers and had just withdrawn his token financial support from the *Canadian Forum*. The *Forum* had endorsed a United Packinghouse Workers strike against McLean's firm.

Writing very knowing art reviews for the *Varsity* newspaper and editing the University College magazine *The Undergraduate* were quite proper activities also. I skated close to open water, however, in another area. When I became president of the university Cooperative Commonwealth Federation club, I invited Charles Millard to address a public meeting sponsored by the club. I knew Millard would attract a good crowd; he was Canadian director of the United Auto Workers and a leader of the 1937 Oshawa strike against General Motors. After reserving a bright room in the University College Women's Union, I sought advance publicity in the *Varsity*. The editor, Larry Smith, was also in modern history and he more than obliged. On the morning of the meeting, the *Varsity*'s front-page headline read 'Hepburn Must Go' – the topic of Millard's speech. Premier 'Mitch' had tried to crush the Oshawa strike by sending in his 'hussars' – a body of special police. He was still battling the Congress of Industrial Organizations (CIO) and the 'communist threat' in Ontario. And he read the *Varsity* (or had it vetted for him) carefully. At 9:30 that morning President Cody's secretary summoned me to Simcoe Hall 'immediately.' Cody huffed and puffed about his devotion to free speech. He then told me that he was at that very moment discussing with the government the need for a new science building. The premier had called him at 9:00 a.m. about the *Varsity* story. He was sure I would understand that our Millard meeting could not be held in a university building. A policemen would be at the Women's Union just to make sure. I had forgotten that the pompous old cleric had been minister of education in the Tory Hearst government in 1918 – and thus a friend of WK. At the door of his office he admonished me: 'If your grandfather knew what you are up to he would turn in his grave.' Well, the *Varsity* had also carried a box taking note of Cody's birthday. I wished him a happy birthday and left. In the 1960s, as the campus rang with the happy cries of Bob Rae, Michael Ignatieff, and other occupiers of administrative offices, I felt a bit nostalgic about the fatherly old campus cop guarding the Women's Union in 1940. Our meeting was held off campus.

I had not yet learned, in 1940, the first requirement of self-knowledge: never take yourself too seriously. Despite the evidence of this present exercise, I think I now understand that beautiful injunction. In any event, I was all too serious about my membership in the Cooperative Commonwealth Youth Movement (CCYM). The president of the CCYM was J.S. Woodsworth's daughter, Grace MacInnis. I had met Grace and her husband, Angus, at Blythwood Road and been captivated by her enthusiasm – and forgave her for co-authoring that disastrous pamphlet *The Fifty Men Who Own Canada*. When I joined the Eglinton (North Toronto) branch of the CCYM in 1939, the debate about cooperating with the communists was over – settled in favour of strict adherence to parliamentary socialism. We thrashed out the hot question of the war, however, with acrimonious zeal. In September a slender majority of the CCF national council defeated Woodsworth's demand that Canada stay clear. M.J. Coldwell, supported by David Lewis, Grace and Angus MacInnis, and others secured support for a very pragmatic policy: economic support of Britain, but no expeditionary force from Canada. I read the reports of Woodsworth's noble defence of his position in the Commons. He confirmed my pacifist conviction that the new war would settle no more than had the previous one. Moreover, I felt that the Coldwell-Lewis position was devious to the point of hypocrisy.

Our CCYM group split on the war question much as had the CCF across the country. We all worked enthusiastically for the party in the 1940 federal election, however, and I came to know some colourful young labour union people such as Fred Dowling of the United Packinghouse Workers and Eileen Tallman of the Retail, Wholesale and

Department Store Union. Dowling would become Canadian director of his union, and Tallman in 1947–50 led the toughest organizing drive ever undertaken against a Canadian department store. In the end Eaton's defeated her – through intimidation and steady turnover of their sweated employees and with the aid of very skilful lawyers. A slender, intensely committed young woman, Eileen was not only an avid unionist but was deeply opposed to the war. Between us we concocted a hair-brained antiwar action. Typing out a one-page argument for refusing to enlist, we mimeographed several hundred copies. Next, we made a list of the most frequently borrowed books in the public libraries. Touring the various branches, we inserted copies of our statement in as many of these books as we could find on the shelves. We were lucky that no notice seems to have been taken of our clandestine adventure. Other than filching three pennies from a stationer's pile of newspapers when I was about five, I think this is the only Criminal Code offence I ever committed.

In June 1941 a ninety-seven-year-old Sir William Mulock took my hands in trembling fingers to confirm that I was graduating. In a day of precise ranking, I was fourth of the four first-class graduands in history. Because of a hard-to-forgive failure of high-school guidance (regarding a half credit), Beverley had one year more to complete her degree in psychology. A decison was required.

In a fit of uncertainty I took a job in the market research department of J. Walter Thompson. In this Toronto branch of an American advertising firm we juggled the results of door-to-door product surveys – so they would prove what the account executives wished their clients to believe. At least this was my assessment of the operation. I also saw enough of the Babbitt-like bonhomie and hard drinking at 80 Richmond Street West to put me off the 'business world' for life. Even apart from the two-month live-and-learn charade at JWT's, I suspected that I was psychologically ill-equipped to deal with the bottom lines of trade. My other experience of the 'real world' of business was as a travelling salesman. In the summer of 1938 I visited nearly every city and town in the Maritimes as a traveller for the Canada Seed Company. This firm was a subsidiary of Steele-Briggs, then Canada's largest seed company – and its president was the father of my close friend John Steele. Well, that's the way things were, and probably still are. A stripling of nineteen, I set off in a spanking new Chevrolet armed with a route guide to all the hardware and grocery stores that carried the company's seed packets throughout the three provinces. My job was to collect and ship back to Toronto the unsold packets and percentage charges, and take orders for the following year.

What was a relatively simple task ended in financial failure. My salary was $15 a week, and all travel costs were chargeable to the company. So indifferent were my records, however, that when I got back to Toronto I was actually slightly in debt to Canada Seed. Yet that Maritime journey gave me much. Belting along the mostly gravel roads, I could scarcely resist stopping to sketch – along the Cabot Trail, the Cavendish shore, the ports of Nova Scotia, the gorgeous valley of the Saint John River. But then other sad, often scary sights intruded venomously into the idyll. In the depression-scarred towns there was more bare wood than paint. In a café at Caraquet in New Brunswick, I found only salt cod and potatoes for lunch. In Glace Bay, Stellarton, and many other ravaged towns, I could feel something close to hatred: for a skinny teenager scooping up the profits and driving in his shiny car with the Ontario plates. More than a third of the stores on my list were closed. The black ruins of the Cape Breton mining towns I related to the tough policies of Uncle Charlie's Dominion Steel and Coal Company. I returned to Toronto more deeply concerned of the need to 'overthrow capitalism.'

Graduation left still unresolved a question much more immediate than what long-term future I should plan for. A few of my friends had enlisted; two had already been killed. With all other male undergraduates I had been compelled to attend weekly drill sessions in the COTC and a nearly worthless two weeks 'under canvas' at Camp Niagara. I still believed the war was wrong and would settle nothing; but that conviction was under constant assault. In September 1941 I juggled with three options for the immediate future. The first was suggested by a cousin-by-marriage who was advertising manager for John Labatt's: to edit his company house organ *The Arrowhead*. The second came from my uncle Hilton Tudhope, who kindly offered to settle me on the bottom rung of A.E. Ames. The third opening appeared at a boys' residential school, Pickering College, in Newmarket, 30 miles north of Toronto. Uncle Hilton never forgave me for saying no to a decent salary and respectable future – I think he blamed the 'communistic' influence of my parents. Gordon Jack, at Labatt's, understood my refusal perfectly, although the beer salary would have been roughly four times that of Pickering's $1800 a year.

Joseph McCulley, the headmaster of Pickering College, was a tall, fleshy, and imposing person who enjoyed immensely the company of men and boys. He was later to become commissioner of federal penitentiaries and, after that, a respected warden of Hart House. His school, founded by Quakers, eschewed corporal punishment and was mildly progressive. Being private, the teachers needed no certificate. Somewhat in the manner of Choppy Grant and Terry MacDermot, Joe (even senior students such as John Meisel called him that) chose his staff for reasons other than an official stamp of approval. While many of the masters were long-term devotees of Pickering, quite a few others were transient. At various times Charles Ritchie and John Holmes taught there. The fine Toronto pianist Reg Godden commuted weekly to direct the music program. Fred Hagan, just graduated from the Ontario Art College, gave inspired direction in arts and crafts.

I began a lifelong friendship with Hagan. He had grown up in Cabbagetown – long before Ontario Street was captured by the white-paint crowd. A vigorous, passionate artist, Fred had already mastered the various paint media and was on the way to becoming one of our foremost stone lithographers. He was also a splendid craftsman. In after-class hours I learned from him a love of woodworking that I now indulge with some abandon. I think we both succumbed, too, to the beauty of our Newmarket setting. Pickering's main building was red-brick Georgian with an elegant white-pillared portico. It occupied the highest point on the edge of town, facing a welcoming lawn whose elms and maples coloured the lingering autumn. To the east stretched 200 rolling acres of school property. On duty weekends in the fall and spring I took some of the boys sketching there – in the winter we donned skis or staged hockey practices on the frigid outdoor rink. Most weekday evenings Joe held court in his large, comfortable study. The beer was plentiful, and a fairly regular group of masters was on hand. Not an original thinker, McCulley nevertheless could lead discussion very well and also moderate, when necessary, the enthusiasms of opinionated youngsters like myself or Ron Ide – who later became a creative pioneer in the establishment of TV Ontario. I also admired McCulley because he had faced down sharp criticism from potential benefactors when he hosted annual meetings of the LSR at Pickering.

In a strange and direct way my teaching in Firth House, the Pickering 'Prep,' led me to stop dithering about the war. In my class of fifteen, nine were British war guests. These boys, ranging in age from twelve to fourteen, had been sent to Canada, riskily by sea, to keep them from greater risk at home. They were all better educated than their Canadian classmates. But, apart from that, they were a daily reminder of what was going on in Europe. And they were very lonely. One gangling youngster, Martin Kibblewhite, hid his precocity and his homesickness behind bottle-thick spectacles. But one day, overcoming shyness, he walked to the blackboard on which I had just written the title under an excellent drawing of 'Tyranosaurus rex' and calmly inserted the missing *n*. We got along very well.

On 7 December 1941 Martin's mother came up from Toronto, where she was clerking in Birks jewellery store. Bev was also visiting for the weekend, and on the Sunday afternoon we were having tea with Reg and Norah Blackstock. 'Blackie' was the charismatic director of Firth House – a romantic idealist who in the summers ran one of Ontario's best boys camps at Lake Mazinaw. While we were chatting about Mazinaw, the news of Pearl Harbor burst upon us. After the first shock, Mrs Kibblewhite sighed with audible relief – the American make-weight was secured once again. I knew then I could not just sit out the rest of this gruesome tragedy.

My pacifism was not religious; I was, in fact, obnoxiously agnostic. Because my antiwar conviction sprang from political-economic conclusions, it was more vulnerable than that, say, of George Grant. I remained persuaded that the roots of war lay deep in the amalgam of capitalist-imperialism. Britain, France, and, above all, the United States, I was sure, had evaded all the opportunities of collective security – from Manchuria to Spain and the 'failed' anti-Hitler alliance with Russia – because of obscure but real economic purposes. But finally the cumulative horror of a Europe in thrall to a system with uglier roots than mere capitalism could not be blinked. Racial totalitarianism, West and East, added a dimension of 'original sin.' Although this was a notion I had always sneered at and would not seriously grapple with for some years to come, on a purely emotional level I saw that a choice between two wrongs had to be made.

I finished out the school year at Pickering. Our wedding took place in mid-June in Trinity College – a week after Bev's graduation. Once again, despite Uncle Hilton's misgivings, the trickle-down was there. Aunt Edna gave us a cheque that provided a trip to Montreal – in circumstances that now make me wonder whether the intervening years have actually witnessed progress. At the foot of Bay Street, we boarded the lovely old steamer *Kingston*. A dance orchestra played as we sailed sedately across to Rochester. Next morning we meandered through the 1000 islands and docked at Prescott. There we boarded the *Rapids Prince*. The shallow-draft steamer shot the rapids en route to Montreal.

This hair-raising bit of navigation took us through foaming water and within feet of partially submerged granite – an excitement not equalled by 30-foot Atlantic rollers. Several days at the elegant, long-gone Queen's Hotel rounded off a perfect honeymoon.

My approach to military service was bedevilled by one self-afflicted disability and one inherited. The first was the naive rejection of influence or even of any advantage conferred by a bachelor's degree. I actually tried to practise democracy – although I should certainly have known better by then. Thus I did not follow the route of the COTC to a nearly automatic commission. Instead I strolled down to the main Toronto enlistment centre, naked as it were. There a medical officer discovered the second shortcoming: I was slightly over 6 feet and weighed in at 129 lbs. He gave me a 'B' physical rating, and I was taken on as a private in the Royal Canadian Ordnance Corps. At the Toronto depot I discovered that the RCOC looked after procurement and distribution of nearly everything required by the army – from clothing to tanks. I spent the summer and fall learning ordering and accounting procedures that were supposed to keep track of this staggering range of equipment. Infinitely tedious.

In December I enrolled for a senior NCO training program – thinking this could be the way in which a democratic army might discover and reward merit! I was given three unpaid stripes and packed off to Camp Barriefield at Kingston. The only exciting event in three frigid weeks was when the Bren gun I was learning to use chattered sideways across the ice-covered butt and continued firing along the line of other trainees. None of them was hit. Most were corpulent old sweats from the permanent force – warrant officers enjoying a respite from dull duties in other camps. They spent each long night in the sergeant's mess – while I was studiously memorizing the mimeographed lectures on RCOC organizational details. Back in Toronto I found the course results posted on the depot bulletin board. I had come top of the pack – such as it was. The reward was swift. My prized sergeant's stripes were removed and I was dispatched to the Ordnance depot at Camp Borden as a private. Mine not to question why – and in some respects Borden resembled death.

Some 50 miles north of Toronto, Camp Borden sprawled across sandy hills and was a general-purpose training centre. Hundreds of wooden huts, hangars, and halls housed maintenance equipment, tanks, trucks, ammunition, and other stores, and an average of about 20,000 soldiers. I grew to hate the pot-bellied coal stoves in winter and the swirling sand the rest of the time. For nearly three years this ugly environment backdropped sporadic efforts to do something about a very unpleasant situation.

Considerably disillusioned by the Barriefield fling, I beavered away in the Ordnance accounting office. In six months I had three stripes back and then added a crown to become a staff-sergeant – my pinnacle of army achievement. And all the while I had to instruct a stream of officers-in-training in the niceties of Ordnance R and I – receipts and issues. Hoping to wiggle past the obstacle of my physical rating, I consulted the depot's medical officer – about adding some weight. His only advice was to drink a quart of beer before dinner each evening. This, he said, would not only add calories, but would stimulate my appetite. It seemed to do neither – although I had plenty of company in the sergeant's mess. Another prescription I tried – milkshakes enriched with heavy cream, an egg, powdered milk, and a dollop of sherry – produced only nausea.

In early 1944 my roommate and I decided to try a different route. Bob Lamb, a talented teacher, was also a skilled mechanic. He ran an important service section in the tank and truck maintenance hangar. We both felt that, once slotted, as we were, we were not likely to be moved. Although I had determined by then not to question army decisions, we agreed rather fecklessly to seek a loophole. At the RCAF Borden headquarters we asked if we could transfer – and were politely refused, without explanation. After another year I wound up at the Central Ordnance Depot in Ottawa. The alleged purpose of this posting I still find difficulty believing. It was to track down two 'discrepancies' in RCOC ledgers. One was the disappearance from the books of two Ram tanks, which had last been heard of on their way to a proving ground in Texas; the second was the 'disappearance' of a freightcar load of 75 mm shells. I never found any acceptable record of either loss. On 19 September 1945 I was discharged in Toronto.

The bare bones of this tale are bad enough. The actual experience of ennui and embarrassment was much worse – while I remained safe and sound, friends and one relative were being whisked overseas. The relative was Ernest Sirluck, and responsibility for our relationship lies at my door. We had become friends while sharing, with six other University of Toronto students, a bell tent at Camp Niagara. A graduate of the University of Manitoba, Ernest was already launched on a PhD program in English with seventeenth-century specialist A.S.P. Woodhouse at Toronto. On the middle weekend of the painfully dull two weeks, I invited him to join Bev, my sister, Lesley, and me for an evening at Blythwood Road. Ernest and Lesley hit it off immediately – and were married a few weeks after our own wedding. During one of the long months at Borden, Ernest began his training as a cadet officer. The four of us spent a short weekend together at a quite luxurious old house on a hill in Barrie overlooking Kempenfeldt Bay. Barrendale Hall was for officers only, but token resistance to admitting a mere NCO was easily overcome by the haughty persuasiveness that Ernest was later to deploy before students and faculty colleagues. Shortly after, he went overseas as an intelligence officer – a selection I always thought most appropriate and enviable.

While I was at Borden, Bev's degree in psychology paid off handsomely. She took a job at Toronto's Juvenile Court: giving intelligence tests to young offenders and interviewing their parents in homes scattered about the city. This she did on foot and by streetcar. Her salary paid for a small, pretty apartment on Eglinton West. Most weekends I was able to come down from camp. Because bus and train routes were extremely leisurely, I bought a car – actually, a museum piece, which I wish I had kept. Dubbed 'the Rocket,' this 1925 Packard Victoria cost me $265. Stored on blocks for some years, its unworn Goodyears alone were worth much more – yet they were secure against theft because they were far too big to fit any other vehicle. At a time when most drivers were reduced to synthetic tires which froze flat on the ground during winter – or blew out on the highway – the Rocket's tires made up for its ancient design and finicky six-cylinder motor. Its stately perpendicular elegance was enhanced by silk window blinds and a coffin-size trunk at the rear. It was a gas-guzzler, and I usually had two or three passengers to supply much-needed ration coupons. I was always anxious to have Bob Lamb along: he knew how to adjust an oft-soldered carburetor float that tended to jam on the hills around Allendale. In town, Bev never wished to be left long if I parked somewhere because no one passed the Rocket without stopping to stare. The great pleasure of these many weekends and of the two-week furloughs spent at Cedarhurst was always shadowed, however, by awareness that I had no little maple leaf on my volunteer service ribbon.

4

While I was at Pickering I had travelled down to Baldwin House each Friday afternoon to attend Ralph Flenley's graduate seminar in historiography. His seminar was much better than his undergraduate smothering of medieval Europe. I was invariably late and Flenley was invariably tolerant. A great many evenings at Borden I had spent reading – mostly in books ancillary to the historiography course. When I emerged into another wonderful Toronto autumn in September 1945 I had no lingering doubts about where I should head: right back to Baldwin House to enrol in the graduate history program. Despite what I knew about the tribulations of Frank Underhill, George Grube, and the others, including the still abysmal levels of faculty salaries, a warm glow surrounded my vision of the 'academic life.' The Department of Veterans' Affairs made wide the way by payment of fees and a small living allowance.

Dick Saunders's seminar on the Enlightenment I found as absorbing as I had his first-year lectures and tutorials in 1937–8. Probably the least 'recognized' member of the history faculty, Dick lacked all sense of self-importance, yet combined his thorough scholarship with a sharp, critical ability and a teaching manner that was provocative – and dangerous to the unprepared. I did my major paper for him on Abbé Fénelon. I suppressed my first thought of doing an illustration à la Catherine the Great, but I remember his chuckle when I reported Fénelon's response to critics who implied that his evangelistic travels about France with a Mme Guyon cast doubt on the purity of the abbé's doctrine of *pur amour*. Fénelon's explanation was that he and his *religieuse* enjoyed a 'supersensual interpenetration.'

Much less fruitful was a seminar in American history – the whole of it. George Brown was present (presided would be too strong a word) in the first term. As he drowsed through the two-hour sessions, the less generous among us wondered how much U.S. history he had read beyond Charles and Mary Beard. Richard Preston, in second term, picked up the pieces very effectively – even though the subject was not his major interest. Donald Creighton's seminar on dominion-provincial relations I relished because it provided a strong counterbalance to everything I had imbibed about Canadian history from Underhill – and, I suppose, because I was well aware of the bubbling tensions between the two men. In addition to their profound political differences, their battles over curricular matters were enlivened by Creighton's festering resentment of Underhill's 'jump-start.' Underhill had come to the department in 1927 as a full professor; Creighton came in the same year as a lecturer – who was also in debt. The gap in rank remained until Creighton was made a professor in 1945 – without, of course, equalling Underhill's salary. Creighton had published *The Commercial Empire of the St. Lawrence* in 1937 and considered Underhill to be more journalist than scholar. Fortunately for me, Creighton's jealous hatred for Underhill did not extend to 'Underhill's students.' I've never quite understood how I managed to emerge relatively unscathed from between these two powerful grindstones.

My final seminar was with Frank Underhill – in nineteenth-century British political thought. By this time Underhill had pretty well completed his startling recantation – of socialism and isolationism. He was taking leave of the CCF and was especially hostile to the labour union influence represented by David Lewis. In a storm of personal guilt, he reacted violently to most of his previous assumptions. Or perhaps he was rediscovering feelings that had lain dormant beneath his 'progressive' historical articles and his socialist politics. He had always been (I discovered later) as much interested in Hobbes as in Locke. Now, as the world was getting ready for the Cold War, he was immediately attuned to the seismic shifts in American political writing. Persuaded that power in an imperfect and increasingly totalitarian world was essential and that the requirements of that power would have to be lived with, a new role for intellectuals must be accepted: that of ensuring that the power of the West would be used humanely, as opposed to the older role of holding all power suspect. As he had earlier adopted Charles Beard and Frederick Jackson Turner to his interpretation of Canada's Clear Grits and western progressives, he now employed the pioneers of American consensus history and Cold War liberalism to justify his political *volte face.*

One of the first of these consensus thinkers was Pendleton Herring. Underhill strongly endorsed *The Politics of Democracy: American Parties in Action,* noting that Herring understood 'that the existing party system is the best way of conducting politics in our contemporary North American democracy ... He doubts if American unity is strong enough to stand the strain of open conflict between such parties as the British Conservative and Labour parties.' As early as 1943 Frank had recommended Herring to all Canadian 'hot gospelers, either of the left or the right, who imagined that in the large-scale complex society of the United States or Canada we are ever likely to have parties in power putting into practise rigid dogmatic principles or action.' Three years later he spelled out the new bottom line: 'The real division in the world today is not between socialism and capitalism; it is between freedom and totalitarianism.' Underhill had reached the 'end of ideology' before that legend of the Cold War American liberals was spelled out by Daniel Bell, Reinhold Niebuhr, Arthur Schlesinger, and the others who, in 1961, would become the courtiers of Camelot.

In the seminar I was still not fully aware of how deep was the change – until I read the comments Underhill wrote on my seminar paper on J.S. Mill. I had argued that Mill, especially in his final revision of utilitarianism, had become a socialist; and, further, that this evolution was the natural outcome of nineteenth-century English political thought – a position that Frank had earlier held. He now commented: 'Mill's inherited individualism saved him from ever falling down and worshipping any collective abstraction – the state, the proletariat – and so there is no element of totalitarianism in his later thinking, as there was in that of nearly all the socialists except the Fabians. The individual is still the measure of all things. This keeps Mill in the essential English tradition.' Well, yes, I thought, but the 1930s Underhill would not have put it quite that way. The ground was being prepared for what would be, by 1950, an open confrontation with my academic father-figure. In the meantime, and even later, there would be absolutely no personal friction.

The two graduate school years could not have been more eventful. In December 1945 our first son, Christopher, was born. The Eglinton apartment suddenly became very small, but I was seldom in it during the day. I had chosen, on Underhill's suggestion, an MA thesis topic and spent most non-seminar hours in the old reference library at College and St George – reading the brittle, yellowing pages of the Toronto *Globe* for the 1880s. Underhill was beginning his search for Canadian liberalism, so my thesis title had come easily: 'The *Globe* and Canadian Liberalism, 1880–1890.' In the summer of 1946 Lesley and Ernest shared the Cedarhurst cottage with us. Ernest was deep in his doctoral thesis about John Milton's struggles with natural law. As he cogitated on the possible connotation of such notions as 'collegium,' I banged out my thesis chapters on a Royal portable – with frequent pauses to look out across Lake Simcoe. Unlike me, Ernest has always taken an extremely cautious approach to life's little problems, viewing each of them carefully from all angles. One day he had – unusually – preceded me down the steep bank to the beach and was stretched out on a short dock. When I came down I hit the dock on the run and dove into the water, just clearing his prostrate form. Emerging, I heard his warning: 'Ken, remember you are no longer eighteen!' Right. I was almost twenty-eight. My thesis was examined and passed in October.

Pressed for warm bodies to deal with the influx of returned servicemen, the history department resorted, for the first time, to teaching assistants. In September 1946 I was appointed part-time instructor and put in charge of three tutorial groups. Awesome. Impressed as I was with my lack of serious qualifications, I nevertheless felt a sort of equalizing satisfaction: so many ex-officers treating an ex-staff-sergeant with some respect! And other excitements crowded about. In the fall of 1946 we exchanged our apartment for a classic old house at 13 Lowther Avenue. Eleven rooms, semi-detached, Toronto Victorian, this brooding 'town house' must have appeared in one or another of Albert Franck's warm autumn oils. When we moved in, the place was redolent with the musty aroma of its original Axminster carpeting. It still flaunted several functioning gas lights; the kitchen and the bedroom above it drew heat only from a huge coal-fired cooking range – in which we roasted (for seven hours) the best Christmas turkey we ever had. Lowther was host to many good evenings that year. Maurice and Betty Careless, Stewart and Velma Reid, Roger and Kay Graham, Gerry and Janet Craig, Norman and Eleanor Beattie were among the grad students and young lecturers who maintained a good noise level – on the base of a fruit punch laced with Niagara red. We 'bought' Lowther with $1500 that Dad gave us – and a mortgage for the balance of $5500. The minimal mortgage payments were further lessened when we rented third-floor rooms to two young men. One of these, Ross

McLean, became a close friend and later a pioneering producer at CBC. At the time, Ross was dating June Wrong, granddaughter of the history department's founder. We sold Lowther for $9000 when we pulled up roots in September 1947. For many years Paul and Joan Fox were to live there, renting from a later owner.

That year, too, I became president of the graduate history club. John Cairns, who has always possessed a much stronger sense of responsibility than I, was secretary, and my predecessor was Stewart Reid. Stewart was already displacing Frank Underhill as my most respected academic. At the very time when Underhill was recanting, Stewart blew fresh, unrepentant gusts of conviction – passionate conviction. Ten years older than I, he was a graduate in English and history from University of British Columbia. He was a Clydeside Scot – with absolutely everything that implies. He had taught high school, and finished his university years by operating pari-mutual machines at racetracks. Abhorring pretence in any field, he was blatantly critical of fools – in academe or political life. I think his dearest heroes were Keir Hardie and J.B.S. Haldane. In appearance and manner he resembled no one more than Tommy Douglas – a bonnie wee fighter. For whatever reason, we took to each other instantly. Stewart was appointed lecturer in 1946 while finishing his doctoral thesis on the British Labour Party. Underhill was his thesis supervisor, although he consulted often with Donald McDougall, for whose lecturing he had much respect.

In the spring of 1947 Roger Graham and I passed our general PhD exams. We celebrated with Canadian champagne at Lowther, supported by the Reids and the Carelesses. I had just selected a thesis topic: 'James Shaver Woodsworth: From Social Gospel to Social Democracy, 1874–1921.' Roger had also chosen his, on Arthur Meighen. It was a noisy evening. Presiding, from a great distance, was W.C. Graham. Roger's father, Graham was principal of United College (now the University of Winnipeg), and was very soon to hire Stewart Reid and me. All our paths would intertwine across the next decade – and beyond.

Chester Martin had tried hard to veto my thesis topic. Because Woodsworth was only five years dead, the subject was scarcely historical. I've often wondered if this was the full reason for Martin's attack. In any event, Underhill rallied sufficient support and the topic was approved. Having finished the PhD requirements, save for the thesis, I was blithely innocent about the future. The country's universities were crammed with 'highly motivated' ex-service people, and a good many bottom-rung openings presented themselves. None of these was at Toronto. The University of Toronto, with a degree of confidence which appeared to others as arrogance, believed that its own graduates should serve an apprenticeship somewhere in the 'rags and ends of Confederation' before returning (if ever) to the promised land. Thus I narrowed the choices to three: Dalhousie, McMaster, and United College in Winnipeg. For two good reasons I chose Winnipeg.

Stewart Reid had already accepted an offer to become head of United's three-man history department. A.R.M. Lower, who was leaving United for Queen's, suggested my name for the junior position in the department. Had I known then the mind-boggling terrors of Manitoba's climate, I might well have chosen Hamilton or Halifax. But I didn't know, and the prospect of learning the trade in a department headed by Reid attracted me strongly. The fact that Winnipeg had been Woodsworth's home base, and the Manitoba archives housed much source material for my thesis, swung the decision. Principal Graham made the formal offer by phone from Winnipeg. When he asked my religious affiliation I replied, 'Anglican, but I only use it for filling out forms.' I imagined I was being disarmingly candid, but Graham took the flippancy in his stride and confirmed the appointment. A dedicated churchman and Old Testament scholar, Graham had taught for some years at the University of Chicago. He had taken on the thankless job of running the United Church college in 1938 – and I would be only one of many tribulations that he suffered in that cash-strapped school. My starting salary as assistant professor was $2700.

My sole 'teacher training' came as lecturer in a six-week Canadian history course that summer. Armed with my own student notes and diligently mining Creighton, J.B. Brebner, Lower, and McInnis, I kept about two lectures ahead of the unsuspecting crowd of teachers who sweltered with me in the Household Science Building on Bloor Street. Although extremely nervous, I was bolstered by a non-objective approach to history and recollection of the styles I had most admired. I also learned to roll with the punches. In the first lecture I advised the class against writing down everything I might say. As I spoke I watched three nuns in the front row scribbling furiously.

Winnipeg, even in its best autumn colours, was a shock. United College, set flatly at the corner of Portage and Good, compounded the horror of its bastard Romanesque lines with building blocks of very pale yellow. The few trees bordering its Portage front seemed undernourished imitations of Ontario elms. Had I, like Margaret Laurence or

J.S. Woodsworth, approached the college and the city from the West, all this might have been imposing. As it was, it took several years before I felt real warmth in what Millar MacLure was to call 'this God Damned whistle stop on the prairies.' Unlike MacLure, I learned quickly to suppress too-easy 'eastern' pejoratives.

The first visual tremors subsided when I recalled what I had learned about United's remarkable record. For seventeen years Arthur Lower had exiled his feisty historical scholarship there; his *Colony to Nation* (complete with three different spellings of Laurier's given name) appeared in the same year as we arrived. Arthur Phelps and Watson Kirkconnell had for many years bestowed academic kudos upon the dust-blown scene. Even Jack Pickersgill, God save the mark, had taught history there in the 1930s. Carleton Stanley was just beginning his teaching-in-retirement. And beyond these accomplishments, when United was Wesley College, lay its long association with the social gospel, prairie progressivism, and the CCF. Woodsworth had been 'Senior Stick' student in 1896, Salem Bland had taught at Wesley – and been fired in 1917 – and Stanley Knowles had studied theology there.

United was still a small college. In addition to university-level teaching, its theology department was the main western training centre for the United Church ministry, and it also offered profitable courses at the senior high school level. It was an odd mélange with a high friction potential – much higher than we could have imagined in the autumn of 1947. About 1500 students composed what we thought of as a promising liberal arts college loosely federated with the University of Manitoba, which counter-signed, as it were, United's BA degrees. I was soon to learn how turbulently opposed were the idealized and entrenched visions of United's proper role: the church's hope of Christian education; the social-stabilizer function cherished by the businessmen and lawyers on the church-controlled Board of Regents; the prairie radical tradition; and the liberal arts utopia we brought along in our Toronto baggage.

Stewart Reid and I bedded down for a few early September days in the echoing student dormitory. We had come ahead of our families, in search of affordable housing. Tryggvi Oleson, the only other member of the tiny history department, guided us. He had grown up in the Icelandic community of Glenboro. A Manitoba patriot, prominent in the Icelandic Association, he was intermittently engaged on a thesis in medieval history for Bertie Wilkinson. Short, bandy-legged, and rapidly balding, Tryg's puckish face was seldom without a warm glow. He was never without a pipe, which made his voice a growling, throat-clearing rumble. I knew how poor we would be when I watched Tryg use his charge card to buy two boxes of wooden matches at the Bay. With high good humour, however, he led us through street after street of houses we couldn't afford. I finally chose one on Montague, a few doors from Oleson's. Montague was in River Park, a still unfinished development at the south end of Osborne Street. Few of the young residents had laid sod, so the entire area sported straggling reaches of grey gravel streaked with gumbo and yellow clay. The only time I can remember Tryg being really touchy was when he proudly escorted me to the Assiniboine River, a block away. Viewing the dreadful vista of soggy banks and tangled scrub oak, I said it called to mind a painting of the battlefield at Mons.

A down payment of $1500 'bought' us number 458. A small stucco bungalow whose spruce frame was so green that the rafters crackled like rifle fire once the serious winter weather came upon us, it nevertheless saw many of the most convivial, stimulating evenings I can recall. But it was an awfully long way from Lowther Avenue. When Bev arrived with Christopher in mid-September, I shuddered, although I needn't have. She took it in her stride. She even said it was 'pretty.' And she prepared at once to reach out for new friends, to relish the excitement of a new life. Without her unfeigned interest in people, in friendship, I think Winnipeg would have defeated me – as some of its leading lights would try hard to do.

Bev and Tryg's wife, Elva, got along from the start. We quickly came to know a wonderful clutch of medical families. Ernest Sirluck's sister, Gladys Bruser, was married to one of the originators of an experimental doctor's cooperative, the Mall Medical Group on Memorial Boulevard. Quite coincidentally, one of David Bruser's colleagues at the Mall, Paul Green, was married to a Torontonian with whom we had mutual friends. Bertha Green and Gladys Bruser each entertained us as soon as we were settled in. Their group of mostly Jewish friends became ours also. By the time we were blown out of Winnipeg in 1959, those friends had become the principal reason for regret – beyond, even, the breakup of our hopelessly idealized vision of a liberal arts college.

5

For the first three years at United, Tryggvi Oleson, Stewart Reid, and I shared a large overheated office on the second floor. This was pretty chummy. The 'open concept' gave little privacy for talking with students, and lots of scope for our own conversation. My weekly teaching included nine lecture hours and four or five tutorials. I lectured in the European survey course, Canadian, and a wildly improbable History of the Americas. Course descriptions and examinations were arranged jointly with the historians at the University of Manitoba in Fort Garry, just south of the city – with which United was loosely federated. Kenneth Belton, a distinguished medievalist, headed the Fort Garry department, which included W.L. Morton, Richard Glover, and Stuart Webster. We all got along famously despite the competitive hostility of United's dean of arts and a sense of insecurity that afflicted quite a few of our colleagues in other departments. We three suffered from no such doubts.

Olafur T. Anderson, our dean, we quickly identified as the outward and visible sign of a serious frailty in United's self-perception. A native of Gimli, Anderson was a heavy man who had no doubts about his combative powers. The very model of a modern sergeant-major, he brought to his teaching of mathematics the virtues of the parade square. Through formulaic drilling of his classes he achieved high exam success rates, and expected no less from others. His loyalty to the college as an institution was exactly what was later to be found wanting in Harry Crowe. That pride and loyalty led him to demand faculty discipline of a sort unimaginable – save by a willing suspension of disbelief. He required the taking of attendance in every lecture. Nine times a week I was supposed to call the roll in classes of up to sixty-five. By the end of the first year I simply stopped doing it. Unfortunately, I never asked Arthur Lower what he had done about this duty – but I can make a good guess. My close friend Gerald Prodrick fared less well. He came to teach economics in 1947. Halfway through the year, OT noticed that Prodrick's roll-call records were spotty. He also recognized a sensitive target and barracked him so mercilessly that Gerry left at the end of the year. Prodrick, after a short stint at the World Bank, moved into library science and a fulfilling career at the University of Western Ontario.

Our own battles with Anderson, and lesser skirmishes with his docile faculty minions, continued. Indeed, they set the scene for the ultimate showdown in 1958–9. Anderson's anti-intellectual antics climaxed each spring when he convened his troops in the dismal varnish-smelling board room to review final examination results. Here was naked competition. In each course he compared the failure rate of United's students with that of the Fort Garry students – all of whom wrote exams that were set and marked jointly. Lecturers whose failure rates were higher than those at the university could look forward to discussing the problem in OT's office. Anderson, in fact, expected us all to adopt his drill-master's view of good teaching, and also his unquestioning loyalty to the college.

Anderson epitomized an understandable, nostalgic view of United, a prairie church college deeply rooted in the community and instinctively resentful of eastern notions about higher education. We felt that OT had not been unhappy to see people like Lower and Phelps leave for Ontario, where they belonged. He felt secure in the compliant teachers such as A.R. Cragg, who dictated his lessons in psychology (students called it Craggology), or Victor Leathers in French: I always regretted that Leathers (who looked like a down-at-heel Hercule Poirot) never invited us to view his art collection, which, I was told, consisted largely of photoreproductions from *Life* magazine. David Owen, the one-man philosophy department, expressed his unquestioning fealty to higher authority on every possible occasion. These were Anderson's NCOs. Together with the other ranks they were frequently called upon to beat back high-handed introduction of Toronto notions, such as regular tutorial groups or emphasis on critical thought as opposed to systematic regurgitation of prescribed material – the sure route to low failure rates.

In 1949 Millar MacLure joined the faculty as chair of the English department. He must have appeared to OT as yet another, and serious, threat to the prairie-Rotarian conception of the college. Millar looked as if he could model for a *fin de siècle* cartoon of 'the aesthete.' Tall, thin, and elegant, he delighted in drawling out laconic observations on the lack of civilization he noticed all about him. He had no intention of gracing the Red River valley a moment longer than necessary. But for three years he lectured brilliantly on English literature, complementing Carleton Stanley's learned and wide-ranging performances. MacLure's special field was the seventeenth century; he had just finished a thesis on John Donne's sermons. He and Stewart Reid did not hit it off very well. Stewart found Millar too mannered; MacLure thought Reid too intelligently matter of fact. But Reid's fine lectures on the English Civil War meshed well with what was on offer from MacLure. There were some fortunate students in those years at United.

MacLure and Stanley left at the same time – MacLure for Toronto, Stanley for final retirement. Stanley's retirement party – a tea, with hardback chairs lining each wall of an assertively barren room – I take as the starting point for a brief elaboration of a cultural rift more subtle, deeper even, than that across which we and OT's crowd glared at each other. Looking once more into that chasm I find it painful; I know, however, that it was there and that this separation made it virtually impossible to prevent catastrophe in 1958–9. A hundred matters, each insignificant in itself, dug deeper each year.

One such matter was Charlie Pye. He had been the college 'engineer' since 1920 – when he was appointed after promising to save money on the heating bill. He made good on his pledge by stuffing the huge old furnace with any discarded combustible he could lay hands on. On several occasions that building had to be emptied because dense acrid smoke from old tires filled every corridor up to the men's residence on the third floor. Following one such hubbub the registrar, Wesley D.G. Runions, posted notices: 'In the event of fire, evacuate out the window.' Variations of this injunction circulated among us for some time. Elizabeth Morrison, the dean of women, saw another splendid side of Pye's no-nonsense personality. The women's residence was connected to the main building by a long, dimly lit tunnel: a too-convenient trysting spot. Weary of encountering smoochers in the shadows, Morrison suggested to Pye that he install adequate lighting in the tunnel. Ever alert to cost-cutting, Pye put forth an alternative: 'Whenever you catch two of them, put your foot on the boy's back and call for help.' Betty took it in her stride: 'Mr. Pye, it's far too cold in that tunnel to take your coat off, let alone what you're suggesting.' And Charlie was a great mingler at every college occasion. At Stanley's farewell tea, after the presentation of a cup and saucer, he slapped Carleton soundly on the back, calling out in full voice: 'Well, so long, old sport.' Amusing, but it was cumulative.

Lingering Methodist social strictures seemed both oppressive and hypocritical. No smoking at faculty wives' meetings; no alcohol at any faculty occasion. The incubus of no-frills rectitude and loyalty clung tightly despite inexorable changes. On one Sunday each year in the city's United churches, ministers gave sermons on the value of higher education. Faculty and senior students were expected to attend, one group to each church. The service over, each 'volunteer' received a list of about twenty church members. We then called at each listed household to solicit contributions for the church college. I did this twice. The second time, in Kildonan, most of the homes I visited seemed to merit contributions more than did the college. It was easier for me to quit this gruesome duty than for the students. On education Sundays, Wesley Runions toured the men's residence to rouse slumbering delinquents to their religious obligation.

The veil over this happy, abstemious family was rent in a quite startling manner shortly after the arrival of Principal Graham's successor in 1955. Wilfred and Eileen Lockhart decided to start off on the right foot by entertaining a mixed group of faculty and board members in their home. Eileen quite definitely presided, referring to her husband at one point as 'the boss.' Fruit punch and coffee flowed freely. Senator J.T. Haig (who had been on the Wesley-United Board of Regents since 1906 and was its chairman) instructed me in the virtues of hard work, institutional loyalty, and care with the pennies. We and the Reids were the last faculty members to leave. As Mrs Lockhart closed the door, Stewart heard her call out to her remaining guests, 'Good, now we can have a drink.'

Our daughter, Allison, was born in August 1948 – and this was the only full summer we spent in Winnipeg. Ninety-degree weather and swirling city dust nearly matched the shocking grip of winter's 'dry cold.' But the satisfaction from teaching and research, together with an 'integrative' social life, took the edge off discontent. It was all quite contrapuntal. For the first couple of years a great many of the students were veterans. They brought a certain punchiness to class, a minimal regard for deference. In the first January I took to wearing an ancient ankle-length coonskin coat, topped off with bearskin hat and gauntlets. Dogs used to bark at my heels as I ran for the rickety wooden structure at the end of Osborne Street. The vets called me 'the Coat.'

But I blessed the family friends who had sent me the outfit from their own chilly venue in the Ottawa valley. Most of the vets were my age or older. We frequently met for after-class talk fests in Tony's, the basement snack room not far from Pye's three thumping boilers. One day, at the end of term, a rather knowing student chimed in: 'What are your politics? We've been trying to figure that out and I've bet you're a Liberal.' Since I had recently been lecturing on the Winnipeg General Strike of 1919 and had certainly not deliberately dissembled, I was puzzled. I didn't spell it out for the provocateur because I felt fairly sure he knew the answer.

Whatever philosophy of history I brought to those early lectures was pretty nebulous. I hope I showed an interest in how things had really happened. As to why they happened, I walked up close to Marx and then walked away. I pronounced the 1919 strike the most obvious case of class war in Canadian history: a result of unrestrained industrial capitalism. But I couldn't take the next step – the interpretation of the strike as failed revolution, as a lost opportunity. Canada's Marxists – later historians as well as some half-baked Socialist Party of Canada members at the time – painted the strike as inevitable and revolutionary in nature. And it followed that all measures of reform, all attempts to use parliamentary democracy to move steadily towards greater social justice, would simply dissipate the workers' consciousness of class. I was repelled by this 'impossibilist' argument, especially by the inevitability that informed the Marxist dialectic. All I had absorbed as an eavesdropper at Blythwood Road, in reading the history of British and European socialism, and in tangling with the idea of progress impelled me to reject both monocausalism and inevitability.

As I pieced together Woodsworth's odyssey, I could scarcely miss the shining significance of the individual actor in history: a child of his age, but no automaton dangling from the determining 'means of production.' I did err in glossing over some frailties in Woodsworth. He was a bit vain, more than a bit patriarchal, and, by today's judgment, a racist (although he modified sharply his early acceptance of Anglo-Saxon superiority as he looked ever more closely at the immigrant contribution and potential). He was, perhaps, too sure he was right. But he was no believer in absolutes. He accepted the influential role of ideas, of a moral legacy – but not any determining force of environment or economic organization. He could, and did, pillory capitalism and imperialism as the causes of class exploitation and war. But in his own life – in his letters, speeches, tireless organizing, and penultimate stand in the special war session of the Commons in 1939 – he made very clear that individual convictions need not be determined by material influences.

While Woodsworth eschewed exact and mystical creeds, he remained profoundly religious. This bothered me. Religious faith, let alone actual church-going, had been openly rejected by my parents – along with the British monarchy. But if not faith, where did one locate the driving forces? I settled for what J.S. Mill, borrowing from the French philosophers, called *bienfaisance*. Mill argued that the rationalist, utilitarian notion that 'the greatest good of the greatest number' is achieved when each person preserves his best self-interest needed further elucidation. To this original utilitarianism Mill added a codicil. As society progresses, people expand their definition of self-interest to include the well-being of others. This revised utilitarianism, I thought, explained the evolutionary nature of British, and therefore, Canadian socialism. Its superficiality became apparent to me as I revised lectures in North American history and plunged into a course in Europe since 1815. Mill's later utilitarianism, as a theory of historical progress, or just of history, didn't carry one far in dealing with Napoleon, Bismarck, Stalin, Hitler, or Senator Joseph McCarthy. It didn't really stand up well as explication for Woodsworth. By the mid-1950s I would reject it almost entirely.

Some other notions of historical causation, particularly the role of 'determinance,' seemed to need much more thought than I had given them previously. In the late 1930s and 1940s, for example, 'environmentalism' very nearly dominated the writing of American and Canadian history. Originating with the American Frederick Jackson Turner, the 'frontier thesis' purported to explain the course of American political, social, and economic history. An uninterrupted westward-moving frontier developed notions of individualism and democracy which lie at the centre of the American experience. The frontier also created sectional interests that led to the recurring political battles between the urban East and the small-town farming West. This simplistic determinism has, of course, been replaced by other 'determinist' interpretations. At the time, however, it was eagerly appropriated by many Canadian historians to explain the main lines of our own political history – from the 1837 troubles to the progressive movement, and even the CCF. As I dug into the sources on Woodsworth, I saw more and more rents in the fabric of this monocausalism.

To begin with, the Canadian and American frontiers had always been quite different: not only the differences in geography (a thousand miles of Precambrian rock between the 'East' and the 'West' in Canada, for example) but the obvious roles played by ideas, by constitutional traditions, by divergent views of the relationship between order and liberty, and by quite distinct conceptions of democracy, egalitarianism, and the importance of continuity. Indeed, I concluded that the two 'frontier experiences' were the products of their points of origin more than they were the shapers of the two nations.

Pondering the shortcomings of monocausal history – Marxist, frontierist, and other – I thought I saw a link between single-cause determinism and the frequent, too-easy use of 'inevitability' in much historical writing. How often even the most celebrated historians used this crutch! After various 'certain points' (take your choice), the English Civil War and the French, American, and Russian revolutions were all 'inevitable.' So, too, were the American Civil War, the Canadian Rebellions, and, above all, the 1914 war. Quite suddenly, historical inevitability became an overriding concern for me. Not a problem easily resolved, it was obviously closely related to other questions, such as the uses of history, the extent to which actors in history are free agents – and thus back to 'progress' and motivation.

Teaching, I discovered, goads one to examine one's basic assumptions much more forcibly than does mere study. As I revised a lecture on the Reformation, I realized that I was gliding over Luther and Calvin without really thinking about their startling propositions; not an uncommon experience in survey courses. Erasmus seemed to deal pretty satisfactorily with free will, but, in doing so he pilloried predestination. So what did I really think about Calvin? I read *The Institutes of the Christian Religion* and discovered that the French lawyer was a good deal more rigorous about God's consigning every person, at birth, to election (salvation) or damnation (hell). No person was free to choose evil (if of the elect) or good (if of the damned). Moreover, predestination was not just a matter of God's standing outside time and thus having foreknowledge of what everyone would do and where each would end up. He made an 'inscrutable judgment' on each person. And to nail down this preposterous proposition, Calvin wrote that even to suggest that God's foreknowledge, rather than an actual judgment, explained predestination was to reveal that one was of the damned, not the elect. Well, each time I dealt with the Reformation I asked those who considered themselves to be Calvinist to raise their hands; a nasty but galvanizing trick. I next asked whether any of their confessors thought they might be of the damned. None. I then asked, after explaining 'foreknowledge,' whether they accepted that this was the proper explanation of predestination. Every single one.

This dalliance with theology confirmed, for the time being, my rather noisy agnosticism. But it also glued my attention to the apparently careless use of secular inevitability by so many historians, particularly the frequent 'nearly inevitable.' I concluded that to present anything as inevitable made everything inevitable – unless the chain of cause and effect could be broken. Why, then, study history? Beyond the philosophical conundrum, I sensed that inevitability, as interpretation, was not only an intellectual cop-out but often served a political purpose. In the case of American history, which I was delving into with growing enthusiasm, the inevitability of the Civil War, for example, not only relieved historians from assessment of blame but served as a political aid in bandaging the long-festering wounds of that conflict. Even more 'useful' was the concept of America as inevitably 'liberal.' Developed in the 1950s by the 'consensus historians' (a euphemism for conservative), this ludicrous concept (with variations) embraced the notion that John Locke's political philosophy so dominated American thought in the late eighteenth century that it became frozen as the *only* possible basis of political life in the United States.

The many problems raised by the consensus historians became a focal point for me in the 1960s and 1970s. In the meantime I toyed with two particular aspects of determinism: each suggested the political uses of history. In the United States, Louis Hartz announced that socialism could never find a legitimate role in that country because of the inevitable dominance of Lockean liberalism (read democratic capitalism). Without endorsing all of Hartz's tortuous explications, Richard Hofstadter brought his powerful artillery to support Hartz's conclusion, if not all its preliminaries. Hofstadter finally summed up his argument thus: 'In the U.S., third parties, like bees, having stung, must die.' Pervading virtually all American history and political science textbooks, this pronouncement underpinned the effective 'doctrine of the lost vote': vote for a socialist and you lose your vote. I judged this to be a convincing instance of a historical interpretation itself becoming a political factor.

A second aspect of the inevitabilist consensus orthodoxy was that its proponents staked an exclusive claim to objectivity. I had early on begun to suspect that objectivity was an illusory notion. I now became pretty sure that whenever a historian paraded his work as completely objective, he was probably a defender of the status quo – and probably an apostle of inevitability to boot. About this time I read a *New States-man* review of H.N. Brailsford's biography of Harold Laski. Brailsford reported that Laski used to begin each course by announcing: 'I am a socialist. From time to time I will say things with which you disagree. If you wish, come to my office and I'll show you where you're wrong.' I thought this was exactly right. Although I never put it quite so provocatively, I have always made perfectly clear my position on objectivity: it is neither possible nor desirable. Forgive me for this lengthy digression; it could and maybe should have been longer. I'll return to its subject matter later.

Whether we were to have a long stay at United or not, I felt compelled to finish my thesis as quickly as possible. Each day, either between lectures or at the end of the afternoon, I shivered the short distance from the college to the archives in the Legislative Buildings. It seemed always to be winter. The broad stretch of Memorial Boulevard and the treeless lawns on which the 'Golden Boy' looked down from his unbelievable perch on top of the legislature's copper dome were a kind of target for the vicious gales from the Arctic. Wrapped in my furs, I nevertheless felt fearful of breathing too deeply. At 30 or 40 degrees below zero the scene was nearly always fascinating. Frequently, moisture in the air was frozen into tiny crystals. Through this ice fog the sun's long rays shimmered in frigid beauty. Entering the exotic, polished stone halls, I spent the first few minutes of each visit pressed tight against one of the thumping radiators.

During the winter of 1949 I often joined W.L. Morton, from the Fort Garry campus, for coffee breaks. He was coincidentally checking quotations and footnotes against primary sources for *The Progressive Party in Canada*. Bill was a heavy-set man, kindly of eye and thorough in his scholarship. A native of Manitoba, he always seemed to me a bit exotic as a westerner. A tweedy pipe-smoker, he spoke with precision and a memory of Oxford. Stewart Reid, sniffing affectation, remarked during one academic showdown that Bill 'fought like an enraged mouse.' Stewart was unfair in this respect. When 'high noon' rolled up at United, Morton gave strong and public support to academic and personal freedom. I was surprised to find that Bill, the leading historian of prairie populism, was not only conservative but also Conservative. Perhaps my surprise sprang partly from still not recognizing my own conservatism. It seems to me that the study of history brings out the conservative in most people. Even the most radical profess to discover values that have been lost and need recovering, conserving.

When Morton's *Progressive Party* came out in 1950, I reviewed it for the *Canadian Forum*. Lauding it for its thoroughness, I couldn't resist pointing out that the book's title belied its central thesis. In chapter after chapter Morton documented the refusal of the Progressives to form a political party. He quite rightly argued that devotion to constituency independence was a principal reason for their disappearance. When my review appeared, Bill told me without rancour that the publisher had insisted that 'party' rather than 'movement' would be more marketable. He was more amused than was another, closer friend, one of whose books I reviewed in the mid-1960s. In the midst of some positive remarks, I made one modest criticism. Our relationship fell into chilly indifference for several years. I have since declined several book review requests.

By the end of 1948 I had covered all the Manitoba archival material on Woodsworth's career to 1921, the year he was elected to represent Centre Winnipeg in Ottawa. In addition to reading the Winnipeg dailies and labour press, I had talked to the surviving members of the 1919 strike and mined the papers and memoirs of many of Woodsworth's contemporaries – including the unsorted papers of John W. Dafoe. I was shaken by the Dafoe record. Touted by Frank Underhill as Canada's best newspaper editor, Dafoe had thrown his *Free Press* unquestioningly behind the highly organized businessmen of Winnipeg in 1919. It was not surprising that Dafoe should see eye to eye with his Sifton benefactors. It was more than a little disturbing to find him out in irresponsible misrepresentation. Although all the strike leaders were either British or Canadian, the *Free Press* referred to them variously as 'bohunks,' 'aliens,' and 'foreigners' and joined the other Winnipeg papers in the cry: 'Deport the aliens.' The *Free Press* had, in short, joined a conspiracy to suppress what I had concluded was a straightforward, non-violent attempt to secure higher wages and the right to collective bargaining. I had documented the closely meshed class action by which all three levels of government synchronized the campaign to smear the strike as revolutionary and thus to crush it with police and army. The research had deepened my commitment to democratic 'socialism' and also to pursuing further the 'truth' about Canadian society. When I glanced through the post-1921 Dafoe papers, I was not surprised to find that he suspected that David Lewis was a communist. But time smoothes out everything; Dafoe's entry in the *Canadian Encyclopedia* perceives 'a man of the centre, he always denounced extremes of the left and right.' Oh?

The 'man of the centre,' I knew full well, was Woodsworth, not Dafoe, nor any of the well-heeled members of the Citizens' Committee of a Thousand who orchestrated the events leading to successful use of state violence. I had followed JS through the private turmoil revealed in his diaries, letters and actions, to his conclusion about the 'objectivity' that leads to support of the status quo. He early identified the 'sin of indifference': the great 'sin of the middle class,' the sin that led Dafoe and his fellow editors to weep over inconveniences suffered by 'innocent bystanders.' Woodsworth had resigned from *that* middle class: from its sanctimonious compact with war and empire, profits and privilege. He had lived in the midst of poverty. He knew that to fight democratically for social justice *was* to be a man of the centre: the centre between unbridled exploitation and violent revolution.

While I was drafting the first thesis chapters, I also thought a good deal about how to make our Winnipeg experience as brief as possible. No easy answer appeared, but I pursued two obvious longer-term 'solutions.' The first was assuredly desperate. I wrote to fourteen American universities in January 1949. All the replies were courteous; some offered dim future possibilities. Paul Knapland wrote from Wisconsin: 'We shall, however, keep your application on file, and in case a vacancy for which you are trained occurs, we shall give very careful attention to your candidacy.' By the end of January I knew any flight from Winnipeg would not be southward. A year later Senator Joseph McCarthy fired his first big cannonade in Wheeling, West Virginia, and very shortly I was actually pleased with my sheaf of rejections.

My second approach produced a surprisingly quick result. I took three weeks off thesis drafting to write an article analysing the 1919 strike, Woodsworth's role in that struggle, and his political victory in the 1921 federal election. Without much confidence, I sent one copy to my father and one to Underhill. Dad made helpful suggestions about style; his own model remained Arnold Bennett and he reminded me, once again, that the adjective is the enemy of the noun. Frank's reply was of the kind to which I had become accustomed – very few specific comments, but loaded with encouragement: 'The more I think of your article, the more I admire the skill with which you manage to give the labour interpretation of the Winnipeg Strike without offending other people's prejudices.' Considering that Frank was then deeply suspicious of union leaders in general, this guarded approval was all I needed. I shot the article off to the *Canadian Historical Review*, which printed it in June 1949 as 'J.S. Woodsworth and a Political Party for

Labour.' Joy unbounded, but a lot of publishing was still needed to prevent our perishing on the prairies.

In the spring of 1949, not long after the Red and Assiniboine rivers had jostled their ice jams into Lake Winnipeg, we set off for the East. We took the Burlington Zephyr to Chicago, where we visited with the Sirlucks. Ernest had joined the English department at the University of Chicago in 1947. My parents had not taken well to the simultaneous departure from Toronto of Lesley and me, so we spent much time discussing their plight, especially their selling the Cedarhurst cottage and contemplated sale of Blythwood. Their shared depression seemed almost self-flagellation. I suspect that this emotional turmoil was what led to Dad's coronary attack and early retirement from McKim's at the end of 1950. I planned to spend the summer breaking the back of the thesis. In other circumstances we would have settled in at Cedarhurst, but, as it was, we rented a tiny bungalow in north Toronto. Living in town for the summer, although I hate city summers, was what I should have arranged to do even had Cedarhurst been available. I spent profitable hours in the United Church archives and in long conversations with C.B. Sissons and, especially, Lucy Woodsworth.

JS's widow lived with her sister-in-law in modest quarters on Bain Avenue. A strong-featured, soft-spoken woman, Lucy Staples intimidated me as much by her penetrating, humorous gaze as by what I came to know about her high intelligence and extraordinary life of sacrifice. I regret, now, that she doesn't appear much more prominently in *A Prophet in Politics*. More intellectually disciplined than her husband, she quite deliberately chose the role of nurturing both him and their children. I think she knew that intellect is not enough. Thus she held things together, making sure that her husband's fiery commitment should not be dampened by mundane domestic matters. On the few occasions when she visited us she insisted on reading to Allison and Christopher – and drawing out the moral implications from their children's books. And she could take risks – as when she lent me JS's diaries, letters, and scrapbooks. I'm not sure I would do the same for a thirty-year-old in search of a PhD.

In the church archives I had to read the record of William Ivens's 'heresy trial.' Ivens was expelled from the ministry in 1918 for preaching the social gospel and too active support of labour unions. He was one of the leaders arrested when the general strike was crushed in 1919, and I had been particularly pleased when I secured his papers for the United College library in the early autumn of 1949. The unsorted collection was in several cardboard cartons. In the library stacks one unusually hot September afternoon I noticed that the door of the back entrance was held open by one of these cartons. Margaret Graham, librarian and the principal's niece, had placed it there in disregard of my earnest appeal to keep the papers completely secure. A depressing start to another long winter. But there is nothing like a marathon to make time whistle past. By mid-April I had completed the thesis and mailed it off to Toronto.

On top of the usual trepidation, I knew that Frank Underhill had been seriously ill during the winter – and had been unable to read closely the draft chapters I had been sending him seriatim. When Ralph Flenley, then head of the Toronto department, wrote in March that Frank would not be able to read the final two chapters soon enough to meet the time requirements for an exam on 23 May 1950, I nearly panicked. Flenley wrote: 'Underhill and I discussed the question of the last two chapters and he thinks you had better put these in their final form without their having been read here. I agree.' I would be flying blind. I was trying to anticipate the possible lines of questioning when I received the penultimate assault on my nerves. The membership of the examining committee read like a University of Toronto who's who. The chairman would be Northrop Frye. The members: Chester Martin, Frank Underhill, George Brown, Donald Creighton (the possibilities here seemed horrendous), S.D. Clark, Edgar McInnis, Ralph Flenley, Maurice Careless, and Alex Brady. A composite guillotine, it seemed to me.

Suppressing our shared anxiety, Bev and I prepared for the second of our many summer trips east. We were more than ready. The winter had seen a near tragedy. In February, Allison, at eighteen months of age, was stricken with virus croup. As her trachea narrowed, each breath sounding like a high-pitched foghorn, her doctor prescribed but one treatment: bed, in a steam-filled room. Bev and I took turns each night keeping watch on the boiling kettle. One thesis chapter, as a result, emerged permanently wrinkled. At 2 o'clock one morning Allison began to turn blue and the doctor, having previously warned that, above all, she should not be in cold air, said, 'take her to the emergency at Misericordia.' When I took her out to the ambulance, it was minus 35 degrees Fahrenheit. At the hospital, a surgeon who looked about seventeen advised an operation to open her trachea – which was on the point of closing completely. The success rate, he told me, was about 50 per cent. I have had pleasanter nights.

After several weeks in hospital while the virus burned itself out, we brought Allison home and looked hard at the future. Could we face more Winnipeg winters, more of OT, Pye, and their unlovely cohorts? The answer was no – despite our attachment to a widening group of friends in the West. So we put our bungalow on the market. Almost at once a retired United Church minister bought it. I should have known better. When we asked him to delay occupancy until 1 May, he refused. So we stored our furniture and, for several weeks, lived in the Greystone Arms – an elegant mansion built by the man who had did-dled the Manitoba government for a lot of money during construction of the Legislative Buildings. The too-eventful academic year closed with a bang – and a bit of poetic justice. As we were preparing to drive east on 2 May – in a seven-year-old Plymouth my father had donated – mighty ice jams clogged the Assiniboine and the Red in the heart of Winnipeg. As the water rose, it washed over the Pembina highway. We drove out of Manitoba by way of Fort Frances. Even there a reluctant spring had pushed the Rainy River across the highway as we splashed our way into Minnesota. When we finally reached Toronto, a letter informed us that the great Winnipeg flood had pushed muddy water over the ground-floor level of the Montague bungalow – which its new owner had been so anxious to occupy. Our 'decision' about Winnipeg had been endorsed from on high.

6

Smell has much to do with a sense of place. Dry prairie air fails to carry the wonderful aromas of spring and summer. Each time we came east and drew in the moist air of the Great Lakes, perfumed and slightly hazy, we felt easier, at home. Sometimes we tried to resist the comparison – but always failed.

In Toronto we stayed several weeks at Blythwood before renting a second-floor apartment in an old house on Cottingham Street for the summer. In the lilac-filled morning of 25 May I made my way to the place of execution – a dignified mansion that housed the graduate school on Hoskin Avenue, now the site of Massey College. I recall only one of the endless questions bowled at me down a very long table: S.D. Clark's. He wondered if I had considered a Freudian interpretation of Woodsworth. I later learned that this is the sort of thing to expect from 'extradepartmental' examiners. At the time, sweaty with fear, I toyed with possible answers. I settled for the best one: no. The ordeal was ended, save for fifteen finger-twisting minutes on a hard chair in the hall awaiting the verdict, which was 'OK.'

At lunch, after the exam, Frank Underhill told me to expect a call from the departmental chairman, Ralph Flenley. Too good to be true. Yet Ralph did phone and we arranged to meet for lunch in Hart House the next day. What followed, I still do not really believe. I forgot the arrangement – until late in the afternoon. I called Flenley to apologize. He received the apology frigidly and signed off with the remark: 'Perhaps some other time.' And so, I thought, back to Winnipeg.

Still reluctant to accept the verdict – clearly my own fault – I plunged into another round of applications. Fourteen more American universities put my letters on file. But at the Learned Societies' meetings in

Kingston I met George Spragge, and this led soon to a cliff-hanging career decision. Spragge, who had been one of my masters at Upper Canada College, was now in charge of the Ontario Archives. He invited me to become his assistant. I asked for time to mull over his offer and, just at that point, received a letter from United. Principal Graham was pleased to tell me that my salary would soar from $3000 to $3200. 'This,' he wrote, 'will be a measure of recognition for your achievement of the Ph.D. degree and will make clear your status as second man in the Department.'

Fortunately, Spragge was out of town; but silently I had said yes. We actually signed an offer to purchase a charming house in rolling country about 10 miles north of the city. That night Bev read my mind and said: 'You don't really want to leave teaching.' Next morning, we cancelled the purchase offer and, with extreme luck, retrieved our small deposit.

During the summer I began the research that would lead to a full biography of Woodsworth – the thesis having carried him only to his first election in 1921. We made several junkets north to pine-and-rock country and also day excursions to the Toronto islands – grieving slightly over the disappearance of Nitschevo and many of its handsome companions. I felt nostalgia, but no disapproval. A good balance was being achieved among yacht clubs, acres of parkland, and a small community of unpretentious homes.

The furore of the exam and nerve-wracking decisions already a memory, in late August I unloaded in print some of the nagging doubts I felt about the early years of the Cold War. NATO was a fact. China had 'fallen' and would henceforth be known as Red China. In June 1950 the United States jumped the UN gun and the Korean War was under way. The rhetoric of Reinhold Niebuhr and of the McCarthyites was spilling over into Canada: it was but feebly countered, even by the CCF. The children of light were bidden to roll back the children of darkness. Above all, the West was torpedoing every effort to control (let alone abolish) atomic weapons. An unthinkable war of annihilation (possibly mutual) seemed more and more likely. I felt a deep fear that we had committed ourselves to a knee-jerk response to the requirements of what Frank Underhill called 'our American century.'

Because I can now see the article ['The CCF Failure in Foreign Policy' – I used the pseudonym S.W. Bradford for some reason I can't recall] published in the *Canadian Forum* in September 1950 as the distinct beginning of my unbroken fascination with American history and with

Canadian-American relations, I must say a little more about it. When I wrote the article I felt we were in the midst of a dangerous resurgence of the imperial motif in America. The basic American expansionist impulse had always run in tandem with both populism and progressivism. At the same time, progressives, socialists, and pacifists in the United States provided by far the best critical analysis of American society, and especially of its foreign policy. Canadian socialists in the CCF seemed indifferent to the threat of American domination, clearly perceived by Americans on the left, not only of Canada but of the West's response to the Soviet Union. It seemed clear to me that we were relapsing into a second colonial period – so soon after emerging from the first. Worse, the new American imperialism relied ever more blatantly on military superiority. Atomic weapons technology would be held in trust and feverishly 'improved' by the West – even though the jealously guarded atomic monopoly was already broken. Harry Truman, Dean Acheson, and others had achieved in NATO and the Pan American Union the foundations of a military alliance system to confront (and, as we now know, roll back) the Soviet empire. The Open Door policy, first enunciated after the Spanish-American War as justification for demanding free entry to every country for American trade and investment, came to full life again in the Marshall Plan. For all its generosity, that plan excluded command economies; it was the economic-ideological counterpart of the military expression of George Kennan's containment and Truman's roll-back policies.

In my article I referred to a dispassionate report by the American Friends' Service Committee which stressed the need for realism in the confrontation between the two imperial powers, strengthening the United Nations, and seeking ways to cooperate in alleviating postwar economic distress – especially by permitting East-West trade in Europe. I also mentioned proposals by British and French socialists for a neutralist 'third force' positioned between the two imperial combatants which would promote aid rather than arms, and which would recognize that communist influence was nourished by social-economic conditions and by repression of independence movements in Europe's Asian and African colonies. I stressed that we were now called upon to support the world's most reactionary regimes: Chiang Kai-shek in Formosa, Syngman Rhee in South Korea, the French in Indo-China, and many others. I quoted the New York Times (March 1950) and the Herald Tribune (November 1949) on Rhee's plans to reunite Korea by force. Nowhere in the article did I imply that communism was not to be resisted; rather, that an atomic monopoly, military alliances, and support of suppressive regimes was not the best way to counter its spread.

Frank Underhill reacted violently. He had once told my mother that too often I thought with my heart; in the following issue of the *Forum* he let me have it with both barrels, and very much from the heart. He opened by saying that 'if one admits the article's sincerity, one has to add that it persistently beclouded most of the real issues.' He warned 'Mr. Bradford' (having found out who he was) 'to consider the kind of company he is getting into ... the French-Canadian nationalists ... and the Labour-Progressive party with their fellow-travelers.' Enjoying his new role as America's man in Toronto, he chided 'our Canadian Communists' for their 'tender solicitude for the British connection.' In a splendid side swipe, he added that 'they'll be recruiting an Allan Mac-Nab–John A. Macdonald international brigade one of these days to fight against the American Franco in Washington. And Mr Bradford had better watch out or they'll be wanting him to join it. They would, I suppose, put him in a special scout company, to be raised mainly from among Canadian historians, with Captain Lower and Lieutenant [!] Creighton in charge.' He then elaborated the already familiar Cold Warrior thesis: there was no possibility of pursuing the policy I had suggested 'because Russian policy has forced a polarization of world politics into two armed camps ... The communists have shown that there is no limit to their ambition short of world domination and that they think their ambition is realizable because of our weakness ... Until the threat of Soviet totalitarianism has been removed, freedom is a more fundamental issue in our world than socialism.'

As I read Underhill's passionate piece I recalled a lunchtime conversation we had had just two weeks previously. He called off our warm discussion with the remark, 'Just put it down to hardening of the arteries!' Well, it wasn't that; the battle would rage throughout the 1950s and 1960s. That it never affected our friendship, however, was shown in Underhill's letters to me during the academic freedom crisis at United College, and again when the Woodsworth biography appeared in 1959.

Houses have played a large part in our lives. Except for the Montague bungalow, we have always chosen large ones, slightly beyond the reach of my unassisted salary. This risky approach has had several advantages: large living and dining rooms have given Bev scope for the entertaining she loves and excels at; five bedrooms give scope for children and frequent guests; the charm of an older house refreshes the spirit; and I get the seclusion of a study-cum-studio. The latter has always been necessary – principally as a base for writing, not only academic but also modestly remunerative pieces for magazines, newspapers, and radio. A personal loan from Bev's grandmother plus two mortgages, with which we began again in Winnipeg in September 1950, made me more than ready to engage in extracurricular activity. The abysmal salary scale at United was an added spur. So, after a brief, intensive survey of Winnipeg real estate, we settled on a three-storey, brown-shingled house at 739 Macmillan Avenue in Crescentwood. That the Red River gumbo had caused it to heave about a bit was of little concern – it was big and quite handsome. Besides, all its neighbours tilted one way or another also, as if some monster hand had plopped them down at random. Over the next eight years, '739' seemed almost an active agent in our deepening attachment to Winnipeg and even United.

Retrospect gives the illusion of pattern. Even resisting the illusion, I see 1950 as decisive, as very much determining its successors. While I continued to explore ways of escaping, I also took more seriously the potential that was still in United. Teaching brought intense pleasure – not least because of the very high quality of many of the students. In Toronto I had been gratified to learn that recommendations from United's history department were accepted pretty much without question. And in 1950 Harry Sherman Crowe joined our department, replacing Tryg Oleson.

Harry told me that the 'Sherman' marked a convoluted descent from the Northern general who scorched Georgia. Apochryphal or not, the two had much in common. Harry immersed himself in whatever problem he faced – especially if he sensed a risk or if he could challenge either pretension or authority abused. Not uninterested in generalization, he was attracted more by people and facts. He sought the keys to history, politics, and university life in personality and character more than in circumstance. His political heroes were Franklin Roosevelt and Tommy Douglas. Not surprisingly, he organized his lectures around leaders and revealing anecdotes. In Tony's basement hideaway he regularly attracted as large a group of students as his cubicle-of-the-day could accommodate. Deliberate and emphatic, Harry always fixed with a piercing eye the person whose views he sought to correct. A political junky, his knowledge of the American electoral map was as exhaustive as his detailed statistics of Canadian constituencies at all three levels. He never disguised his commitment to unionism, the

CCF, or the puncturing of pomposity. By nature he was a general – in love with strategy and tactics.

The college old guard, almost from the time of his appointment, viewed Harry with caution – as if they were preparing the later charge that he was a born 'troublemaker.' Many, of course, were probably jealous. As an undergraduate at United, Harry had been a leader in the Student Council and Senior Stick. In France he had won the Military Cross for his bravery in leading a perilous raid. At the end of the war, he had completed his honours degree and won a University of Manitoba gold medal. He then took an MA at Toronto and, at the time of his United appointment, was enrolled as a doctoral student with the fabled J.B. Brebner at Columbia.

That Harry never completed his PhD both puzzles and illuminates. Arthur Lower, at the end of the United College crisis in 1959, told me that if Harry had acquired the degree, Queen's would have appointed him at once. As with others who've encountered the thesis block, everyone avoided the subject entirely. I now think that Harry simply wasn't interested in sustained intellectual analysis – let alone the paraphernalia of scholarship. Unlike Stewart Reid, who could spend whole lectures worrying the *ideas* of the Levellers, Milton, Cromwell, or the Fabians, Harry was absorbed by the processes and practitioners of politics. He was also deeply committed to various causes of social justice: labour unionism, the CCF-NDP and, later, the survival of Israel. Handsome, heavy set, almost military in bearing, Harry also took immense pleasure in organizing and administration. Ironically, perhaps, he had a thinly disguised authoritarian streak. For all his warmth and devotion to individual and minority rights, I never felt really close to him – even in our frequent convivial moments. Nevertheless, our little department throve in amity. Stewart, Harry, and I came at history, politics, and social relationships from different quarters, but our conclusions seldom clashed. To the college conservatives we appeared, I think, dangerously united, and not a little arrogant.

In the early spring of 1951 a glimmer of hope appeared in the East. Again my deepening ambivalence about Winnipeg and the college was tested. Eric Harrison, acting chair of the Queen's history department in Kingston, wrote suggesting that I go there on a one-year appointment. Rex Trotter, the department chairman, was terminally ill; a lecturer in Canadian and Commonwealth history was needed – until a permanent replacement was decided upon. I agreed, and soon received a letter from Principal Wallace, who put the case in a nutshell: Lower and Malcolm Ross (whom I had come to know and like very much in Winnipeg) had recommended me; the salary would be a thousand more than United's; then, 'there is a strong possibility that an appointment will be made for 1952 of a man who is not available at the present time. But this is not at the moment absolutely definite. This appointment, if you decide to accept it, will give you an opportunity of teaching in the East, and making your contacts in this part of Canada.' The man who was not available at the time was Fred Gibson. He was working in the East Block in Ottawa, and also beginning his painstaking study of the people and practices of Canadian politics. A Liberal and a Queen's man to the marrow, he had the successorship to Trotter tied up tight. I was pretty sure this was the case. Nevertheless, Wallace's assessment of the situation was accurate enough and I leapt at the offer. United made no objection to a year's leave; it would save a few hundred dollars on a temporary replacement.

So leisurely was the pace of university life – and so widely underfunded! Harrison typed his sheaf of letters to me that spring on a rickety portable, and I did the same with my replies. In mid-June he wrote: 'I would suggest that a useful time for your appearance here would be on or about 24 Sep, when registration begins; but we can be more precise later on.' This left me free to earn enough money for the eastward hegira by teaching a summer course on the Fort Garry campus – for $400. In our aging Plymouth, the wonderful drive East would take five days, mostly through the United States, because the Canadian route was still unpaved. However, because we never paid more than seven or eight dollars a night for a cabin that could house the four of us, and gas cost about 30 cents a gallon, we would manage quite well even without credit cards. Despite, too, that I had just had my first lesson in the vagaries of the magazine trade.

In May I had submitted to Jerry Anglin of *Maclean's* an article on J.S. Woodsworth. Anglin wrote that he had 'just read the article with enjoyment and I think you have shown considerable facility in adapting yourself to the popular profile style.' He, however, had just moved to *Chatelaine*. He passed the article on to Pierre Berton, who had replaced him at *Maclean's*. In June Berton wrote to me, saying: 'Some of the material is quite interesting ... but, I'm afraid that the article falls considerably short of our requirements in the Flashback series.' Well, I could live with that, and began to revise the piece. Before I had done so, a Flashback profile of JS appeared in *Maclean's* written by Blair Fraser. A great deal of the material was extremely familiar. Much later, in Toronto, I accepted Berton's request to do a half-hour TV discussion with him in a series he was putting together on the Great Depression. I had done quite a bit of TV work by then and was familiar with the going rates. I did not think it necessary to ask about the fee. A few days after we had taped the program I received in the mail a cheque for one dollar. One treasures these little experiences.

The prospect of a year in Kingston wiped out resentment. The limestone city seemed designed to show off Ontario's flaming autumn: the fall of 1951 dazzled us. Bev's mother had tried to line up an apartment for us in advance, but the postwar housing shortage had lingered in the happily underdeveloped, institutional town. She found an excellent place, but was turned down when the owner learned my occupation: she had rented to a professor's family once before. We spent a splendid early September week at a cottage on Loughborough Lake courtesy of a friend from undergraduate days, Maurice Aykroyd. Loughborough is one of the marvellous lakes north of Kingston where the granite of the shield pushed against the limestone in a visible line running beneath the water and up again on the other side – a symbol I still find exciting. Maurice's actor nephew, Dan, would later feel much the same and has created a beautiful Canadian anchor there for himself.

After several forays into town we found a gruesome but affordable flat in an old house on Earl Street. Although dingy and a bit leaky, it was just a few blocks from the university. I had to struggle against a sense of belonging as I walked through the leaves to the principal's late Georgian stone house on the edge of campus: W.A. Mackintosh had just taken over from Wallace and had invited me for a welcoming morning coffee. He sat on a spacious front verandah looking across sloping lawns to snatches of Lake Ontario (or the St Lawrence – no one, as far as I know, has discovered the dividing line, and I prefer to call the whole, from Amherst to Cedar Island, Kingston Sound). Mackintosh, a distinguished economist, was warmly avuncular towards his sessional visitor. Those *were* the days!

On the third floor of the 'new' arts building, which was actually an aging limestone monster, I shared an office with Arthur Lower. Well, 'share' isn't quite the word: I had a small desk in a corner of the large drafty room. Arthur, a big, heavy man, filled this and any room he entered either with his never-muffled voice or, because of extremely limited vision, by banging into furniture. Superbly self-confident, intensely nationalist, he exuded a secularized Protestant rectitude (which turned out to mean Liberal) derived from his home turf, the rolling WASP farmlands around Barrie. After our preliminary chat, he came into the corridor with me and in booming tones said, 'Ken, there's a lot of second-rate Englishmen down that hall.' This probably included a rising star in the English department, George Whalley, who, though not English, should have been.

Life with Lower was never placid. Each conversation was an occasion for pronouncements on Canadian, or any other, history; on Louis St Laurent's French Canadianness (about which Arthur claimed to know much more than he did); or the dullness of Queen's undergraduates – which he said was because so many of them came from Smiths Falls. Of course, we argued long about the CCF, but we agreed completely on the importance of rigorous academic standards. Gruff to the point of rudeness much of the time, Arthur was the soul of kindness with us. We were often at the Lowers' white frame Horizon House, which perched on high ground overlooking Collins Bay. His diminutive wife, Evelyn, had come to Canada as a war bride at the end of Arthur's service as commander of a patrol launch in the Straits of Dover. I imagine she underestimated the rigours of her Arthurian venture. Their honeymoon turned out to be a long canoe trip, about which she recalled telling her husband she would not face another portage until they had brewed a good pot of tea. When they moved to Kingston after their eighteen-year sentence in Winnipeg, Arthur resumed his nautical ways in a series of unseaworthy boats. Evelyn, whom he quite inappropriately called 'Bill,' was his crew. One Sunday off Collins Bay, Arthur blew them both out of their cedar-strip 'cruiser' when he tapped out his pipe in the oily bilge. Bev and Evelyn got along so well that I sometime wondered whether they exchanged condolences.

Eric Harrison and his wife, Elizabeth, who was a talented artist and poet, were equally hospitable. They lived in an off-beat little mews beside the yacht club. When Elizabeth presented Lower with a superb portrait of himself (she called it, privately, 'Fighting Protestant'), they invited us to the reception. Eric made a point of introducing me to a visitor from Ottawa, J.W. Pickersgill, thinking, no doubt, that because Pickersgill had taught at United College, we could at least exchange anecdotes. 'Pick' looked sideways at me, jerked his shoulders a couple of times, and turned his back. I was pretty miffed. Now I feel pleased to have been cut by the politician who gave fresh meaning to the word 'cynicism' and capped his career in the corridors of power by beginning the deconstruction of our railway system.

During the first term a small group met regularly for lunch in the faculty lounge: Malcolm (Mac) Ross from English, Frank Knox from economics, Glen Shortliffe from French, and Alex Corry from political science. We were often joined by John Deutsch. He was with the federal Department of Finance, but was also one of the effective links between Queen's and the Ottawa mandarinate. In our lunchtime chatter, Shortliffe, Ross, and I noisily assaulted the Liberal establishment from a CCF position while Deutsch smiled and Knox played quizzical Scot. Ross was then mulling over ideas that he later published as *Our Sense of Identity* (1954). Shortliffe had an acid wit and leftish politics, and had become one of the CBC's sharpest political commentators, though this had got him into deep trouble in 1949. He had accepted a senior post in an American university, resigned from Queen's, and taken off for the United States border. There he was turned back. Senator Joseph McCarthy's minions had not appreciated the *Weekend Review* broadcasts of this obvious Red. Principal Wallace immediately reappointed him. Friends interceded with someone in Washington and told Shortliffe he would now be admitted should he wish to take up the American appointment. In an interview he said simply, 'I've decided to stay in the free world.' And he did, to our great gain.

In mid-year the bliss was broken. On the way back from a family Christmas in Toronto, we stopped at a shoddy restaurant in Trenton. Ten days later, Bev, Allison, and I came down with infectious hepatitis. Our doctor prescribed complete rest, consommé, and fruit juice. Allison and Bev obeyed and got off lightly. I was in a quandary. How could I quit duties as a one-year visitor? I continued lecturing. In mid-January I went into a coma and was whisked off to Kingston General Hospital. In the following days I turned from yellow to bronze, my skin peeled from head to foot, and I dropped to 100 pounds. The wonderful internist, Malcolm Brown, told Bev that there was no known treatment and the chances were 50–50. I recall tears as I looked at a skeleton in the mirror. Then my liver began to recover, and Brown defied the received notions about hepatitis by ordering a regular diet of steak. I was sprung in three weeks, but much subdued by Brown's severe warning: do absolutely nothing for six months.

Our friends at Queen's, in the department and beyond, smothered my embarrassment with their kindness. I gave no more lectures and even declined an invitation to read a paper at the spring meeting of the Canadian Historical Association in Quebec City. Missing this opportunity to fix one more rung in the ladder of escape was bitter. To fill in many hours of late winter, I scribbled out a long article on the Commonwealth for an American encyclopedia. The payment enabled us to replace our aged Plymouth with a not-new 'fluid-drive' Chrysler. My decadent affection for big, heavy cars deepened as we indulged ourselves with short picnic drives along the St Lawrence and among the neighbouring Precambrian lakes.

Hepatitis hits one's metabolism pretty hard. In my case, a functional change left me 25 pounds heavier than I had been when we stopped at the Trenton eatery. By May, I weighed what I always should have and had never felt better. But Dr Brown ran up bright warning flags: vegetate for the summer or risk a lethal relapse. At this point Eric Harrison told us about Garden Island.

Every Canadian refers, more or less frequently, to 'the island' and takes comprehension for granted. It could be off any coast, big or small, in any lake; it is still, simply, 'the island.' This little conceit is inadvertent. We affected it in 1952 and it quickly became second nature and remains so to this day. Garden Island is 65 acres of limestone lightly covered with arable soil. From Kingston, 2 miles to the north, it is indistinguishable from Wolfe Island – fortunately, few Kingstonians even know of it. Wolfe is a 22-mile-long dairy farmer's dream from which Garden is separated by narrow water – a side-arm of the fur-trader's Bateau Channel. Originally, save for Indians who occasionally camped on it, Garden was part of La Salle's seigneury. In 1792 Mrs Simcoe sailed to 'pretty Garden Island' for a picnic. In the mid-1830s an enterprising lumber merchant from upstate New York came by and noticed a very shallow, sheltered bay on the south shore of Garden – from which one can see many miles down the St Lawrence. The merchant's name, D.D. Calvin, was exquisitely appropriate; he was designed by God to demonstrate the Protestant ethic. In his mind's eye he instantly saw the economic potential, and in several quick steps acquired the island. By the end of the 1830s he had established lumber, rafting, and shipbuilding industries to expedite the rape of the shield.

Buying logs at river mouths (eventually as far off as the upper Great Lakes), skippers of Calvin's bow-loading sail and steam ships brought them to the island's back bay. Scattered about the shallow water were large, stone-filled cedar cribs. After the logs were squared, raft-builders, using the cribs as work bases, bound their timber into rectangular 'drams' – which could be further integrated into huge rafts. Complete with shelter cabins, square sails, food, and crews, the monster rafts were then nudged down by company tugs to the first of the St Lawrence rapids. There, the raftsmen separated them into their component drams. Each dram with its tiny, expert crew set out to shoot the tumultuous rapids, finally fetching up at Montreal. There the drams were reassembled and the stately rafts made their way to teeming docks at Quebec City. Again the rafts were sundered, and the timber sold on the spot to agents from Liverpool.

Old DD profited mightily. Garden Island he ran as a kind of back-woods feudal lord. His industrial village came to number 500 people (which exactly equalled the number of troops briefly bivouacked there by Colonel Bradstreet on his way from Oswego to capture Fort Fronte-nac in 1758). Calvin made his island a self-contained community. His varied workshops milled the lumber and forged the square spikes and nails that went into the dozens of frame buildings that housed his work-ers and, in two lanes of elegant houses, the managers. Throughout long winters his men built the tugs and timber ships, ever larger, required in the trade. One of the biggest, the *Garden Island*, was sold abroad and finally foundered somewhere off India. DD managed every detail of his little domain. For his mixed workforce – well sprinkled with Irish and French Canadians – he built a schoolhouse, a mechanics' institute, and a general store-cum-post office, and maintained a farmer to produce most of the islands' vegetable needs. Garden Island scrip was redeem-able at the company store, where much of the merchandise from pots and pans to toys had been crafted in the island workshops. As his capital grew, DD invested in such mainland enterprises as the Kingston and Pembroke Railway and the Tory Party. He was reeve of the township and sometime MLA. When he died, Sir John A. came to the island for the funeral service. His son, Hiram, carried on. The tale is told of Hiram meeting the island boats as they brought employees back from a Satur-day night in Kingston. If he spied a telltale bulge in a hip pocket, he would rap it smartly with his cane – and calmly watch the whisky dribble down onto the wharf. The Calvins were Baptists.

In 1914 Hiram's sons went off to war, taking wives with them as far as England. At the same time, the already sagging timber market col-lapsed. As an industry, Garden Island folded. Hiram deeded the island to a private company, Garden Island Ltd, with the shares divided among his progeny. Thereafter, and despite kaleidoscopic policy shifts, the island has been mainly a summer retreat. Its semi-feudal past lingered as the first of a long line of non-Calvin tenants took up summer residence in 1917. No one may own property; there are no leases, simply a letter each January from the current manager asking if one wishes to rent again the house occupied the previous season.

Throughout the 1920s and 1930s many of the oldest village houses and some of the workbuildings had been lost to fire, or cannibalized to sustain those that remained – about fifteen. Apart from three large Calvin houses, all had lost their paint and taken on the wonderful silvery warmth of pine long beaten upon by wind and rain. In the words of Principal Wallace (who summered for a few years on Garden), the island had become a 'decadent Jalna.' We have now been tenants for more than forty years. This little excursion into that rise and afterglow of Upper Canadian capitalism becomes a necessary backdrop to much of what follows. Just a year ago one of my grandchildren retrieved from the constantly shifting clay of the back bay a halfpenny piece issued by the Bank of Upper Canada in 1857; it lay beside a raftsman's clay pipe made in Montreal.

When the Harrisons introduced us to the island in 1952, they already had status. Arriving from England, impecunious, in 1936, they had spent their first two Canadian winters in a frame house perched on the rocky windswept shore. Eric reached Queen's by walking across two miles of windswept ice to Kingston. A few fir trees were implanted to mark the safe route during blizzards. Slender and rather dashing in appearance, Harrison supervised occasional cricket games in the rough-cut grass of the island meadow in the golden St Lawrence summers. When he heard about the happy sentence imposed on me by Dr Brown, he told us of a possible sublet. Professor W.M. Conacher of the Queen's French department would be taking his wife for a visit to Ireland and would rent us his place for six weeks for an affordable $65. 'Connie' had come to the island, as the first non-Calvin, in 1917. We had met his son, Jim, several times at Toronto departmental parties given by Maurice and Betty Careless. Jim and Muriel Conacher would become our closest island friends. Jim closely resembled his father: tall and spare, with a hoarse yet penetrating voice. When Bev phoned Connie to ask about the key, he replied: '*Key*? There's never been a key as far as I know.' It was our first taste.

On the Queen's birthday in May, Blossom McDougall shepherded us on a preview picnic to the island. She was a voluble monarchist; her husband, Lorne, a Queen's economist, was a pre-eminent apologist of the Canadian Pacific Railroad. On both subjects we had achieved a standoff, seldom breached during many summers. Captain Dougan (Lyle only to his oldest acquaintances) took us across in the steel workboat he used for moonlighting as a water taxi. His regular job was transporting pilots to and from freighters as they entered or left the

St Lawrence channels and canals. Dougan lived with his French-Canadian wife in an insulated brick bungalow perched on the Kingston shoreline. Available for pilots (and, increasingly, for islanders) twenty-four hours a day, he was seldom out of his clothes. When the St Lawrence Seaway opened, Dougan's official duties dwindled as the ever-larger ships veered south of Wolfe Island to the new main channel. To accommodate his growing water taxi trade, he bought and refurbished a powerful 26-foot mahogany launch, probably a veteran of the cross-river prohibition trade. This vessel he drove with a skill that seemed to us to approach total abandon. Riding the crests of 6- or 7-foot waves, he would occasionally stroll to the stern to make some adjustment – quietly amused by the fearful regard of his passengers. He liked to discourse on politics, with a cynical Conservative seasoning. Once, towards the close of his career, I asked what he thought of Joe Clark. 'Well, Mr McNaught,' he mused, 'there's not much greatness there.' On his retirement, the islanders gave him a garden party and a purse containing $600. Mrs Dougan, his guardian of the fares, opened it on the spot, flicking through the bills with a wet thumb.

The Conacher house, two-and-a-half storeys, semi-detached, and sheathed in silvered pine, looked out across the water to Kingston. No floor was truly horizontal; a kitchen hand pump drew water through a pipe that snaked across the limestone shelves to the lake. The back door, as Connie had said, was held more or less shut by an old branch propped against it. Enough for now. During six weeks of sun and wind, I occupied a deck chair most of the time while the grass grew tall. Christopher and Allison were also in heaven; we had perch for breakfast most days.

In mid-August, again following Dr Brown's advice, we booked passage on the SS *Keewatin* – to save a good three days of driving on the trip back to Winnipeg. We put the car and ourselves aboard at Port McNichol and cruised across Huron and Superior for two days and a night, to disembark at Fort William. The passing of those lordly upper lakes passenger vessels I take as no mark of progress.

Driving off the shield into the vast flatland of the Red River 'valley' brought instant foreboding. But as we drew up at 739 Macmillan and greeted Stewart and Velma Reid, who had been our tenants for the year, the shades began to dissipate. Feeling extremely well, I looked forward almost eagerly to what might yet be done at United. And much was done in the following six years – until a melange of inept, narrow-visioned clerics and businessmen pulled the plug.

7

As Winnipeg autumns go, which is pretty damn fast, that of 1952 seemed propitious. Two young men arrived from the East; I knew at once they would shoulder academic muskets on the banks of the Red.

Richard Stingle came to teach English. The black Scot in Dick swamped his drops of German blood. Growing up in Timmins and Kirkland Lake had hardened his heart against most bosses; he had fought for unions and the CCF in rowdy mining towns, and then put himself through the University of Toronto. At Victoria College, Northrop Frye captured him with myth and archetype – tools that Stingle used brilliantly in literary analysis and teaching. When he became dean of men at United in 1954, he introduced some formalities that irritated the dean's crowd, but expressed Stingle's profound respect for form. In religion, Dick was high United Church; this, too, Anderson's acolytes saw as eastern affectation.

If Stingle, sharp of eye and tongue, was strong medicine for the teachers-by-rote, no less was Michael Oliver, who, with his ebullient, sophisticated wife, Joan, arrived at the same time. The Olivers positively oozed Montreal. With a McGill MA in political science, Mike had begun doctoral work on Henri Bourassa and Quebec nationalism. His father, like F.R. Scott's, was an Anglican rector; Mike was already well along the political-cultural trail marked out by Scott. His height of about 6 foot 5 often brought forth another memorable drollery from Wesley Runions: 'We all look up to Michael Oliver.' But we didn't; Mike formed the coterie of those who were reviled for too frequently calling attention to how things were done in the East.

In the following autumn, W.G. Dean arrived to establish a Department of Geography. Bill, after his Toronto MA, had done Arctic research and had been working in Victoria for the BC government. Quiet, almost bashful, he was nevertheless his own man. To his definite ideas about the function of geography in explicating historical and contemporary political-economic circumstances, he added a superb organizing ability that would later result in two of Canada's most distinguished atlases. He and his very Ontario wife, Betty (St Catharines born and bred), added much to the cohesiveness of those who dreamed of a first-rate liberal arts college. When Bill left for the University of Toronto in 1956, he was succeeded by John Warkentin. A Manitoban, John had begun doctoral work at Toronto; his wife, Germaine (with a Toronto BA in philosophy) was recruited to teach English – because of a sudden enrolment bulge. Each Warkentin was committed to a careful balance between teaching and scholarship – a view of academe that gained growing support from several appointees in these years. Viljo (Bill) Packer and his librarian wife, Katherine, came in 1955. With a new PhD from Cornell, Viljo became the German department; he exuded professionalism and a concern for organizational detail, not unlike that of Harry Crowe, with whom he would shortly engage in some crucial correspondence.

I have let slip the hawsers of chronology. Sequence seems less important in the five years following 1953 than the feelings of community that imperceptibly attached us to the city and the college – or, perhaps, to our idea of each. Long winters when the sun pierced through fogs of ice particles suspended in the air, and when you knew that no car would start if it were left more than a couple of hours without its engine block heater plugged in, brought a kind of grudging excitement – at least until the weariness that struck in March or even April. I never got used to watching Chris and Allison strike out for school at   30 or 40 degrees, coats flapping open as they disappeared between the snowbanks. For several years Allison thought the name of her city was Winterpeg. And, of course, in those days the Chicago of Canada really was isolated. The nearest big city, St Paul and Minneapolis, lay some 500 miles to the south. Indigenous cultural activity flourished. Bev worked with the women's committees of the Art Gallery, the ballet, and the symphony. As a member of the Winnipeg Little Theatre board I pushed, successfully, for the appointment of John Hirsch as director. I had come to know and admire Hirsch through the CBC, a connection resulting, I think, precisely because of the size, isolation, and importance of what was still the prairie capital.

No week passed during those winters without at least two evening parties. Beginning around 9 o'clock, these were not only congenial frost-killers – although they certainly saw a good deal of anti-freeze downed – but, more often than not, generators of serious discussion. Bev made '739' a principal centre for such gatherings and enjoyed cross-fertilizing our several circles of friends. Through our friends of the Mall Medical Group – the Greens and the Brusers – we became part of a largely Jewish covey. The high-decibel level of the parties subsided only when Sam Freedman, who became chancellor of the University of Manitoba and Manitoba's chief justice, cleared his throat to tell a distinctly off-colour joke. I always thought of Sam as a super-intelligent Jack Benny; certainly he was the finest after-dinner speaker in the country, with none of Leonard Brockington's Churchillian magniloquence. Nor had he any of the self-importance of his vastly overrated journalist brother, Max. Monty Israels, a CCF lawyer and perennial mayoralty candidate, was an honorary Mall member, as were Gloria and Wilf Queen-Hughes. Gloria's father, John Queen, had been imprisoned for his part in the 1919 strike and was elected to the legislature while still in jail; later he had been an ILP-CCF mayor. Gloria was a bawdy, ebullient feminist. Wilf had been with the Winnipeg Grenadiers at Hong Kong in 1941; the ravages of Japanese prison camps, while evident and eventually lethal, had in no way tamed him.

With the doctors and lawyers we often mixed in some of our United coterie, and also friends from the Fort Garry campus: Clarence and Babs Barber (economics), Murray and Nancy Donnelly (political science), Dick and Connie Glover, John and Barbara McEwan, and the Olesons (history), James and Colleen Reaney and John and Barbara Peter (English). Tryg and Elva Oleson brought us into their cohesive circle of Icelanders; indeed, we and the Reids became honourary 'goolies' – a near pejorative, which I use with affection. Their parties called for stamina. From Gimli, Glenboro, and villages scattered about the province they retained, in Winnipeg, as healthy a respect for winter as they had for books. When Tryg opened his door to guests, his glistening face disappeared at once in a cloud of steam as the overheated air of the house rushed out to meet the icy night. Inside, the favoured antidote to the climate was Shea's beer, with chasers of rye or akvavit. As spirited political discourse dissolved into song, Thor Thorgrimsson would oblige Stewart Reid by leading in 'The Road to the Isles.' Around 2 a.m. Palmi Palmason, who played with the Winnipeg Symphony, would reach for his violin and favour us with the Icelandic national anthem – by far the most depressing work of its kind. But by then, who cared? Well, I did, a bit: Palmi seldom put enough resin on his bow.

Another interlock was with the CBC people, especially those in the Talks and Public Affairs department. Isabel Wilson (Donald Creighton's sister), Bernard Trotter (son of Rex Trotter of Queen's), and others visiting from the East provided occasions for yet more parties. Network is too strong a word, but something of the sort did evolve. Winnipeg's isolation we overcame not just by involvement with its people and institutions, but by hospitality to the peripatetic minions of central Canadian culture, and by frequent correspondence with those who didn't travel. Publishers' representatives abounded, and they had expense accounts. When not dining with us, they hosted meals in their rooms at the elegant old Fort Garry Hotel. These friendships led to much underpaid reading of manuscripts. My friend from toddler days on Sheldrake Boulevard, Don Ritchie, travelled for Gage. His firm wanted to do a two-volume history of Canada, having conducted a rather optimistic market survey. They had lined up an excellent Maritimer for volume 1 and asked me to do volume 2. At the outset they had some doubts about the authorship, for, as Don wrote to me: 'The ghastly part is that W.S. MacNutt of UNB is being pointed out as the best man for the earlier phases, and *MacNutt and McNaught* sounds like stammering.' A contract was actually drawn up, but it aborted as storm clouds formed at United.

At the same time another Toronto flashback produced some new friends and a little more bread and butter on the table – and the table was scarcely groaning. By 1956 my United salary had inched up to $5000 – lightly iced by promotion to full professor. The flashback was to 1946–7. Ross McLean, one of our two third-floor tenants at 13 Lowther, was financing his education by work at a Toronto radio station. He was a tall, good-looking lad with a mop of dark hair flopping over his horned-rim glasses: quizzical, imaginative, energetic. Over beer in the back yard, with the top of the Park Plaza not quite hidden by an apple tree, we talked into the warm evenings and became good friends. Later, from Winnipeg, we watched Ross's CBC enterprises flourish as he developed pioneer TV magazine shows, particularly *Tabloid* and *Close-Up*. We always touched base with him on our annual passage through Toronto en route to Garden Island. In 1953, when Ross heard that his CBC colleague Michael Hind-Smith was posted to Winnipeg to inaugurate a TV talks department for the prairie region, he asked him to give us a call.

When the Hind-Smiths came to dinner, they seemed to us outrageously young. Michael and his wife, Joan, the ink not dry on their UBC parchments, sparkled with entrepreneurial enthusiasms. Joan, blonde and vivacious, was learning the techniques of market research; Michael, dark and heavy set, already with the judicious eye of a well-groomed CEO, spent much time analysing U.S. and British public affairs programming. We introduced them to our thriving party circuit. Michael and I invariably tangled on the issue of public and private enterprise. Although a 'public servant' in the CBC, and a devoted one for a while, he was a devout free-marketer. I should have been able to predict (perhaps I did) his later skyrocketing into the world of Power Corporation and cable TV. One evening in the spring of 1954 we were joined in a particularly sparky conversation by John Hirsch. The following day Hind-Smith invited me to try out as host of CBC Winnipeg's first foray into TV public affairs broadcasting. He, Hirsch, and their colleagues planned a weekly half-hour panel discussion program to be called *Roundtable*. Hind-Smith would produce it; Hirsch would direct it.

Everyone so young, so eagerly professional: John Hirsch and Hind-Smith were both twenty-four. Hirsch, a war orphan, had come to Winnipeg in 1947 from Hungary. Sponsored by a brilliant school-teacher, Sybil Shack, and Sybil's mother, he quickly mastered the language – and had just emerged from the University of Manitoba with the gold medal in English. Lanky, passionately theatrical, his ideas demanded such fast release that he frequently sprang from his chair to crouch, long arms waving about, in front of whoever needed instructing. Sybil, proud and loving, watched the performance with quiet amusement. We all became close friends; Sybil Shack was to be a regular, highly reliable participant in *Roundtable* sessions. John Hirsch and Tom Hendry would found the Manitoba Theatre Centre the year before we were blown out of Winnipeg. Hirsch's later achievements came as no surprise at all.

My tryout in 1956 produced no disasters. So, for four successive seasons, I chaired weekly *Roundtable* panel discussions in what is now called prime time. The CBC paid me $50 for each evening – I think this rose to $75 in 1957. If the pay was minimal, so were the studio facilities. The CBC inhabited a scruffy little building at Portage and Good, just across the street from United. This first studio was about the size of our living room, blazing with klieg lights, equipped with a single camera and a long desk with chairs behind it for me and the three panellists.

We had to wear solid blue shirts so that they would appear white to the primordial camera without blinding the viewers. Beneath heavy makeup, sort of non-porous mud-packs, all faces were streaming by the end of each half-hour. In front of us, Hirsch moved about with simian agility urging some life into the inherently rigid setup. I learned quickly to understand his frantic signals; fortunately, because the broadcasts went out 'live' to Winnipeg's black-and-white receivers and goofs were irretrievable, what saved me from panic during the first few broadcasts was a snobbish disdain of the new medium. Virtually the only preparation I made before each broadcast was to take a solid hour's nap. We did not own a set until late 1954, so Bev saw the first few programs at the homes of various friends.

For the whole four years of *Roundtable* I did not once meet either of the head men of CBC's prairie region, except accidentally at social occasions. James Findlay, the regional director, and his second in command, Dan Cameron, I soon discovered, were timid people, anxious to maintain distance and proper lines of communication: that is, they assigned to the producers such dirty work as vetoing topics or panellists. The successive producers were Mike Hind-Smith, Spencer Moore, Ken Black, and Paul Wright. Each went to his reward in the eastern valhalla of media power. Because they were 'from away,' transient in Winnipeg, they drew heavily on me for the names of likely panellists. Our discussion topics ranged across the three levels of Canadian politics to international affairs, education, and social-economic issues. Several days before each program I met with the producer to define a topic and choose the guests. We soon had a list of dependable panellists, most ticketed as right, left, or centre. The majority came from our social-academic 'network' or from the local pool of journalists – from which Peter McClintock of the *Winnipeg Free Press* joined in most frequently, complete with trace of brogue. Sybil Shack, Anne Dumoulin, and Jean Edmonds gave some 'gender balance' before the notion was even hinted at.

On air, my job was to hold the ring and provoke when necessary. I was never privy to ratings; indeed, I don't know that such things existed at the time. A lot of people must have watched *Roundtable*, however, and I found myself addressed by name by store clerks at the Bay. Apart from the ego boost, this made me a bit nervous. It was so easy. As with the too-early promotion to full professor, the *Roundtable* stint gave me the feeling of a largish frog in a pretty small pond. It also, perhaps ironically, strengthened my self-confidence – which would soon be tested not only in the college but also in the CBC, prairie region.

Two incidents, in particular, alerted me to the spongy quality of the Winnipeg directorate. One blizzardy February night – not fit, as W.C. Fields put it, for man or beast – we found ourselves lacking one of the panellists, fifteen minutes before starting time. The guy in question was a prominent lawyer whom one of the top men had met in some Wellington Crescent mansion. He was also a celebrated drinker – and that night he was soused. When he blew in from the storm, I saw that he shouldn't be allowed anywhere near the studio and phoned Murray Donnelly as a quick replacement. Murray lived nearby and could have made it, maybe two minutes late. But word came down that the drunken guest was to go on – no matter what. He did. An adroit cameraman panning quickly back and forth allowed the merest glimpses of the slouched figure beside me. I asked the sodden social pillar the odd question, which I immediately answered for him. When I told all this to Bev, she said she hadn't noticed any of the potential horror – nor, apparently, had any other viewers. That night, as the brass caved in, 'social concern' gained a new unlovely meaning.

The second incident demonstrated equally questionable concern for *vox populi*. We had set up a press-interview format: three journalists and the mayor, Steve Juba, who was the ultimate self-made man: folksy, popular, he was also an MLA. We had agreed on a number of questions to be put by the reporters. One question concerned one of Juba's election promises: slum clearance and new housing in the centre of Winnipeg. When asked why he had done nothing about this, the mayor replied that he had proposed a Sunday sports bill to the legislature. Another reporter repeated the question and got the same reply. I then, most unwisely but truthfully, said that Mr Juba didn't seem willing to answer, and we moved to the next question. In the following days the CBC found itself awash in hostile letters, as did the newspapers. Nearly all condemned the arrogant, socialist professor who had publicly insulted the mayor. Again the nervous nellies swung into action: I was removed from *Roundtable* for several weeks. Irony followed upon this wrist-slap. Ted Byfield, who had been one of the panellists at the Juba fiasco, called at our house with a most surprising apology: he had forewarned Juba about the key question. The mayor had been prepared to stonewall.

As the queen said of a much later year, 1958 was *annus horribilis*. Or, maybe, *mirabilis*. Because I was later to resign twice from the editorial board of the *Canadian Forum* and from the Fair Play for Cuba Committee, I wonder a bit, now, about that earlier year when I resigned from my two main occupational bases: United College and the CBC. Did I show a character flaw, a need to flee nasty situations? David Lewis seemed to think so; or, at best, to suspect poor judgment. One snowy March evening in 1960 we went to dinner at George and Sheila Grant's house on Farnham Avenue in Toronto. George had just resigned from York University, having refused to prescribe a philosophy textbook written by Marcus Long. David and Sophie Lewis and George's feisty sister Charity were the other guests. Conversation touched, naturally, on the question of resigning-on-principle. David lit into me for abandoning United (which I had in 1958) rather than staying there trying to re-establish the principles of academic freedom and the privacy of personal letters. When he allowed that I had been merely self-righteous, Bev took over and they had a knock-down battle: expediency versus principle. I think David was unusually touchy that night. He was painfully aware of his reputation for manipulating CCF conventions and masterminding the marriage of the party with the unions, which was then being consummated. He also resented the implication of undue deviousness in my account of his part in undercutting Woodsworth's 1939 attempt to hold the CCF to its neutrality plank. *A Prophet in Politics* had come out in 1959. As we left the Grants', David found that his car refused to start, so Bev and I drove Sophie home while David waited in the snow for help. Tearfully she asked us to remember how much David had sacrificed for the CCF and to overlook his outburst. I did not doubt David's unlimited devotion to democratic socialism, nor do I now. George and I never discussed the resignation-on-principle question despite our shared experiences since the first tussle over the Upper Canada College cadet battalion.

Back to my final showdown at the CBC corral. When Paul Wright became producer of *Roundtable* sometime in 1957, Mike Hind-Smith's original policy of a wide range of topics, from international to very local, finally died. Wright seemed to concur with regional brass that CBWT should concern itself only with strictly Manitoba issues – that the bigger ones could be better handled from Toronto, on the national network. To no avail I argued that the views of informed Manitobans on national and even international questions might well differ from those of easterners, and that it should be a special concern of CBWT to air such views.

An equally troubling tendency of the regional directorate became, for me, insupportable. Substantial interest groups wielded a veto on topics and panellists. Two startling vetoes precipitated my resignation. Much public discussion of the high cost of burials had arisen in 1958. We scheduled a program on this clearly local issue. It was cancelled at the last minute, as was a second attempt. Wright told me on each occasion that the brass had intervened because the Winnipeg Undertakers' Association refused to provide a spokesman. After several weeks, a Winnipeg TV panel did debate the funeral question: Citizens' Forum organized it from the East. A second overt kowtowing to private pressure came at about the same time. A strike by Canadian Pacific Railway firemen blossomed into a national issue and was of special concern in Winnipeg, which still boasted the country's largest freight yards. The local head of the fireman's union agreed to take part on a program *Roundtable* had scheduled – after getting assurance from Toronto that the strike was of local as well as national importance. Again, the program was hastily cancelled; the CPR had declined to participate. At the same time, a full panel discussion of the strike emanated from Toronto over the national network. A week later we argued it on *Roundtable* – without the local head of the firemen's union.

It was too much. I wrote Findlay a long letter of resignation reviewing these and similar experiences, and concluding: 'It is with a very real sense of disappointment and of concern for the future of publicly-owned television in this region that I submit my resignation. Since I believe strongly in the necessity of a really independent and effective system of non-commercial public broadcasting in this country I sincerely hope that the situation which I have described may be altered in the future.' Of course I had no such hope, but I sent copies of the letter to the CBC chairman, Davidson Dunton, and to Alex Corry, who was then a member of the board. Dunton's reply was a model of circumspection. Alex offered to bring the matter up at the next board meeting: 'There is an issue of policy here that should be aired.' Mike Hind-Smith, to whom I had sent a copy of my letter, wrote from Ottawa endorsing my action, but with a well-founded tone of scepticism: 'I'll be interested in knowing whether Frank Peers [then head of Talks and Public Affairs] or the Toronto brass ever see hide or hair of your letter.' Well, I would be, too – academically.

All this kerfuffle took place during the seismic federal election of 1958. Correspondence always included predictions – or reflections. Mike Hind-Smith, just before the election, assessed Diefenbaker accurately: 'He's really one of the most stunning political pitchmen I've ever seen.' Mike predicted 170 Tory seats. Alex Corry, the day following the election (1 April), wrote: 'If I were a person given to surprise in political matters, I would now certainly be astonished ... I regret this enormous majority and am inclined to think that it controverts Professor Lower's thesis on the staid sobriety of the Canadian people and shows them suckers for hot gospel ... On purely personal grounds I was distressed to see Mr. Coldwell and Mr. Knowles defeated.' So were we. Stanley Knowles had become a good friend. Several days before the election, he had been with us at 739, the perpendicular creases in his gaunt face deeper than ever. But the only exact prediction of the landslide I know of came in a letter that Harry Crowe wrote to Viljo Packer from Kingston. In this brief missive, which was to result in Harry's dismissal from United, the substantive portion predicted 208 Tory seats.

My relations with the CBC, beyond the prairie region, continued unharmed, if less intense. I chaired some TV Citizens' Forums, did some radio book reviews for *Critically Speaking*, and a series of *Weekend Reviews* – of the sort Glen Shortliffe had found so risky. My favourite was early on, in May 1955. I called it 'The Shocking Dearth of Communists in Our Universities.' I remember a fine feeling of release as I wrote it. McCarthyism had come and gone, and Elvis and conformity expressed the staggering complacency of a pre-*Sputnik* West. Disarmament foundered on the shoals of 'our' technological superiority; Niebuhr seemed to have won, as we plunged further into the Cold War seldom questioning our own values. Almost a preview of the 1980s. I had my only serious quarrels with Stanley Knowles over the CCF's continuing support of Canada's membership in a NATO that had congealed in a purely military, destabilizing confrontation with the Soviet Union. In the radio talk I argued that stupefying student conservatism reflected professional 'objectivity' – usually a celebration of the conventional:

We examine universal empire, universal Papacy, divine right monarchy, communism – all in turn to come up with the expected answer that our modern democracy ... is a very beautiful thing ... It seems incredible that if communism, as a really basic criticism of our political-economic assumptions, were presented in all its historic aspects – and without prejudgment – that some young minds wouldn't, at least temporarily, accept it ... Liberty, like Christianity, is always a dangerous doctrine – and liberty in education is no less dangerous than liberty in political society.

Among quite a flutter of letters was an approving telegram from

Mike Hind-Smith, beginning with 'Break out the Red flag.' The letter I most appreciated came from two United graduates then living at Chaffey's Locks on the Rideau: 'Your voice is one that is encouraging to hear – and we are glad to find that our college still has independence, vigour and provocation.' I was beginning to feel the same way, then.

Tentacles of belonging touched us in many ways. Chris and Allison throve on skating, school, and parties. But one day they asked us, 'Why don't we go to Sunday school as most of our friends do?' We knew the answer: we're agnostics and don't want to indoctrinate you. Yet the question nagged. Finally we agreed that we were pushing them in one direction without letting them know about the other. So one Sunday in 1954 I took them to nearby St Luke's Anglican Church – thinking to meet them at the end of their class. I found, of course, that children sat with their parents before going downstairs halfway through the service. I was trapped. Worse, I was moved by the music, the liturgies, the sermon. Thereafter, Bev and I both went with the children to St Luke's. By midwinter we joined the adult confirmation class. In the spring we were confirmed – after I had been baptized. Bev had been christened in Ottawa.

This may seem all very sudden, but it was only superficially so. Damascus had not shimmered in the distance. I had been ruminating as I prepared or updated lectures, especially those in European and American history, and as I worked through the final phases of Woodsworth's life – and death. The Heavenly City of the eighteenth-century *philosophes* and the inevitability of progress lost much of their certainty. Rereading such writing as Charles Cochrane's *Christianity and Classical Culture*, R.G. Collingwood on the nature of history, and Herbert Butterfield's arguments that the real end of history lies outside history, I reacted pretty skittishly. In particular, I began to doubt J.S. Mill's notion that some instinct of *bienfaisance* impelled most people to perceive that their own self-interest coincided with that of their community. This foundation stone of rationalist convictions about 'the nature of man' and progress appears to lack supportive evidence. Hiroshima and Nagasaki were no more; the first hydrogen bombs had been successfully 'tested'; and our triumphant leaders proclaimed that original sin afflicted only the godless communists. If, then, *bienfaisance* lacked a moral imperative, a sanction as it were, almost evil, why 'believe' in it?

Canon Jack Clough, in powerful, intensely personal sermons, completed the demolition of my shaky rationalism. In his confirmation classes at St Luke's I fought manfully against surrender to something I had been brought up to disparage. In the end he won. No one is ever free of doubt, he argued; faith does not strike like lightning. Act *as if* the Christian message were true, and faith will, God willing, follow – as the night the day. Well, I think it worked. Jack himself was far more important than the mere arguments he advanced. He lived his faith as surely as had Woodsworth. He had been chaplain of the Queen's Own in Toronto and went into battle with them – refusing to carry the revolver to which he was entitled. He understood the importance of the free individual, the impossibility of perfection, and the need to strive for it – with the help he knew was available.

Regular Sunday walks through bone-chilling brilliance, to and from St Luke's, were oftened followed by a pre-prandial drink with Mike and Joan Oliver – who taught us the delicate art of mixing Old Fashioneds. I came to know Bill Morton much better while we were members of the vestry – he as rector's warden. Chris and Allison were belatedly baptized. Allison took up horseback riding, not infrequently at –30 degrees. Chris joined the choir; when we left Winnipeg for good, he was head chorister. And so the warmth of belonging grew – to be gracelessly smothered during *annus horribilis*.

Belonging – to the city, to the college – remained, however, in tenuous balance with yearning. Our communication with the East remained very close indeed, and not just by letter. In February 1955 Eric Harrison wrote: 'If you would like to come east again this summer, I would offer you the excuse of a pass course in American History concocted for the purpose of enticing the McNaughts to take a tenancy on Garden Island.' Queen's summer school would pay $600; rent on the island: $225 for the entire season. Thus we became tenants in our own right, and have remained so until now.

Miss Hilda Calvin, spinster daughter of Hiram, who managed the island for the family company, alotted us the School House. Built in the late 1830s, it lacks any foundation other than thick pine beams laid flat on the pebble-suffused clay – which is itself but a thin layer covering Garden Island's limestone base. Over 150 years have produced interior undulations that we call charm. During our first three seasons in the School House I cleared dogwood and thorn bushes from our half-acre property – giving access to the back bay for boating and to the rock shelves on the north side for swimming, and contemplation of Kingston's domes and spires. In a cock-eyed corner of the living room I built a book shelf and desk. During the past forty seasons I've spent most mornings writing in that warm, sunny corner. Harrison 'concocted,' in all, three successive summer courses, and timetabled each to fit the Wolfe Island ferry schedule. The *Wolfe Islander*, or the smaller *Upper Canada*, stopped in at the island several times a day; twenty-minute trips on the top deck gave 'a lift under the wings of the spirit.'

And each September came the five-day drive back to Winnipeg, colours ever brighter, children clamouring for candy stops. Island fancies faded into winter plans as we drove north from Pembina. One college event each year I anticipated with growing interest: the Macalester-United student exchange visits. Initiated by Arthur Lower, this November conference alternated between Macalester College in St Paul and United College and was intended to encourage interest in international affairs, history, and political science. Faculty members selected promising students, agreed on a topic, and held preparatory sessions – complete with reading lists and exhortations to read. Delegations travelled back and forth by bus or train for the weekend affairs – which featured student papers, keynote speakers, and much joviality. Faculty members and students billeted each other, and we came to know several Macalester families very well. Donald and Irene Warner we found particularly compatible. Don had written perceptively on the Canadian movement for annexation to the United States and was a good Democrat, just left of FDR and Truman. He was also a Catholic, teaching in a Presbyterian college. Late one evening, peering through thick, slightly misted glasses, he observed: 'Macalester is a Christian college. We prove it every spring by having a crucifixion.' I should have taken more seriously his cryptic warning.

In September 1954 I had agreed to be keynote speaker in St Paul. The conference topic was 'Canada and the United States in the United Nations.' In that culminating year of McCarthyism (the Wisconsin senator had unwisely taken on the army), Macalester, like most American campuses, felt very edgy about the national witch hunt. I was a bit nervous about my paper and kept biting back the dyspeptic remarks that frequently occurred to me. The material and interpretation grew out of a seminar I had launched on the history of Canadian foreign policy. In the seminar's first year I had three students. One of them, Ramsay Cook, was, with good reason, known as 'Red.' He let me get away with nothing – and still doesn't. In the course of our discussions I found myself ever more impressed by the lines of continuity in the evolution of Canadian self-government, and also by the way in which we tried to manage our relations with the imperial power of Britain and the United States. The themes of tolerance, accommodation, and pragmatism, though the copy-book was often blotted, seemed startlingly salient, especially when compared with the calamitous self-righteousness of American manifest destiny. In the Macalester paper I sketched some historical comparisons, and then dealt with glaring differences of approach to the threat of Soviet communism. In brief, I pointed to the imprudence of confronting the danger exclusively by military-ideological means and alliances with reactionary regimes dotted around George Kennan's perimeter of 'containment.'

On the train to St Paul, David Blostein, a brilliant third-year student, showed Mike Oliver the paper he had prepared on the U.S. attitude to the United Nations (a Macalester student would read one on Canada). Mike, prudently, advised several deletions from David's unbridled analysis. Overhearing this discussion, Bev told Mike: 'Let David leave it as it is.' From the seat behind us, an over-serious Howard Pawley concurred with Mike. David made no corrections. At the end of his reading at Macalester, all hell broke loose; unlike their professors, the St Paul students were John Foster Dullesites to the last soul. Blostein's talents (he was a concert-level violinist) led him to write and produce in the following year a musical rewrite of *Romeo and Juliet* – which the visiting American students liked much better than his St Paul paper. His stage production depicted fearsome rivalry between two street gangs in Brooklyn. Following rave reviews in Winnipeg, he sent the script and score off to New York. There was no serious response. Six years later, *West Side Story* hit the Broadway boards. David is the only student I've allowed to graduate while still owing his final paper. That spring he asked whether I thought he should go on with the violin or into graduate school. Perhaps because of my own abortive tussles with a violin, I recommended the ivory tower. I think he's forgiven me.

In St Paul my paper went down well – at least with faculty and the Canadian student delegation. Afterwards, Kenneth Holmes, Macalester's senior history professor, startled me with a most improbable suggestion: Why not submit the paper to *Foreign Affairs*? Well, this most establishment of American quarterlies had certainly not occurred to me. However, I sent it off and received a quick reply from the assistant editor, Byron Dexter – with some helpful proposals for minor changes. I realized how 'judicious' I must have been as I read Dexter's letter: 'Your paper discusses frankly differences of Canadian and American approaches to the United Nations and to the general problem of security from Communist aggression which are usually unmentioned, and does so so sensibly and moderately that your paper is a real

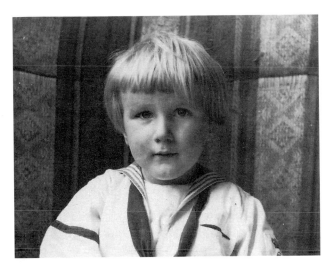

A serious two-year-old Ken in Toronto

The young sailor pays a visit to the *Bluenose* in Toronto harbour, 1936

Wedding Day, 13 June 1942: Ken McNaught and Beverley Argue at Trinity College, Toronto

LEFT: Sergeant McNaught of the Royal Canadian Ordnance Corps at Camp Borden, 1943

BELOW: 'The Coat' – Ken in the buffalo-skin coat that earned him a measure of notoriety among United College students

Ken with Arthur and Evelyn Lower and friends at Garden Island in the 1950s

Ken and son Andrew fishing from the broken-down pier on Garden Island

LEFT: The TV Pundit – chair of the CBC 'Round Table' in Winnipeg, 1954–8

BELOW: The McNaughts in 1957 – Christopher, Ken, Allison, and baby Andrew on Beverley's lap

The author's delight – a book table selling Ken's biography of J.S. Woodsworth in October 1959

The social critic – Professor McNaught addresses the Ontario Federation of Labour in the early 1960s

A 1966 reunion of United College 'exiles' – Beverley McNaught, Peggi Morrison, Walter Young, Dick Stingle, Betty Dean, Fred Harper, Bill Dean, Ken McNaught

Ken, any evening, any summer, from 1952 to 1996 on Garden Island

Ken and Beverley at 'Canada Night' in the Nuffield Flats, London, 1964

contribution to a better understanding.' A short while later the dignified old editor, Hamilton Fish Armstrong, wrote to say the article
would appear in the July 1955 issue. Frank Underhill, who read every
worthwhile American and British journal, wrote in July. After a mild
rebuke in which he observed that it is only our governments that are
cynical – as a people we are, like the Americans, too moralistic [he
believed in George Kennan] – he relented: 'But this is the best article
I've read for some considerable time.'

An equally pleasing and characteristic letter came from Arthur
Lower, who was doing a stint at the University of Wisconsin: 'I am glad
to know that you had this bit of good fortune. If you can get Americans
to recognize your existence, Canadians may begin to recognize it.'
Arthur was edgy for a particular reason: 'I have just read Mr [James]
Eayrs' review in the CHR of my *Most Famous Stream*. If he is typical,
and I hope he is not, I'm afraid I must write the younger generation off,
for it is plain that he just has not guts enough to be *anything* and so
takes the usual weak-kneed intellectual's recourse of just pouring a
tea-coloured liquid over everything.' At the time, Arthur was trying to
pry open a position for me at Wisconsin, 'as I know what a hell United
College can be.'

That spring and summer of 1955 were fairly blissful. In June, David
Farr, whom I had first met in Underhill's graduate seminar, wrote to
say I had been elected to the Council of the Canadian Historical Association. A week later, H.S. Bailey of the Princeton University Press
asked me to review Lester Pearson's *Democracy in World Politics*.
Underhill thought the review was too critical; at the time he read it he
had just accepted Pearson's offer (on Jack Pickersgill's suggestion) that
he become curator of Laurier House. I was amused, yet knew perfectly
well there was no interconnection. At the beginning of July I agreed to
write a long article on Canadian–American relations. This, plus the
Pearson review, several other reviews, and a Queen's summer course,
provided a nice balance to life in the School House. Occasionally I
mulled over the frequent jibes of my business friends in the real world:
'So you're off again for a four-month holiday.' And then I thought,
despite near penury, we really are pampered – doing exactly what we
most like doing and at a pace of our own choosing.

Back in Winnipeg, the old feeling of real attachment again alternated
with tantalizing eastern possibilities. In September, Underhill wrote
about his Laurier House appointment: 'I jumped at the chance since I
am at the retiring age-level now and also haven't looked forward with

great joy to continuing in the present department with Don Creighton as head ... I'm a bit doubtful as to how you stand with Creighton but it would do no harm, I should think, for you to write him making enquiries.' Well, I did just that; and received a quick reply whose salutation amused me: 'My dear Ken, shall we drop the formalities? I shall be glad if you would call me by my first name.' Underhill's letters, to the very end, began, 'Dear McNaught.' The 'anti-Brit' Underhill clung to British usages; the anti-American Creighton moved easily to North American informality. Creighton's letter that autumn told me that while there was no immediate opening, he would treat my inquiry as 'information which may be useful should a particular set of circumstances arise.' Was he prescient?

8

In the summer of 1955 Principal Graham died at his summer retreat on Lake Simcoe. We had never felt close to the Grahams, though we admired his struggles to wrench from the Board of Regents greater efforts in raising funds for a church college whose academic standards Graham wished always to advance. His tolerance of our assertive idiosyncrasies was remarkable, but not infinite. A friend reported telling him of my confirmation and of his response: 'Oh, well, he'll be all right, then.'

Perhaps long immersion in Old Testament study had led Graham to place too high a value on kinship and personal loyalty. He was deeply affronted when, in 1953, Stewart Reid, Harry Crowe, and I initiated a United College Association (UCA). We had read a good deal about the British Association of University Professors and the equivalent American association and had supported the founding in 1951 of a Canadian Association of University Teachers. We had a twofold purpose: to secure faculty representation on the Board of Regents and to force salaries upward. The two aims were, of course, related, but not mutually exclusive. United's salaries were still abysmally low even compared with the generally depressed Canadian averages. In 1956 my first communication from Graham's successor told me that I was promoted to full professor, with a salary of $5000. That figure was the floor for assistant professors at our sister Victoria College in Toronto. We believed that with faculty members on the board, we could strengthen Graham's hand and also move towards the ideal of faculty self-government – although this ultimate goal was muted. Graham had viewed our action as a vote of no confidence in himself.

Although several of the old guard refused to join the 'union,' most became members. I was especially pleased that Gordon Blake, United's economics department, decided to join. Blake and I had met in 1946 as members of Alex Brady's huge graduate seminar at Toronto. When he and his wife, Sibley, came to United in 1949, they bought a commodious house just a block away from us in Crescentwood. We socialized a lot. Although Gordon and I became, I felt, close friends, he seemed always to withhold something of himself. Tall, slender, and rather elegant, he had a nervous facial twitch that slightly disconcerted one in conversation. Most of the Blakes' friends were in business, so whenever I tried to engage Gordon in debate about public ownership and such things, he would smile and change the subject. His aura of privacy turned aside my unguarded readiness to put all the cards on the table. Still, I enjoyed his enigmatic, almost military mien. I record these details because, in the ugly events that lay just ahead, Blake's role was the most nearly tragic and to me the greatest shock. Long after the event his wife is reported to have said, 'Gord backed the wrong horse.'

That wrong horse, in the person of Wilfred Lockhart, came to replace Principal Graham in the autumn of 1955. Lockhart arrived with good academic credentials (PhD, Edinburgh), a reputation as left-of-centre during a ten-year stint as chaplain, first of Hart House and then with the Canadian Officers' Training Corps at Toronto. He was chairman of the United Church's Board of Colleges and had been, since 1942, pastor to the wealthy congregation of Kingsway-Lambton Church on the outskirts of Toronto. Lockhart brought with him a wife, Eileen, who was to show some personality resemblance to Marie-Antoinette, and a spanking new Buick donated by his Toronto congregation, with whom he was immensely popular. While the new principal made sympathetic noises on the salary question, he showed little vigour when confronted by an obdurate Board of Regents. We soon suspected that Eileen was of stronger mettle, when she took over detailed direction of redecorating the main college building; or when, on a 'pastoral visit,' she jocosely reprimanded a noisy Oliver youngster: 'You should know better, when the boss's wife is visiting.'

A year after he arrived, Lockhart faced a tough dispute between the faculty association and the Board of Regents. Although he quavered, he made it clear the regents must prevail. The incident followed on Ottawa's decision to make a substantial grant of money to universities for the specific purpose of improving salary levels. When United received its puny $57,000 from the federal grant, Lockhart and the board decided that a substantial chunk be devoted to sprucing up the main building. As chairman of the UCA's salary committee, I requested a meeting with the regents. Dick Stingle, Harry Crowe, Mike Oliver, Viljo Packer, a nervous Ed Eagle (the Classics department), and an inscrutable Gordon Blake accompanied me to the board room to present our salary brief.

At the head of the table governed the crustaceous Senator J.T. Haig, finishing his last year as chairman of the board. Our immediate purpose was to have the regents reverse policy and apply the entire grant to salaries. In support of our case I quoted from the House of Commons Hansard, which recorded speeches by Prime Minister St Laurent and several leaders of both parties, all of them stressing the single purpose of the grant. J.M. Macdonnell, Tory financial critic (and regular host to the University of Toronto's Historical Club), had remarked: 'Other grants to universities with a view to Capital expenditures will be discussed and that need not be gone into now.' It took a good deal of bravado for me to quote Haig's own remarks in the Senate: 'The additional money ... is being allocated to the increase of salaries and endowments for professors, a provision that must be made if these men [!] are to be retained in the positions they occupy.' I was particularly proud of this bit of research, and equally astonished by Haig's rough-edged response: 'Young man, don't believe everything you read in the Hansard.' And that was that. Years later I discovered that Lockhart had told the board that he had been put in 'a somewhat intolerable position.' I've concluded that Eileen Lockhart very likely had a hand in her timid husband's 'decision.' She took too much delight in supervising the refurbishing that resulted. Among other improvements, the outside of the main building was scrubbed and yellow-hued floodlights trained upon its architectural horrors. Stewart described the whole effect: the building had been faced with chicken shit.

Despite this hullabaloo, our lives, both academic and social, became steadily richer and more rooted in the college. I took several of the daily morning chapel services – nervously, because I had not yet memorized a creed and was even shaky on the Lord's Prayer. To the amusement of Reid and Crowe, I ran a non-credit seminar on Christianity and history in which I proved Christianity to be the source of the most valid idea of progress. I also became 'president' of the 1958 student graduating year, whose spring dance, largely on Dick Stingle's insistence, required white ties and long dresses for the faculty – to the disgust of most of the old guard. Disapproval arose also when the Reids

correctly sent their daughter to the Fort Garry campus, rather than
enrolling her at United, and when we sent Chris to St John's-Ravens-
court for his final two years of grade school. Dick Gordon, Ravens-
court's headmaster, had offered a bursary, and we were more than
happy with the school.

In 1953 I proposed to Stewart and Harry that we collaborate on a
book of primary source readings in Canadian history. Such volumes
were common for American and European history but none, apart
from some single-themed collections in constitutional and economic
history, existed for Canadian history. Stewart undertook the first section on discoveries, New France, and western expansion; Harry would
do a middle section; and I took over at Confederation. Stewart and
Harry each drew their material from widely scattered published works.
Hoping to nourish the project with some unpublished matter, I spent
the summer of 1953 in Ottawa. We rented a small house at Brittania
close to the water – where I left Bev and the kids each day while I
ploughed about in the archives. To speed things up I borrowed a portable dictaphone; there were no easy copying services then. As I worked
through the Macdonald, Laurier, and several other collections, I
crouched low over the big volumes to muffle my voice as much as possible. Despite having a contract with Longman's, Green, our only subsidy was a $900 Social Science Research Council grant – split three
ways. As a result, I spent many of the following winters' evenings tran-
scribing from the playback. A highlight of that hot Ottawa summer was
daily lunch with Heath Macquarrie. Big, heavy set, full of sardonic
good humour, Heath always showed up with a furled umbrella –
already in training, perhaps, for the Senate.

A Source-Book of Canadian History finally hit the market in 1959.
Stewart had finished his relatively short section first; Harry bogged
down in a mix of political activity and his doctoral thesis for Columbia,
which he never quite completed. In the final phase I funnelled a lot of
my archived nuggets into Harry's section, and the manuscript went off
to Longman's in 1957. Taking account of readers' reports took some
time, too. However, the book was well received and a second edition,
with an index, unwisely avoided in the first, appeared two years later.
At that time we agreed with Longman's to do a second volume devoted
entirely to the twentieth century. But by then Crowe and Reid were in
Ottawa, and I was in Toronto; we each had too much on the plate. Too
bad; I have an ancient fourteen-page outline that still looks good.

Ambivalent feelings about United and Winnipeg surfaced sharply in the late winter of 1956. In March, George Stanley, head of the Royal Military College's history department, wrote to offer me a position as associate professor. Arthur Lower had been the prime mover. The salary would be much higher than United's; there would be civil service security; and from RMC's Point Frederick you can see Garden Island. I'm still not certain why I declined; vague uneasiness about a military-conservative milieu, I think. Had I accepted, we would have been spared much heartache, but we would also have missed our most formative experience.

Another consideration certainly intruded. In January I had accepted an invitation from Fred Soward, head of history and international studies at the University of British Columbia, to teach a summer course in Canadian history. Apart from the lure of seven weeks in Vancouver, I hoped that this interlude might lead to something permanent. I suspect Soward thought so, too; but, if so, he changed his mind. He had read the *Foreign Affairs* piece and had drawn imperfect conclusions about my judiciousness. Nevertheless, the summer rewarded us handsomely.

We bought a big used Chrysler in June and set out for San Francisco. Such south-sweeping routes we had chosen on previous drives to the East, dipping into Missouri, Ohio, and Kentucky. That spring, as we banged over some rough mountain roads, I was jittery because Bev was five months pregnant. All went well, however, and Bev was scheduled to make the return through the mountains by train. In San Francisco we visited with a cousin, Robert McNaught, who, as head of ophthamology at Leland Stanford, lived in a stately Spanish house overlooking the Golden Gate Bridge. Most impressive, until Bob unleashed his Republican opinion that the city had declined with the inrush of 'niggers' during the war.

For the summer we had arranged to rent the house of Esther and Earle Birney – who were friends of my parents and also of the Sirlucks. High above Spanish Banks, glimpsing the sparkle of English Bay, the Birney home seemed ideal. It was full of water-colours by Leonard Brooks painted at San Miguel, Mexico – where Earle was, we were told, enjoying one of his frequent trysts. Esther had mentioned that the house had a self-contained basement appartment. She had allowed that the single tenant there would be no bother, but that tenant turned out to be one of her 'lame ducks.' When he opened the door to us we saw a bizarre figure with orange hair, clad only in Hawaiian shorts, and blowing forth fumes of Niagara sherry. With a slight lisp he acknowledged Chris as 'Chrissy,' ignoring Allison and a clearly pregnant Bev. I managed to steer him downstairs, locking the cellarway door after him. Bev's shock deepened as we surveyed the kitchen. The stove was streaked with hardened spaghetti; a cross-eyed Siamese cat prowled among dirty dishes and pots on the counter. Once we had put the house back in order we saw little more of him – save for a few occasions when we forgot to lock the cellarway door. On one of these he staggered up clad in a monk's robe, which he told me he had worn during an unsuccessful novitiate. Worse, he recalled that I had done the illustration for a poem he had published in the Upper Canada College magazine *In Between Times*. Dear Esther. Some years later we read of his suicide.

There were two days of light rain that summer. Two hours of lecturing, daily, left plenty of time for the beach, picnics, and sketching – no problem with subject matter. We also gained some very good friends. Bill and Margaret Robbins and Ted Morrison of UBC's English department provided a socialist base for some convivial occasions, and I rediscovered Bill Duthie from University College days. Bill was building his fine bookstore into the city's largest. He and 'Mackie' lived in Caulfield, just across the Lion's Gate Bridge, in a waterside house with a mountain stream running over a rock wall in the washroom; deep envy. Richard Van Alstyne, one of the summer lecturers from the United States, I found particularly stimulating. Already a senior diplomatic historian, his work on American nationalism and foreign policy was to influence me more than that of any other American scholar. Unassuming, erudite, 'gentlemanly,' Van Alstyne was my first acquaintance of this wonderful American 'type.' I met many more thereafter, and usually felt a twinge of guilt as I mined their work with hypercritical intent. Van Alstyne was, in 1956, mulling over ideas that he would incorporate in *The Rising American Empire*, the first of whose many editions came out in 1960.

Another American summer lecturer, whose name I've repressed, was to be my undoing at UBC. A medievalist (and rabid Republican) from Coe College in Cedar Rapids, he and his wife joined the rest of us at an end-of-session dinner given by the Sowards. During coffee, he and I fell into a noisy argument over the merits of Adlai Stevenson, who had just won the Democratic presidential nomination. Sparks flew as Soward was moving around with liqueurs. Bending close to my ear he said softly: 'McNaught, you'll catch more flies with honey than you will with vinegar.' And that was that. As we journeyed back to Winnipeg, I thought of the luncheon appointment I had missed with Ralph Flenley in 1950.

Underhill, Creighton, and Lower set high standards of concern for their ex-students and colleagues. Their letters still warm my heart. While I was in Vancouver, Underhill wrote to say that he was now on the Senate of Carleton College and had spoken of me to James Gibson, the acting president, and to Claude Bissell, the incoming president of Carleton University. Bissell he judged to be 'a very intelligent fellow himself and everything [about the new university] will depend on how firm and strong he is.' While nothing matured for me at the time, the word with Bissell did no harm for the future. In September, Dave Farr wrote: 'Professor Creighton has asked me to approach you about doing a paper [for the 1957 CHA meeting] ... He suggests you might feel able to do something on Canadian foreign policy.' A very full Winnipeg winter lay ahead. That winter got off to a great start with the birth of Andrew in October. Although Bev was thirty-seven, her doctor had spoken strongly in favour of the venture; it proved to be the least difficult birth of the three, and Andrew at once enjoyed Allison's mothering instincts.

For the CHA paper, I used material and notions gathered for my seminar and for the final stages of the Woodsworth biography. I had finished the biography in 1953 and was in the midst of final publishing negotiations in the autumn of 1957. Before dealing briefly with the convolutions of publishing, and because *A Prophet in Politics* became central to my political and historical thinking, I will backtrack a bit to say something about its gestation.

In the spring of 1948 I wrote to Grace (Woodsworth) MacInnis asking her advice and help in gaining access to her father's papers. Her reply offered some very slender hope: 'Mother is not yet prepared to make Father's personal family letters available. I do not share her viewpoint but I'm afraid I'll have to respect it ... I doubt whether, during Mother's lifetime, it will be possible to publish much about the personal side of Father's life ... The only suggestion I could make is that if you could win her confidence – and I think that could be done only by showing her a chapter of writing about Father – she might be willing to let you have more than anyone has been able to get so far.' In October a letter from Underhill brought a bit more hope:

I had quite a long talk with Mrs. Woodsworth. Grace had consulted with her earlier and she felt she had been too absolute in ruling against anyone having access to her husband's letters. (Sissons had advised her that not until about 40 years after a man's death could a good biography of him be done [Woodsworth had been dead for six years]). I advised her that her best course would be to let you use them for a biography and also at the same time make a calendar of them. She seems inclined to do this. She told me that Lorne Ingle [a family friend and CCF researcher] had approached her with a view to doing a biography of her husband, but I told her that you would be a much more suitable person. So she is going to consult Grace and Angus [MacInnis] and I hope they agree with my advice. She feels that something should be done much earlier than à la Sissons; and I think she will come around to making use of you.

Those two letters impelled me to write the article on Woodsworth and a political party for labour, which I have mentioned earlier. Although it stole time from work on my thesis, its appearance in the June 1949 *Canadian Historical Review* turned the trick. That summer in Toronto I had several long talks with Lucy – and also one with C.B. Sissons. A Classics professor at Victoria, he had recently completed his excellent biography of Egerton Ryerson. He was also a cousin of JS What I didn't know, at the time, was that he and his wife had formed an undergraduate quartet with Lucy and JS at Victoria and that he had been engaged to Lucy. His forty-year rule remained – but not quite inflexible; what I later pieced together came mostly from interviews and JS's side of their correspondence. Underhill had been perceptive when he wrote: 'Sissons says that if you are not a religious man you cannot do Woodsworth properly, but he liked your article in the CHR. He thinks I am a religious man without knowing it [so do I, now], since I liked his Ryerson. So this may count in your favour.' It did. Victoria's grand old man of the day allowed me to read a judiciously pruned selection of his correspondence with JS.

As I was winding down the thesis and planning the further research to extend it into a full biography, Grace threw a thunderbolt. In February 1950 she wrote: 'For years I have played with the idea of writing a book about Father – not a careful chronological thing such as you are doing – but the only sort of thing I had a chance of doing – my own interpretation of him ... I've decided that now is the time to have a shot at it ... Please don't say anything about it for the present ... Have you any advice or suggestions to offer? ... I'd value anything you had time to write ... I didn't expect to be turning the tables on you in this fashion Kenneth, but there it is.' There, indeed, it was. I needed all my slender resources of tolerance, particularly when I discovered that Grace used some correspondence which she had withheld from me. My admiration of Grace, whom I had first met when she was president of the Canadian Cooperative Youth Movement in the late 1930s, eventually prevailed – especially after her moving personal account appeared in 1953 as *J.S. Woodsworth: A Man to Remember*. Lucy applied an interim bandage when she wrote in April, after reading most of my draft thesis chapters: 'Well, your great day with reference to this undertaking, Kenneth, is drawing near. For me your studies have meant re-living those enchanted years during which, whether together or miles apart, we travelled side by side.'

Grace's book came out just as I was finishing the manuscript of *A Prophet*. In a foolish fit of urgency I sent it off to Ivor Owen of Oxford University Press in Toronto. His response shook me: 'You have written a very good book and we feel that it must certainly be published; if possible, by us. The main difficulty is its length.' He suggested I cut the manuscript by 25,000 words because 'this is a book for the Canadian citizen and not for the research library only.' With great pain I made a few compressions (far short of his recommendation) and sent the manuscript back to Oxford. In April 1954 Ivor sent a hand-written note: 'I have read your revised manuscript and like it immensely. I think we will probably decide to publish it ... for quite extraneous reasons there might be a delay before we communicate with you officially. Hence this note, which is so unofficial that I am not even putting a copy of it in any file.' Five months passed. Then came a formal letter advising me to cut the manuscript to 85,000 words (from about 120,000). I rejected this demand. In December the whole miserable charade wound down and Owen wrote: 'I do hope there may ultimately be a chance of working with you on something else.' Some chance.

With unusual prescience I had read correctly the omens in Owen's first proposal to eviscerate and popularize the biography. In January 1954 I took out some insurance; a copy of the original manuscript went off to Marsh Jeanneret, director of the University of Toronto Press. I told him in a covering letter of my unpromising approach to Oxford. In a sober and encouraging reply he wrote: 'Such delays are extremely trying, of course, but perhaps some slight consolation can be taken in the fact that it may be just as well if a little time elapses between the appearance of Mrs. MacInnis's book and yours, even though the two are quite different in purpose and treatment.' I followed his advice, to seek a subsidy from the Canadian Social Science Research Council. This process took a long time, but it was worth it. Frank Underhill was one of the council's readers and he sent me (quite improperly) a copy of his reader's report: the book 'brings out the quality of the man very persuasively, and at the same time gives an analysis of Canadian politics in the twentieth century, which is one of the best that has been written.' Frank's covering note of October 1959 was vintage FHU: 'Ottawa is still in the midst of the hysteria over the royal visit, which appears to be a great success and will put back the appearance of the Malcolm Muggeridges and Lord Altrinchams and John Osbornes in our Canadian society for another generation.' In due course the publication grant came through and the University of Toronto Press swung into almost dizzying action.

Under Jeanneret and Francess Halpenny, the UTP had reached a high level of academic publishing. Francess was well on her way to being the country's most distinguished scholar-editor. In November 1958 she returned the fully edited manuscript to me, replete with queries and comments – all of which were relatively minor and also very helpful. Jean Houston did the final detailed editing, in such exquisite detail that she even caught a couple of incorrect page references to Hansard debates. Page proofs and a request for an index reached me at the end of April 1959. I spent our last days in Winnipeg messing with dozens of index cards covering the dining room table like a quite possible spring snowfall.

Frank Underhill had written his report recommending a publication subsidy just four months after I read my paper at the June 1957 CHA meetings in Ottawa. That session was by far the most explosive I ever got caught up in. I titled the paper 'Canadian Foreign Policy and the Whig Interpretation; 1936–1939.' I attacked fairly savagely the 'received' Liberal version of Canadian history: the relatively non-violent, compromise-by-compromise, parliamentary evolution from 'colony to nation,' at the end of which Mackenzie King had emerged as great because he divided us least (Underhill's 1949 recantation). Reviewing the steadfast King–Lapointe refusal to debate or clarify Canadian policy as war loomed, I quoted Arthur Lower: 'Under the circumstances, the supreme task of statesmanship was to avoid enunciating a foreign policy.' My conclusion was that King's slogan, 'Parliament will decide,' was a mere screen behind which the government's prior decision to 'be at Britain's side' would be sustained by leaving Parliament with nothing to decide. Arguing that all the commitments had been made by the time King summoned the emergency war session of September 1939, I suggested that Canadian unity, and the proper role of Parliament, would have been better served by permitting open debate during those crucial years.

I knew this brash tilting at Liberal orthodoxy would produce less than unanimous applause. Fortunately, Donald Creighton (CHA president that year) had seen to it that Frank Scott was chairman-commentator for the session; also, Eugene Forsey was present and recognized support for his ongoing crusade against the shade of King when he saw it. But after Scott's approving comment had been read, I took a hair-raising pounding from the floor. Fred Soward (quick to recognize the vinegar) led off, followed by Colonel Charles Stacey for the army historical section, and then Frank Underhill: 'Professor McNaught has said all the things I was saying in the 1930s. I was wrong then and he is wrong now.' Well, I had expected worse, and there were many pluses. Both Scott and Forsey (whom I had 'met' at Blythwood when still a youngster) became good friends. The paper itself was published in the CHA Annual Report and, over the next couple of decades, appeared in several anthologies.

The steamy June days of that CHA conference were further hotted up when Donald Creighton delivered his presidential address. With unrestrained verve he castigated the Liberal interpretation of Canadian history – the Word, the Authorized Version, the Sacred Text; an interpretation, he charged, compounded of the American frontier thesis and the Marxian class struggle discerned by the 'pseudo intellectuals' of the League for Social Reconstruction. In black-tie splendour, his brow glistening in the suffocating auditorium, Creighton leaned across the lectern to define his specific target: 'It finally began to be realized that the task of enlarging and perfecting the Sacred Text was a full-time occupation which required the undivided services of specially designated, specially dedicated, and particularly pious clerks. A national Liberal shrine, in short, was imperatively necessary. What building could serve more appropriately than Laurier House in Ottawa? National Liberal Scribes were required to devote themselves to the service of the Word. Who could be more appropriately chosen than those scholars who had dedicated themselves to the lives of the blessed Liberal saints and martyrs of the past?' The only veil across this personal fusillade against Underhill was the pluralizing of 'clerks,' 'scholars,' and 'scribes.' Bev and I had been invited to post-session parties: one for Frank and one for Donald. We managed both. I had agreed with quite a bit of Donald's critique of the 'received version,' but, like everyone else, found the personal vendetta deeply unsettling.

Another shining summer on Garden Island nourished us for a near-enthusiastic return to Winnipeg. During the fall term Stewart Reid and I worked out a detailed proposal for a two-volume history of Canada which would have space for much more social history than could be found in the existing single-volume texts – a new synthesis incorporating specialist studies that had been appearing since 1945. W.J. Gage gave us a contract, and we began discussing the project with congenial colleagues such as Dick Stingle, John Warkentin, and Fred Harper. Our hope was to give a multidisciplinary punch to the work; indeed, we saw it as demonstrating the virtue of a liberal arts college whose disciplinary discussions didn't inhibit mutual enterprise. Our last high hopes were to crumble irretrievably and quickly.

At the end of 1957 Stewart fell prey to prostate cancer. His doctor told him that if he were in his seventies, he would probably survive – to die of something else. But Stewart was just fifty, and he possessed a fiery sense of personal dignity. When his doctor guessed a four-year expectancy unless he would submit to castration, he chose to fight it out on his own terms. The doctor's guess was out by only two years. When Stewart got out of hospital, he and Velma 'celebrated' the arrival of 1958 with a long midnight dinner with Bev and me at 739 Macmillan.

We went ahead planning the Canadian history text, but some of the steam was missing. While I was on the barricades trying to defend *Roundtable*'s independence, contacts beyond the turmoil of Winnipeg continued to multiply. In February, Bill Eccles wrote asking me to be commentator on a paper for the CHA spring meetings in Edmonton. We had found Bill and Jean very congenial during the period when Bill was suffering in the toils of several one-year appointments on the Fort Garry campus. He was beginning his demolition of Count Frontenac, and carried his iconoclastic fervour into social conversation. When he and John Peter, the brilliantly acerbic South African novelist in the University of Manitoba's English department, matched assessments of academe, prudent people took cover.

Of course I accepted the CHA invitation. I had no way of knowing that the Edmonton Learned Societies would be awash in discussions of United College.

9

On 2 July 1958 United's Board of Regents fired Harry Crowe. My first intimation of what came to be known as the Crowe case (I've always referred to it, more accurately, as the Lockhart case) had come to my office on 16 April when Viljo Packer brought in a letter that Harry had written to him on 14 March. I begin with this incident because Harry's letter was, and remained, the only crucial *document* in an ugly sequence of actions, charges, and countercharges that eventually stirred academics across the country and breathed vigour into the fledgling Canadian Association of University Teachers. The all too public battle over that letter also catapulted us out of Winnipeg and back to Toronto. I now find it hard not to look upon those long months from April 1958 to June 1959 as a tragi-comedy: tragic because of smashed friendships and subversion of self-evident truths; comic because of the convoluted machination of small minds seeking (to my mind) revenge and security.

Harry wrote his letter in Kingston, where he was finishing a one-year appointment at Queen's, on leave from United. He and I corresponded frequently that year, during which I was president of the United College Association (UCA). Harry had been secretary the preceding year; Viljo succeeded him, and we both kept him posted on the deepening tension in the college. Afterglow from the board's raid on the federal salary subsidy, and stonewalling of proposals for faculty representation, had been reinvigorated by hefty suggestions that faculty members participate in a large building-fund drive to be launched that spring. On these matters I had commented pretty acidly to Harry; his letter to Viljo offered further reflections.

When Viljo handed me Harry's hand-written letter, he explained that he had just been given it by Lockhart in the principal's office, to which he had been summoned by Lockhart's secretary. Before I read it, Viljo told me that when he entered the office, the principal drew from a folder on his desk the opened letter. Handing it over, he asked if Viljo had ever seen it. Glancing at it, Viljo noticed the Queen's University crest, the salutation 'Dear Viljo,' the date, 14 March, and Harry's signature. He told Lockhart he had not seen it before. Lockhart said the letter had been found in the college hall, by a student, and invited Viljo to read it. Lockhart then remarked that the letter confirmed his view that there was a group in the college caballing against him, which Viljo denied. At that point the principal broke off the interview to keep a luncheon engagement, agreeing to meet with Packer again the following day.

Convinced that Lockhart intended to take action against Harry, Viljo brought his letter to the office I shared with Margaret Prang, Harry's replacement that year. The three of us passed the letter back and forth in apprehension and near-disbelief at the course Lockhart appeared about to take. While the confidentiality of Harry's letter remained the central issue in the following months of bloodletting, it is probably worth printing here in its entirety – if for no other reason than to shed superfluous light on the mental and moral capacity of United's administration.

QUEEN'S UNIVERSITY
Kingston, Ontario

14 March '58

Dear Viljo,

I am most anxious to hear what the U.C.A. is going to do with the freeloaders. This whole business of Swayze and Taylor is most distressing. I can't understand faculty members going out to collect money when the Board told us so emphatically that administration was none of our business. I hope few people answer that impertinent questionnaire. How did it pass?

Ken wrote a long sad letter. He seems most unhappy. I distrust all preachers and think we have abundant evidence that religion is a corrosive force – Graham, Lockhart, Freeman, Taylor, the two Hal[l]steads. People don't seem to have principles unless they are prepared to go to hell.

Unless Pearson catches fire a major political revolution is underway. The Liberal party is falling apart in Ontario. Knowles says they may elect no one in the West; the 'experts' around here are now talking in terms of 6 to 10 seats staying Liberal in Ontario. I have an irrational foreboding of a Conservative sweep of unprecedented proportions. Diefenbaker has communicated to the average little Joe as has no one else in our time – not even Aberhart in Alberta. I would not be surprised to see the Conservatives get around 4 million votes despite Pearson's appeal and the Tories' daily offences against intelligence. Our Irish Catholic neighbours have voted Liberal since Alexander Mackenzie but this time they are flocking to Diefenbaker. 'He is a good man'; 'he increased the Old Age Pension'; 'he is one of us'; 'he is a great leader.' Ugh! It is going to be rough on reason. Pearson is like Stevenson in 1952 with one difference: the Democratic machine in 1952 still did a job. David Croll has been drafted to run the show in Ontario and is reported to be 'stunned' by the lack of preparation and spirit. I have another irrational feeling. So many people hate the Liberals so much and are so excited at the prospect of really cutting them down that a portion of the CCF vote in 1957 will go PC this time. I can hardly wait for the first Gallup guess.

Keep up the good work and thanks for keeping me in the 'know.'

Love, lamentations. Best to family,

[Signed] Harry

I've always thought the most revealing passage in the letter was Harry's sharp prediction of the 1958 election outcome. Since Lockhart put a different, ominous spin on it, several of us – Viljo, Stewart Reid, Dick Stingle (who was on the UCA executive), and Margaret Prang – assembled at 739 Macmillan that evening to discuss the matter and alert Harry. We heard Viljo's brief account on the phone to Harry and then his gasp: 'You *laugh*?' Harry's last laugh for some time.

Viljo met again with Lockhart the following day. The principal altered his account of how he had received the letter. Drawing from his folder a blue envelope and a sheet of paper, he handed them to Viljo, saying that Harry's letter had reached him in that envelope, together with the sheet of paper – on which was typed a message: 'Found in College Hall. We [!] think you should read it. Some staff loyalty???' Viljo reminded Lockhart that on the previous day he had said a student had found the letter and given it to him. 'That was the only reasonable explanation,' the principal replied. Well, it was clearly unreasonable. To Lockhart's visible annoyance, Viljo said he would report the matter to the post office. Later investigation by the postal authorities confirmed that the letter had been properly delivered to the college. A police investigation concluded that someone in the college had stolen it. Theft would certainly not have posed any problem: all faculty mail went, unsorted, into a wire basket on a counter in the registrar's office. Nor would it require the skill of a rocket scientist to conclude that a Queen's University envelope, addressed to Packer, was from the ex-secretary to the current secretary of the UCA. Moreover, anyone reading just the opening sentence could not but know that the letter was about UCA affairs. Viljo's second interview with Lockhart came to an end when the principal told Packer that he was retaining photostatic copies of the letter.

In Kingston, Harry had no doubt he was being pressed to resign. He was also enraged by Lockhart's invasion of his privacy. On 25 April, replying to a report I had sent him about old guard rumours to the effect that he had always been a 'trouble-maker,' and assuring him of 'our' support, he wrote to me: 'I haven't looked forward to a letter as I did this one for a long time ... I don't know how I am going to eat after Sept. 1 but I am certain that if there are grounds for the indictment of Lockhart and I fail to bring him face to face with the grim consequences of indictment that the chances are less that I will be eating than if I do ... I am sure that the causes of job security and of academic freedom are the same ... You ask, what am I doing this summer? Teaching at Queen's and R.M.C. to pay legal fees.' Fortunately, there would be no legal fees. Harry had asked a friend, Colonel J.E. Wilson, QC, to act as an intermediary and adviser. Wilson, even after Lockhart refused to relinquish the photostats to him, wrote to Harry: 'The main thing is to put to rest any further ill will on the subject and I am hopeful that this can be done to the contentment of everyone concerned.' At Queen's, Harry received similar advice, from Alex Corry, Stuart Ryan of the law faculty, Malcolm Ross, Glen Shortliffe, Eric Harrison, Fred Gibson, and others. Yet, even while he was agreeing to pursue his academic and civil rights within the profession rather than in the courts, Lockhart was penning an ominous communication.

Lockhart's letter to Crowe (23 April) included this passage: 'Your letter [to Viljo] is a profoundly disturbing document. After reading it I have had to regretfully come to the conclusion that personally you have no sympathy with the avowed purposes of the College, and that you have no respect for or loyalty to the administration.' Harry wrote to me the day he got Lockhart's lament: 'I have just received what amounts to an invitation from Lockhart to resign [and] expect that if I don't I will be fired later in the summer when the building fund drive is over.' Colonel Wilson told Harry not to reply to Lockhart's letter; instead, Wilson himself met with the principal on 7 May, seeking to 'resolve the difficulties informally.' Lockhart told him it was already too late; 'the matter' would go before the Board of Regents the following evening. Clearly the principal, although denying he had shown Harry's letter to anyone, had discussed its contents with quite a few people. On 7 May he called a special meeting of the college's general faculty council to discover ways of dealing with rumours that 'were circulating beyond the campus and which would ruin the building fund campaign.'

That surcharged faculty meeting should have stopped Lockhart in his tracks. He told how Harry's letter had come to him and what he had done with it – and that rumours which 'could only have come from the faculty' now forced him to submit it to the board. Stewart and I protested that the issue was not the 'rumours' but the facts – which Lockhart himself had disclosed. Others queried Lockhart's proposed course of action – but not enough to stop him. Stewart Reid pointed out that if the letter – or Lockhart's summary of it – were placed before the regents, Harry would be on trial *in absentia*. When Stewart offered to represent Harry, as chairman of the history department, the principal sidestepped and revealed that he himself had written to Harry. Asked if he had received a reply, he said there could be no answer; and at this point the dean of theology dropped a clanger. He challenged Packer to show 'good faith' by reading Harry's letter to the meeting. Viljo refused. Dean Freeman then said that when he 'first read the letter' he felt that anyone on the faculty was duty bound to take it to the principal. Oh?

All this is agony, but we're talking fierce personal antagonism here: hatred that alone explains why a clear-cut ethical blunder exploded in a frightening disregard of academic and civil propriety and a year-long endeavour to set aside the essential issue by resort to tortuous procedural squabbles and feints at 'reconciliation.' Thus, I owe it to Harry to record part of a letter that he wrote to me on 9 May. I had told him of Lockhart's file and his remark that Harry had been expelled as a student 'for immorality' in 1942. Harry wrote:

My recollection of 1942 is very clear. So is Dr. Lower's [Arthur was head of the history department at the time]. He is outraged by this. In 1942 Marshall [Harry's brother] wrote a letter to George Freeman [Dean Freeman's son] which Mrs. Freeman removed from their mailbox (It is an old United College custom). This letter was full of profanity. Mrs. Freeman took it to Principal Graham who wrote Marshall a censorious letter. Marshall replied telling him to go to hell. Marshall and I both registered at the University. [Later] O.T. Anderson told Graham I was going to register at the College for the 2 or 3 months before I went off in the army. Graham, mad as hell at Marshall, had a faculty committee set up to see if I should be allowed into a fifth year for 2 or 3 months. Graham apparently told them I spent all my time on politics and military training and wouldn't do any work. They decided I shouldn't be allowed in. *I was a member of staff before I knew of this!* Graham and I had exchanged words about my spending time reading army books and working for the CCF. About that time we had one *most unpleasant* session. But I was never expelled or any other bloody thing. *Now Freeman* obviously has told Lockhart a cock and bull story. Mrs. Freeman firmly believes Marshall and I talked George out of the ministry.

Harry also pointed out that it was Principal Graham who urged him to join the faculty in 1950.

So the moment when the faculty could and should have stopped the whole gruesome farce was lost. Following the council meeting, we phoned Harry to report that Lockhart would take 'the matter' to the regents the next evening. On the advice of his general staff at Queen's, Harry sent a telegram to Allan Watson, the chair of the Board of Regents, noting Lockhart's misuse of his letter and the rumours that were circulating about the matter 'I have done nothing whatever to initiate.' He wound off the telegram: 'I find it exceedingly hard to believe that information obtained in this manner will be presented to the Board of Regents and I would find it even harder to believe that the Board of Regents should consider it proper to act upon such information. If, however, I am incorrect in this judgment, and if action adverse to me follows, full publicity will inevitably be given to all the facts in this incident.'

Harry sent me a copy of this telegram, and I gave it to the principal during an hour-and-a-half meeting with him on 8 May. The regents were to meet that evening. Having failed to convince a faculty council majority to put Lockhart back on a course of decency, I hoped a private conversation, away from the blood-thirsty dean and their loyal cohort, might induce him to pull back from the brink. I had misjudged him. I don't think Lockhart ever did understand the issues of academic and personal rights his action, encouraged and even precipitated by his 'seconds in command,' had brought into dangerous focus.

In our far from pleasant conversation, he reminded me that I had never been in a position of responsibility; news to a mere professor. He explained that he might not have done what he did as a private citizen, but that he represented the church and the board and had to defend them. I must have spluttered, recalling Harry's remark about 'all preachers,' because Lockhart then repeated that the letter was not the only thing. 'Crowe's file,' he said, contained evidence that W.C. Graham had taken severe disciplinary action against him because of his conduct as a student. If this rumour (which I knew was already floating around Winnipeg) were true, I asked, why had Graham appointed Harry in 1950? Lockhart acknowledged this to be 'a problem.' Observing that he had never intended action against Harry, but felt obliged to take 'the matter' to the board, he ended our chat. I felt then that I had been talking to a man well out of his depth and seeking shelter. Nor have I ever doubted that Lockhart thought he was doing the right thing: efficiently administering a tight budget and ambitious building fund while taking advice from long-service 'employees' and a business-minded board. He was innocent of any concept of academic independence or its relation to 'tenure' – a precedent-breaking notion perfectly foreign to the casual letters of appointment that formed our sole 'legal' connection with the college. Even so, how could he have been blind to the very nature of personal correspondence?

So the ball was now in the court of Allan H. Watson, a banker with a banker's vision. The regents refused Stewart Reid's request to represent Harry at the 8 May board meeting. They certainly discussed Harry's letter – probably learning its contents through detailed paraphrasing. In a letter to Harry following the meeting, Watson set on foot the Kafkaesque convolutions that embroiled us all in nearly a year of turmoil and insecurity.

Watson's letter, swathed in ambiguity, said the board would gather more information by 'further study and enquiry.' In short order, three lawyer members of the Board called 'unofficially' upon Colonel Wilson. The whole problem could be resolved, they said, if Crowe would 'go elsewhere.' His opinions were 'not very acceptable,' and if he came back 'it would be uncomfortable.' Should Harry refuse to 'smooth things over,' said the lawyers, he could return to United for one year only. In early June, following pressure from some United Church people (including Arthur Lower) in Ontario, Harry met with Dr E.E. Long, the church's general secretary, and two other church representatives to no avail. Lockhart hung on to his photostats and, on 28 May, wrote to Harry: 'Since the matter of your future relationship to the College is presently under consideration by the Board and will be at the discretion of the Board, it will be in order for you to address any correspondence in this regard to its Chairman, Mr. A.H. Watson.' From his bunker in Kingston, Harry kept me posted on all these developments, and I kept him aware of who was saying what in Winnipeg. 'I look forward,' he wrote, 'to your letters like I looked for letters when we were in battle in 1944 and '45. The analogy could be pursued.' At the end of another of his lengthy reports, he observed: 'Just got a long account of life in Moscow from Marshall [who was with the Canadian Embassy]. Sounds very peaceful.'

And by the end of June Watson left no doubt that war had been declared. 'It is to be expected,' he wrote to Harry, 'that a decision finalizing the matter will be made at the next meeting of the Board to be held on July 2.' Harry was pretty sure what would happen. Even so, and with Ryan, Corry, and his Queen's cohorts advising him, he strove to dissuade Watson. On 26 June he wrote a careful letter. After reviewing Lockhart's 'unauthorized reading, retention, photostatting and employment' of his private letter to Packer, he gave a clear warning – which the college loyalists later portrayed as evidence of 'aggressive belligerency':

I will tell you frankly that I have been urged by colleagues at United College and by a number of outstanding members of the academic community across the country, including executive officers of the Canadian Association of University Teachers, all of whom feel strongly that the basic interests of the academic profession have been gravely affected, to bring forward immediately before the Canadian Association of University Teachers this invasion of the fundamental rights of university teachers. I have also been advised that my legal rights have been seriously infringed in more than one respect and that I should act to secure appropriate legal redress. Despite my respect for the persons who have offered this counsel, and despite my personal sense of outrage, I have thus far declined to act upon their advice because of my continuing primary loyalty to the College, and because of my confidence that the Board of Regents can be relied upon to protect the interests and rights of faculty members.

If, however, I am proven to be wrong in this judgment, and if action should be taken which would prejudice my resumption of duties at United College in accordance with the normal conditions of academic tenure, then I shall be left with no alternative but to defend by every available means my interests as a member of the academic profession and of the faculty of United College. I will do so in the clear conviction, a conviction shared by everyone who has communicated with me on this subject, that the well-being of the College would depend upon the success of my action.

While Harry was never given an opportunity to appear before the board, Watson permitted Stewart Reid to attend part of the board's meeting on 2 July. Stewart told the regents to return the photostats and forget the whole thing. Instead, Watson wrote to Harry two days later telling him the regents 'unanimously agree that Principal Lockhart acted in a responsible manner as Chief Executive Officer of the College in dealing with this correspondence.' Crowe himself was the guilty party, said Watson: 'your conduct has been such that would enable [the board] to dismiss you for cause and without notice.' Every inch the practical man of business, Watson continued that Harry could return to the college for one year, at a salary below the then minimum for his rank, providing he accepted these terms within three weeks. Even if he agreed, however, 'this is formal notice that your employment with the College will end on the 31st August, 1959.'

When Harry wired Watson, seeking clarification of the punitive proposal, the chairman replied that the salary terms might be further discussed should Harry return in September. Watson's reply caused Arthur Lower once again to reflect on his own experience at United: 'Criticism is treason.' Watson, for good measure, spelled out the 'factors governing salary increments: a) Teaching proficiency; b) Loyalty to the institution; c) Measure of co-operation extended in attaining the objectives of the College.' Item (c) no doubt included soliciting for the building fund.

Watson's criteria shredded any known notion of tenure or academic freedom. CAUT, while it had yet to develop specific guidelines for investigating and acting upon tenure infringement, let alone violation of private correspondence, would certainly be involved – the more so because of the way in which his letter had gotten to Lockhart, and because the principal and the regents had rebuffed Harry's several attempts to resolve the situation through Colonel Wilson and in a long meeting with representatives of the United Church moderator. Although the principal was in the East for several weeks (for the fund-raising campaign) from 3 July, he made no attempt to meet with Harry. As the eventual report of a CAUT investigating committee observed, 'it was the Principal's duty to United College and to his position in United

College to arrange at least one personal interview with Professor Crowe. This assumes the existence of a genuine desire on the part of the Principal and the administration of United College to compose the differences with Professor Crowe.' In fact, the 'CEO' of United thought to wash his hands of the whole thing. Throughout the summer a flurry of letters between Harry and Watson failed to clarify the exact terms on which Crowe might return to the college for one year, except that he must be back by 2 September.

I don't think Gordon Blake ever did understand that the fascinated interest and disgust shown by academics across the country stemmed not from any anti-Lockhart rumour mill. I didn't comprehend then, as I still don't, why he seemed not to recognize the simple enormity of the principal's actions; nor how he could imagine that their consequences could somehow be kept cocooned. My hypothesis, quite unprovable, is that his wartime experience with the Argyll and Sutherland Highlanders heightened the importance he attached to loyalty; his economist's evaluation of corporate life (the model Watson and many other university administrators inflicted on their fiefs) reinforced his insistence on institutional loyalty. In any event, it was the rock of 'loyalty' that smashed our friendship during the unending summer of 1958.

At the early June meetings of the Learned Societies in Edmonton, Underhill, Frank Scott, and people from nearly every campus sought confirmation of the essential facts – always with near disbelief. Harry's plight had become 'the Crowe case' long before the newspapers jumped on it. And it lay behind debate in CAUT council meetings that Viljo attended as secretary of the UCA. Viljo, whose devotion to detail and correct procedures I had come to know well, and rather enjoy, urged the council to adopt the complex procedures set up by the American Association of University Professors for investigating academic freedom and tenure cases. Fearing that lengthy consultation and debate on procedure would hobble CAUT in the likely event of an early request to intervene at United College, the council opted, instead, for a general resolution in support of academic freedom. Viljo, although he would eventually join those who resigned from the college, resented deeply what he considered my support of the CAUT decision. And on this rock another friendship foundered.

By the time we drove east that spring, Garden Island shimmered in our minds, its perfumed welcome a heart-breaking necessity. Again, the island would not disappoint us. I looked forward to the final work on *A Prophet* and the *Source-Book* – the latter now a symbol of the deepened trust among Stewart, Harry, and me. Yet, as Bev and I talked over the looming crisis (to the stupefaction of the three children in the back seat), we knew that the summer would be no idyll. While we hadn't any doubt about the rightness of our moral matters, Bev is a surer guide than I. I knew we were right, but I pondered the past dozen years of vacillating about staying in Winnipeg – under any circumstances. Was I now sniffing an escape route? This question would nag me through to the following November, when soul-searching ceased in a flurry of risky resignations.

Ensconsed in our Garden Island School House, we focused ourselves in daily consultation with Harry. Across the water we could see Royal Military College's Point Frederick, where, as a temporary major, he was teaching a summer course. Either by phone, or when Jean and Harry came across to lunch and swim, we matched information as it came to me from Stewart, who was sweating away at the Fort Garry summer school, or from the convoluted correspondence with Watson and from Harry's sympathizers at Queen's. In midsummer Dick Stingle came for a visit. One evening as we walked down the island lane to the telephone kiosk (individual cottage phones were still to come), Dick stopped short, staring gloomily at the path: 'My God, Ken, what if we win?' What, indeed, did 'win' mean?

Over the water, the Queen's faculty association, of which Harry was a member, had decided that, whatever 'win' might mean, it would not let erosion of academic freedom, tenure, and personal rights slip away unnoticed. On 16 July the association executive resolved to ask CAUT to intervene. Several days later Clarence Barber, president of CAUT and an economist on the Fort Garry campus, received the formal request to have CAUT investigate: 'If after investigation the CAUT find that principles of academic tenure have indeed been infringed, further appropriate steps be considered.' Such steps, the letter suggested, might include 'strong representations to the College and the Board of Regents.' Failing satisfactory action, 'full publicity' of the facts should be given and, if legal action be deemed necessary, CAUT 'should consider Association support for such legal action.'

Members of the Queen's association had, of course, discussed the pros and cons of intervention for some time. Word of the impending Queen's request had certainly reached Gordon Blake: a fanciful version of the whole mess was being circulated as far away as the University of British Columbia. From the Pacific, the noted labour historian Stuart Jamieson reported that John Deutsch (then head of economics at UBC) was spreading 'information' from Blake that Harry had always been a trouble-maker and that a section of United's faculty was undermining the principal and the board by lies and innuendo. I was not surprised to receive from Gordon a copy of a letter he'd written to Harry, dated one day before the Queen's resolution. In it he announced that he had accepted leadership of the college loyalists: 'I think it is fair to inform you that since you have, in my view, regrettably and unnecessarily permitted the affair to reach its present proportion, I intend to take all measures within my competence to oppose any action which you might pursue, which in my opinion would serve to bring discredit upon the institution of which I have the honour to be a member.'

I knew, from Stewart, that Gordon had been consulting daily with Victor Leathers (French), George Taylor (theology), Viljo, and Ed. Eagle (Classics), and that they would pull the rug from any effort I might make to have the UCA executive endorse a CAUT investigation. From many people who were not so blinkered or timorous, I received spirited support. As usual, Elizabeth Harrison's 'Fighting Protestant,' Arthur Lower, urged battle. In mid-July he wrote from California: 'Personally I hope Harry takes the whole thing into the public area and gives it the widest possible dissemination, legal and journalistic. In that way he will be doing the College a service, for he will force a clean-up ... I hope – and here the case goes well beyond the personal – that CAUT will act with decision and boldness; it will be a most valuable precedent.' But Arthur always did come back to the personal. A week later he wrote to tell of inquiries he was making for me about possible future employment and suggesting tactful hints to Harry about finishing his doctoral thesis: a romantic realist.

The personal and the procedural tangled horribly on the Fort Garry campus. Faced with the Queen's request for investigative action, Clarence Barber did not need to guess about the fusillade he would face from United's loyalists should he act upon that request. As an economist, he had met regularly with Blake and their colleagues to arrange course descriptions, common exams, and marking committees. Barber knew well the outrageous competitiveness nourished by O.T. Anderson's sleepless tracking of comparative failure rates and enrolments. The second he initiated CAUT action, he would be accused of using his position vindictively. To his great credit, he acted both decisively and prudently.

Before acting on the Queen's request, Barber consulted officers of the American Association of University Professors. They assured him that AAUP's procedures and guidelines in cases involving academic freedom and tenure had grown precedent by precedent – from the first year of its existence, when it was faced with eleven complaints 'which the first officers considered it imperative to act upon.' The AAUP office also made a poignant comment I must quote:

In the course of negotiations on a particular case, the Association cooperates with the local chapter to whatever extent cooperation is feasible. Frequently chapters make an attempt to resolve the difficulty on the campus before it is brought to the attention of this office. Once this office enters into negotiation with an administrative officer, however, the chapter tends to assume only an advisory role. It is true that chapters have not always been willing to cooperate in these matters ... last year it appeared that Association members on one campus wished to form a chapter primarily to keep the Association from conducting an investigation of a complaint. Obstructions of this kind are very rare, however; on the whole the chapters are more than willing to give every assistance they can.

CAUT, in its first test, would experience one of those 'very rare' obstructions – and emerge much strengthened.

Barber's CAUT executive acted on the Queen's request at the end of July by appointing a three-man committee of investigation. Between then and the committee's Winnipeg hearings in early October, the procedural white water churned ceaselessly. United's loyalists, infuriated by the end-run through Queen's and insisting on 'AAUP procedures,' tried hard to paint Barber's action as unconstitutional – ignoring the fact that AAUP accepted requests for investigations from professors who did not belong to an association as well as from 'chapters' in institutions other than in which the 'griever' had primary appointments. A clue to United's determination to block or impede investigations came in Lockhart's reply to Barber's letter announcing the committee's appointment: 'We will do everything within our power to co-operate with your Association. We only wish to be sure that the investigation is carried out with the knowledge and support of our section of your organization.'

While United's administration was whipping up a duststorm to obscure the only essential (and well-known) facts – what Lockhart had done with Harry's letter and how the Board had acted upon its contents – Blake fired a warning shot across my bows. On 21 July he wrote that any action by the UCA executive, 'or any members of the executive,' to support CAUT action would be 'grossly unconstitutional' unless endorsed by a full meeting of the UCA. This, too, ignored AAUP precedents. Gordon knew, of course, that he commanded a majority in the UCA. I reminded him that the 9 May general faculty meeting, when Lockhart reported what he had done with the letter and that he was taking 'the matter' to the regents, 'was the place and time to express an opinion – not weeks later when the Board has driven Harry close to public action.' Only four of us had remonstrated at that time; Gordon had been silent. I noted that a great many people had raised the question with me and that every one of them had asked: 'Why did the faculty let him [Lockhart] away with it?' I pled with Gordon to use his obvious influence to have the principal and board rescind their actions and make a fresh start. But I erred in listing 'at random' some of the people who had condemned the Lockhart-Watson actions. They represented campuses from coast to coast. Gordon sent a copy of his reply to every one of the twenty-four people, although I had marked my letter to him 'personal and confidential.'

Gordon's letter, clearly intended for the twenty-four more than me, said that if those people were in possession of 'the essential information,' they would know that the CAUT action was unconstitutional and that 'what are being paraded across the country as *infringements on* academic liberty will turn out to be, in reality, *abuses of* academic liberty.' Despite the ambiguity of his phrasing, his position was clear: only the UCA had a right, in the first instance, to investigate. Although I knew that the request to investigate had come perfectly legitimately from Queen's, that Clarence Barber's procedure was also consonant with AAUP procedures (not that this mattered), and that the loyalist purpose was to block CAUT action, Gordon's disrespect of my final personal letter to him shook me. It also confirmed what Stewart Reid had been reporting about the frenzied endeavours in Winnipeg to stop me from giving UCA executive support for the impending investigation. Although I tried to get our executive to endorse Barber's committee (to be approved or rejected by a membership meeting in early September), I failed. At best I could have achieved an even split: Dick Stingle, Viljo, and I in favour, and Victor Leathers, George Taylor, Alfred Longmen (collegiate bursar) opposed. Viljo, however, had temporarily switched sides – because of concern to follow what he took to be AAUP procedure.

I knew that the twenty-four people to whom Blake had written would be puzzled. I wrote to each of them, noting that I had made reference to them in a confidential letter to Gordon, and summarizing what had so far occurred at the college. I received replies from most of them, including copies of their replies to Gordon. I felt I was in a theatre-of-the-absurd; fortunately, I could not then know how much longer the play would run. But that end-of-summer flurry of correspondence certainly swept away any lingering doubts about the importance of the black struggle we had entered. S.D. Clark (political economy, University of Toronto) told Blake: 'It does seem to me that this raising of a question of proper procedure completely misses the point.' Richard Preston (history, RMC) advised Gordon: 'I would have thought that the reason for the existence of a National Association of University Teachers was because there is ample evidence that in the past it has not been diplomatic for the members of local teachers organizations to act alone in face of their own administration.' Bill Morton wrote to me: 'Gordon is very much mistaken and the tactics he is pursuing injure not only his case but himself.' Bert McCready (history, McMaster, and ex-president of CAUT): 'I urged Professor Blake to put his views before the members of the Committee which Professor Barber had set up ... his readiness to do so – or his failing to do so – will be a kind of test of the strength of his convictions.' Malcolm Ross (English, Queen's): 'I am depressed to find that the faculty of your college did not, *to a man*, inform the Principal and the Board that their behaviour could not and would not be tolerated.' Fred Gibson (history, Queen's) sent Gordon a blistering three-page letter, ending with the hope that Barber's committee specifically write Blake to disclose to it the 'essential information' he had hinted darkly was in his possession.

All the letters struck the same note of incomprehension of Gordon's innuendoes, and of support for Barber's action. Some of the most forthright came from Fred Soward (bless him), Jim Conacher, Donald Masters (history, Bishop's University), Margaret Prang, Jim Mallory (political science, McGill), Donald Creighton, and Gordon Rothney (history, Memorial). Norm Ward, whom I had first met at Pickering College, and who was also a close friend of Gordon, wrote the saddest letter, from Saskatoon. He was bemused, anticipating Blake's bleak prospects.

At the end of August, packing for the trek back to Winnipeg, I moaned a bit to Bev. She sympathized, but pointed out that whatever happened, we knew we were right: much more was at stake than the mere question of where we would end up. Nevertheless, I could have done without the publicity explosion I knew was imminent. Harry had just penned his last note from Queen's: 'The Ottawa Journal has Blake's letter and has asked the Winnipeg Tribune for a story. So the whole bloody thing is going to break while I am moving from motel to motel across the Northern States.' Not only Blake's letters; Allan Watson had circularized the faculty with his view of the spiraling mess and appended copies of his correspondence with Harry. The purloined letter, he lied, 'was never before the Board nor was its contents considered by it.'

Sure enough, somewhere in North Dakota, we picked up a copy of the *Winnipeg Free Press*: 'United College Fires H.S. Crowe.' Welcome home.

10

Winnipeg looked so welcoming. The four airline attendants who rented 739 for the summer had left it spotless. Puny but prolific elms already spoke of autumn; the front lawn glistened with golden leaves. But evening gatherings automatically segregated themselves, the conversational focus predictable. A year later, in darkest Westmount, Frank Scott asked Bev what it had all been like. She answered, 'I never felt more alive.' I guess. There was certainly much electricity surging through the halls of old United as we girded our loins to face students and colleagues – both groups deeply divided. Two letters gave me heart as I called the unavoidable general meeting of the United College Association (UCA) for 15 September. Frank Underhill wrote: 'If a professor who doesn't think much of his institution is to be therefore dismissed on the ground of disloyalty to the institution, about half of the university professors in Canada (probably more) would have to be dismissed. At any rate, Crowe's remark on the moral standards of theologians has been justified.' Malcolm Ross wrote from Queen's: 'I'm all for reconciliation. But reconciliation means full restitution, an open apology by Lockhart and a written guarantee from the Board that Harry's future is in no way prejudiced – i.e. *unconditional surrender.*' Variations on the theme of reconciliation would be hummed throughout the winter – by little ministers of uncertain mind.

I am still surprised that Gordon Blake and his loyalist majority failed to turf me out of the UCA presidency. I remained, nominally, in office through all the coming turbulence. In the sombre boardroom on 15 September I read a seven-page review of the summer's events: Gordon rigid with anger, Stewart Reid occasionally risking a wink. Half way through I paused to explain why Harry (technically back for his year's kiss-off) was not present. Two hours before the meeting a board lawyer had handed him written notice that his employment was terminated forthwith. I concluded by recommending that we cooperate with the CAUT investigation. The meeting then passed a resolution prepared, I think, by Gordon and Viljo Packer: the UCA would 'co-operate in an enquiry by any properly constituted investigating committee.' 'Properly constituted' was an escape hatch for the timid. As one loyalist asked: 'Where else could I be a full professor and head of a department?'

Classes began against a background cacophony of newspaper stories about the firing. Several students were children of loyalist faculty members; pro and con groupings in lectures were all too evident. Wendy Lockhart was in one of my courses throughout the nightmare year – which staggered along from bad to worse. Letters flooded editorial desks at the *Tribune* and the *Free Press*; editorial positions were taken in newspapers and magazines across the country. In the city itself, rumour mills flourished. One stormy day Velma Reid and others were hurrying on Portage Avenue. Passing the college, an elderly woman remarked: 'That's where that Harry Crowe was seen tearing up a Bible.' At the *Free Press* Tom Kent stayed mute, telling us that he must await the 'findings' of the CAUT investigation. The *Tribune* continued, throughout the winter, to give the fullest and most impartial news coverage; a cautious editorial in the autumn, however, had offered a pretty good clue about the final outcome. 'Professor Crowe,' said the *Tribune*, 'should realize that the point he wished to make to the public has been made. The board should realize that its side has been given a public hearing. Further pursuit of this course could only be corrosive ... Surely the board will see the wisdom of affording Professor Crowe full opportunity to withdraw from an unhappy situation with dignity.'

Much of the autumnal storm raged right out of Allan Watson's office. Like most prairie disturbances, it threw off dust in all directions. Watson's long letter to the faculty (26 August) had, like Blake's correspondence with me, become the basis of press coverage. In it, the chairman had said that Harry's letter to Packer was never considered by the board: Crowe's attempt to 'intimidate the Principal and the Board' by threats and 'public denouncement,' his 'aggressive belligerency,' was the whole problem. Immediately after he fired Harry, Watson gave a very long statement to the press on 20 September altering his faculty version. The letter had regained its original prominence. 'The attitude toward religion revealed by [the letter] is incompatible with the traditions and objectives of United College.' Moreover, by 'the manner in which he has named in the letter six faculty members, two of whom are deceased and of hallowed memory, Professor Crowe overstepped the limits of decency.' Watson justified this further invasion of privacy by appeal to an AAUP statement on professorial ethics: a professor 'should remember that the public may judge his profession and his institution by his utterances.' That no public utterance was at issue gave a fresh twist to the word 'chicane.'

Clarence Barber's CAUT executive had established its investigation committee by mid-September. Two of the original appointees had withdrawn to avoid any hint of predisposition: David Slater because he was a member of the Queen's Faculty Association, and Martin Johns of McMaster because he had attended meetings of the General Council of the United Church during that council's preliminary inquiry into the college crisis. Whatever Johns might have concluded personally, he would have been compromised by the eventual position adopted by the church council. After interviewing two members of the board of Regents and without hearing Crowe or anyone else from the college, the church exonerated Lockhart and the board, and expressed confidence in both.

CAUT's two-man committee held four days of hearings at the Fort Garry Hotel in mid-October: Vernon Fowke (chairman) was an eminent economist at the University of Saskatchewan, and Bora Laskin was already well known for his work in constitutional law at the University of Toronto. Norman Ward had written to me about the chairman: 'By a coincidence, I was the one who just told Fowke about [the case], and I was at his cottage the day he received his appointment, and dossier ... I don't think the inquiry could have been put in better hands than Fowke's, for he has a stubborn integrity, matched by a conscientious thoroughness matched by few people. Starting out with a general academic interest in the matter, he has been utterly astonished by what he has learned.' Laskin's name had been proposed to Barber by Frank Scott over a mid-summer lunch in the McGill Faculty Club, while they were attending meetings of the Commonwealth Universities Association. Both members had prepared themselves meticulously, gathering all possible documentation, including the bulky Lockhart-Watson-Crowe-Barber correspondence and a sheaf of public statements by all concerned. Throughout the flurry of correspondence between Watson and Fowke preceding the committee hearings, the principal virtually disappeared from sight. Finally, in response to a direct invitation to appear before the committee, he wired Fowke: 'I am instructed to decline the invitation.'

Argumentation during the first two meetings of the committee made clear the Watson-Blake strategy (couched in wonderful legalese by board lawyers) of subverting the CAUT proceedings with the charge that it was improperly constituted. In essence, their demand was for a board of arbitration of the sort used in labour conflicts; they refused to accept any framework of academic tenure or process other than that of the corporate model. The United College Act, of course, gave absolute direction to the Board of Regents in matters of hiring and firing. So the principal, Watson, and the loyalists simply boycotted the CAUT committee. Gordon Blake, with some hauteur, informed Fowke that 'the matter' under investigation 'is not concerned with issues of academic liberty' and 'I had to conclude regretfully that this committee does not meet my personal requirements as properly constituted.' And so said all but one of his supporters – Viljo Packer, whose apparent ambivalence in the midst of all this turbulence escaped my understanding.

I had met neither Bora Laskin nor Vernon Fowke before these four tense days in the Fort Garry Hotel; they had stayed discreetly distanced from anyone but the principals. Laskin already showed the decisive acumen for which he later became noted in the Supreme Court. From beneath heavy brows, his extraordinarily sharp glance missed no nuance in the attempts to obstruct and invalidate the committee made by D.C. McGavin, the lawyer who represented both the board and the principal. Fowke and Laskin simply rebuffed demands to replace their committee with a quasi-legal arbitration procedure. They insisted that their job was not to lay bare the legal situation, nor to 'arbitrate' between an employer and employee, but to discover whether an entirely non-legal concept of academic freedom and tenure had been violated. In the process, they hoped to contribute to the impending CAUT debate on the definitions of those notions and the procedures by which they might be protected. The board's lawyer withdrew after a day of heated discussion – although Watson had several times assured Fowke that the board would cooperate with the committee.

I attended all the committee sessions, as UCA president, as did Harry. The CAUT executive was represented by Clarence Barber and the secretary, George Boyes. All faculty members as well as several board members (in addition to Lockhart and Watson) were invited to give evidence and to suggest others who might wish to do so. Of the faculty, only Stewart Reid, Viljo Packer, Dick Stingle, Elizabeth Morrison (Classics and dean of women), and I were 'witnesses.' Colonel Wilson appeared, as did Peggy Morrison, the college registrar, and two students – one of whom, Joe Martin, had been Senior Stick the previous year. The small number of witnesses was of no consequence: the committee hearings were, in fact, the least important part of its work. Their carefully assembled documentation told the entire story, although the skittish legalism of Watson and his lawyer may well have confirmed opinions that Fowke and Laskin could scarcely not have formed already. Blake's haughty refusal to appear, after several months of dark hints about evidence in his possession, further damaged Lockhart's position.

Fowke and Laskin veiled their disgust during the Watson-McGavin antics; they recoiled in near disbelief, however, as they listened to Peggy Morrison's response to their questions – the only verbal 'evidence' specifically mentioned in their report. Peggy had written, as a United graduate, a strong letter of protest to Watson, with a copy to the principal. Lockhart, who had recently appointed her registrar, called her in to censure and warn her – exhibiting, as the report observed, 'the depths to which he allowed himself to go.' He charged that Stewart and I had asked her to write her letter – which she denied vehemently. He then told her of Winston Churchill who, when criticized by a junior, remarked: 'I don't remember having done you a favour recently.' The principal added: 'I hope you get the full implication.' That Peggy had written as a graduate, not as registrar, in no way diminished Lockhart's insistence on unquestioning loyalty. After all the succeeding attempts at 'reconciliation' failed, Peggy joined the sixteen who eventually resigned. She was appointed to the registrar's office at the University of Toronto, after Bora had spoken about her to Claude Bissell, the new president.

While Fowke and Laskin were writing their report, the stew continued to bubble. O.T. Anderson had died in a car crash just as the committee began its sessions. Lockhart circulated blank ballots on which we were invited to indicate our preferred successor. To no one's surprise, Gordon Blake became dean at the end of October. The principal announced that Gordon had received an 'overwhelming majority' of the 'votes,' without revealing the actual count. The battle in the press, pulpit, and even TV raged on.

Several letters to the editor particularly infuriated Blake's embattled loyalists. Five members of the Toronto history department – Jim Conacher, Maurice Careless, Jack Saywell, Bob Spencer, and Michael

Powicke – sent a stinger to the *Globe and Mail*. Arnold Edinborough, about to leave Kingston to become editor of *Saturday Night*, weighed in with a biting editorial in the *Whig-Standard*: 'What sort of morality amongst church leaders is it that condones not only the reading, but copying, of private mail without the knowledge of its writer?' Norman Zacour, a brilliant young medievalist who had become a close friend when he taught for a year at United, and for several more at Fort Garry, wrote me a spirit-lifting letter from his new position at the University of Pennsylvania. Norm hides his idealism beneath an almost opaque cloak of realism; his letter gave me much to think about:

If you and Stewart leave, there will be no boycotting of United College, simply because the academic profession as a whole (aside from a few notable exceptions) is a gutless one. They have let you down and they will continue to let you down ... which means that you will probably be looking around for more windmills next week ... What a mish-mash of small toads and snakes [at United]! And how they all slither about when the lightning flashes and the thunder rolls! What is so terribly unfortunate is that so many are concerned with their jobs when they never had to be; the college can't fire its entire faculty; this was precisely the issue through which the faculty might have gained ... at least a voice and recognition.

I made three short trips east in November. Each steadied me, helping to suspend disbelief, to reassert the importance of what had to be played out. Mason Wade, director of Canadian studies at the University of Rochester and premier anglophone historian of French Canada, invited me to a weekend conference on Canadian–American relations. Mason was a tall, elegant New Englander, a *bon vivant* who mixed scholarship and conviviality in equal parts – another American to give one hope. Frank Underhill and Claude Bissell were among the performers. In several conversations they mixed their questioning with urgent support.

The second eastward junket proved almost as surrealistic as the Winnipeg environment itself. The CBC asked me to join a panel for one of Nathan Cohen's weekly TV shows, *Fighting Words*. Cohen, a much-feared and erudite drama critic, sported a black cape, a walking stick, and a growly voice that he used to throw forth acerbic comments throughout the program. He (and his producer) chose four guests and a general topic for each show. Our topic was 'liberalism,' or 'liberty' – the CBC archives couldn't assist me on this point. My fellow panellists were the American literary critic Leslie Fiedler, Northrop Frye, and a Toronto journalist. Cohen read short quotations that we were to identify and then discuss. The only one I remember was from Mills's *Liberty* – recollected only because Fiedler admitted to not having encountered the book. Throughout the half hour, Norrie sat virtually silent, staring glumly at the table in front of him.

After the show I drove Norrie and his wife, Helen, back to their Moore Park home. Norrie spoke once: 'Thank God you were there, Ken; I can't talk to idiots.' Cryptic. Helen sensed that I was thinking not of the program but of a 6 November event at United College: the conferring of an honorary degree upon her husband. I had been shaken by Norrie's acceptance of the 'honour' and not surprised when the convocation and Norrie's part in it were announced on a huge billboard on Memorial Boulevard. Helen sought to cleanse the mushy betrayal: 'You must remember, honorary degrees are bestowed by the Senate, not the board.' Indeed I remembered. I knew, too, that only one member of the forty-person Senate had raised a voice in protest at the immolation of Harry Crowe. So much for the centrality of symbols. Frye's principal disciples in Winnipeg, Dick Stingle and Jamie Reaney, attended the convocation, assuring each other that Norrie would 'say something.' Near the end of Frye's address, when not even a veiled reference had been made, Jamie and Dick noisily left their balcony seats. Blake, the new dean, twisted the screw: 'In accepting this honour, Dr. Frye, you must see something honorific in us.' Not very subtle, but who could blame him? I thought of Norm Zacour's letter.

My third flight east came on 21 November – to 'represent' the UCA at the meeting of the CAUT executive council in Toronto – at which the Fowke-Laskin report would be received. For Bev and me the days preceding that third flight (in a Viscount, the most comfortable craft ever to fly Canadian skies) brought us to the Rubicon. The monstrous charade had gone on long enough; whatever the council might decide, we could no longer fiddle around in the vain hope of some impossible 'reconciliation.' We decided to tender my resignation, hope for some offer at another university, or, if necessary, alternative employment 'out there' – to put bread, as Harry said, on the table. One evening at 739 we discussed this with Stewart and Velma Reid and Dick Stingle – to find we were all agreed. Our three letters went off to Lockhart on 20 November.

We each said we could not return to the college in September 1959 unless Harry were reinstated. I added the condition that Blake step down from the deanship, since any new start would otherwise abort. We delayed the effective date in order not to penalize students in mid-year – a concern strengthened by suspecting that more resignations would follow in due course. Lockhart replied on 27 November: 'The Board of Regents does not intend to reinstate Professor Crowe or revoke the appointment of Professor Blake as Dean. I am accordingly instructed to inform you that your resignation has been accepted to become effective August 31, 1959.' At the same time, the board issued a press statement on our resignations. The *Tribune* and the *Free Press* headlined it, complete with photos of all the players, excerpts from our letters, and recapitulation of the whole sordid tale. Lectures the following day weren't much fun. And all of this activity occurred within days of the release in Winnipeg of the Fowke-Laskin report.

Incongruously I was still president of the UCA – which met on November 20 to decide whether to pay my fare to Toronto for the CAUT Council meeting. I was, of course, not present during the debate, but learned that it bordered on the hilarious. Unwilling to complete the UCA's alienation from CAUT by unseating me, or by boycotting the council meeting, the association reached a compromise: my way would be paid, but I must 'refrain from voting or taking part in the discussion following upon the presentation of the Fowke-Laskin report.' OK by me. The previous day, Clarence Barber had written to say 'almost all faculty associations have written expressing unqualified approval of [CAUT's investigation action] ... not one letter has been received from a member of CAUT's executive council or from a local faculty association expressing disapproval.'

The CAUT executive council meeting took place in the King Edward Hotel in Toronto, 22–23 November. The last time I had been in that hotel had been for a 'tea dance' in the Oak Room while I was still at Upper Canada College, when my chief concern was to behave correctly to my hostess and pay attention to the rhythm of Stanley St Johns's great little orchestra. I remember Stan's accepting a request to play my favourite dance tune, 'In the Mood.' Would the council members be as obliging? I knew about a third of them; they had shown unseemly amusement when told of the gag rule, the condition of my presence. But they had all read the Fowke-Laskin report. During the not very lengthy debate, a few questions were raised about the procedure of the investigations – people had done their best to undermine the CAUT operation. Close friends of Wilfred Lockhart, George Brown, and Coleman (mathematics) peddled the notion that the principal was unjustly maligned. In the history department, Brown was a minority of one; Coleman made no headway with Roger Myers (psychology), president of the faculty association. The council endorsed the report overwhelmingly, the news making immediate headlines. My father was particularly agitated by one of the *Globe* headings that week: 'Professors Can Go, United College Says.'

The ninety-one-page report's conclusions, following its play-by-play review of events and documents, were uncompromising [see *The C.A.U.T. Bulletin, Special Issue: Report on the Crowe Case,* January 1959]. Refraining from general definitions, the authors wrote that their mandate had been 'a particular consideration of academic freedom and tenure in the context of a particular set of facts.' They noted that Harry's position had become 'permanent' one year after his 1950 appointment, and therefore he could only be dismissed for 'just cause,' and that 'cause for dismissal, which is a denial of academic freedom, cannot be just cause.' The authors observed that 'the course taken by Principal Lockhart as of May 7 [the faculty council meeting called by the principal] established without any doubt that the only thing then at issue was the contents of Professor Crowe's private letter to Professor Packer ... There is thus a decided unreality in the published reasons for Professor Crowe's first dismissal.' There was unreality in the case of the peremptory dismissal on 15 September also: while the board had seen 'grave inpropriety warranting dismissal in [Harry's] expression of indignation against this invasion of his privacy,' it again used the letter's contents as primary justification. The report judged baldly that both dismissals were 'a trespass on academic freedom and involve as well an invasion of the privacy of personal communication.'

On the question of attitudes to religion in a church-controlled college, the report was concise and definite. No test act was required of United's professors. Thus, 'failure to stipulate or define limitations would warrant a teacher, at least in an arts faculty, in believing that he enjoys the academic freedom which has been traditionally associated with Canadian universities and colleges.'

The report was eloquent: 'It is no part of the function of a professor to speak only in accents familiar to the administration. For a man to be discharged on the basis of the interpretation of his remarks made by the administration would create a situation fraught with perils for academic freedom. To find a discharge made in the face of a remonstrance by the teacher that he has been misunderstood, and without being afforded an opportunity of explanation, makes the offense against academic freedom grave indeed. This is what happened in the instant case.' Fowke and Laskin made no call for censure of United, but in stinging words made one recommendation: 'Professor Crowe has been a victim of injustice, violative of academic freedom and tenure. The story is the sorrier because of the attempt to associate the dismissal with protection or religious principle. Rectification of the wrong done to Professor Crowe demands that the Board of Regents invite him to resume teaching duties ... The offer must, of course, be associated with an assurance of academic freedom and tenure as elaborated in this report.' Perhaps tongue in cheek, the authors refrained from offering 'any suggestion' to Harry as to accepting. For me, unalloyed satisfaction – deepened by getting to know Bora Laskin. On Saturday evening, after the first council session, he invited me back to his home on Chaplin Crescent for a drink. Hair was let down. The impeccable objectivity I had seen in the Fort Garry Hotel gave way to deep concern for everyone who had voiced support for Harry. Not a little black humour laced the conversation.

The returning Viscount landed in a ferocious blizzard – to match the extravagant storms of print that swirled through Winnipeg's newspapers for the whole of December and continued in sporadic gusts for the rest of the winter. Eighty-odd students walked in a sub-zero picket line waving placards demanding Harry's reinstatement. The alumni wrangled and then rallied behind Lockhart. Amidst almost weekly press statements in which Harry, Watson, Lockhart, and assorted ministers refought the whole mess, from procedure to substance, we got strenuous support from beyond the cockpit at Portage and Good. Arthur Lower infuriated the loyal brigade with a long letter in the *Free Press*: 'It is clear that the present principal has outlived his usefulness. It is clear that a thorough revision of the Board of Regents must occur ... What self-respecting man will stay at an institution when government is a despotism?' The faculty associations of Queen's and the University of Manitoba turned up the heat with public demands for reinstatement, as did the Canadian Civil Liberties Association and the history departments of the University of Toronto, Fort Garry, and Queen's. Bill Morton went to bat famously, mourning the death of 'a great department of history.' Most Canadian newspapers ran editorials endorsing the CAUT report. Judith Robinson in the Toronto *Telegram* had read Fowke and Laskin carefully, and her eye had also been caught by news-photos of the student picketers: 'While United College students parade Portage Ave. in the snow, demanding the reinstatement of a professor unjustly dismissed, their elders may do well to read the pages of the report. Read them and weep. Or better, read, then join the picketers.'

Robinson, despite her Tory newspaper, cut no ice with Tom Kent at the *Free Press* or Carlyle Allison at the *Tribune*. Allison's leader waffled its way to a comfortable conclusion: 'The only sensible thing to do is to submit the matter to arbitration' – the labour relations model again. Kent, having assured us for weeks that he would come out strong when Fowke and Laskin reported, simply fizzled. Not publishing Harry's letter, he wrote, 'makes it impossible to weigh the full story or distribute blame to individuals.' Tom even tried to get Lockhart off the hook: 'The Principal ... never at any time recommended Professor Crowe's dismissal.' Noting that Premier Roblin had offered his good offices to 'bring the two parties to the dispute together,' he signed off lamely: 'That is the constructive step which can now be taken.' The great liberal voice of the West had let us down with a crash.

Two genuine liberals would chide Tom – each in his own way. When the Kents arrived late at the Queen-Hughes's New Year's Eve party, Tom almost shivered in the chill. Bev avoided the usual peck-on-the-cheek, saying, 'You let us down,' and turned away. Moving over to the Freedmans, Tom asked: 'What's the matter, Sam? No one here seems to like me.' In his distinctive drawl, Sam answered: 'Tom, it's not your finest hour.' Frank Underhill had written Kent earlier protesting, as he told me, 'the pussyfooting that his paper has been doing on the issue, and telling him that here was an occasion for a liberal newspaper to show itself liberal.'

Some United faculty members had hoped that more than the *Free Press* would accept the CAUT findings. Where, they wondered, was the church? Well, it was everywhere and nowhere. The General Conference had supported Lockhart, as had the United Church *Observer*, whose editor, A.C. Forrest, a friend of Lockhart, called him 'the calmest man in Winnipeg' and dubbed his actions entirely 'responsible.' During the first week of December the president of the Manitoba Conference, Stanley McLeod, presided over extended painful discussions attended by Watson, Lockhart, Harry, Stewart, Dick Stingle, me, and A.G. Dorey, a former moderator. On December 9 Watson announced that this effort at reconciliation had produced an offer to reinstate Harry and that Harry had said no. In fact, McLeod had delivered the offer at 2:15 a.m. on 6 December with an ultimatum that Harry accept or reject it by 9:30 a.m. At 9:30 Harry had declined. The offer required him to apologize for 'any statement or actions of mine that have contributed to the development of the present situation,' and to 'assure the administration of the College of my full cooperation having regard to the principles and objectives of that institution.' It offered to reinstate Reid, Stingle, and me 'on request.' Other oral conditions had been made clear during the McLeod sessions: publication of the letter and an apology to Lockhart.

A huge storm errupted again in the press, keynoted by Watson's Churchillian statement: 'This board does not propose to preside over the dissolution of United College by turning over the administrations of its affairs to a small discordant group of the faculty.' I almost sighed in relief at his addendum: the board can expect the resignation of many senior and valuable members of the faculty if Professors Reid, McNaught and Stingle are retained on staff.' Fat chance. For good measure, he demanded, again, a judicial inquiry.

There were more resignations – but not of the sort hinted at by Watson. One day before Watson's press statement on the offer to Harry, eight-column headlines had proclaimed that Lockhart had handed his resignation to the board. The principal told reporters: 'I now stand condemned and convicted before the public as a result of trial by press, radio and T.V., as a person unworthy to head an academic community, especially a church college. The attacks upon me have been vicious and persistent ... I never at any time took Professor Crowe's letter to the board or faculty, nor divulged its contents to them ... I was profoundly shocked at the statements in the letter.' For the first time I felt sorry for him. He still didn't comprehend the deep reasons for his predicament, nor even the meaning of prevarication. And he was still submissively in the hands of the embattled banker who was directing a damage-control operation with no little success. Watson's refusal to accept Lockhart's resignation came as no surprise, but his strategic master stroke would come on 15 December.

The same papers that announced Lockhart's 'resignation' also carried long stories about other impending departures. The *Free Press* headed its report: '15 Now Have Quit United College Staff.' The story listed the previous resignations: Reid, Stingle, and me at the outset; Mike Oliver; who had written that his move to McGill was confirmed by the principal's actions; and six others: Fred Harper (French), Walter Young (political science), John Warkentin (geography), Michael Jaremko (chief librarian), Margaret Stobie (English), and Roman March (English). All denounced the failure of the board, the principal, and the church to rectify an intolerable injustice; each would withdraw the resignation were Harry to be reinstated in accordance with the CAUT report. The news report then listed those who had given notice on that day: Betty Morrison (classics, and dean of women), Viljo Packer (who had made a clean break with Blake), Gerald Panting (history), Hugh Makepeace (French, and dean of men), and Kay Sigurjonnson (English and French). Marion Martin (French) increased the number to sixteen the following day. Of this group, only Panting made his resignation unconditional. Perhaps Gerry sensed the pit that Watson and Blake were digging. When the press asked Harry if he would return, he said yes, 'according to the report of the impartial investigating committee of the CAUT.' But he added that he would expect the board to withdraw its acceptance of our three November resignations. Fowke and Laskin had properly not made this a requirement. Watson saw the opening.

Lockhart's 'resignation' had brought a dramatic increase in public sympathy for him and the beleaguered administration. Letters to the editor ran heavily against Harry and the 'intransigence.' As the official historian of the college puts it: 'The tide had turned, and from this time forth it was obvious where the Manitoba public stood on the issue' (A.G. Bedford, *The University of Winnipeg: A History of the Founding Colleges* [Toronto and Winnipeg, 1976], 325. Bedford's account of the 'Crowe case' differs from mine, substantially). Many hundreds of postcards with a message inscribed in large type, 'Carry On, Dr. Lockhart,' were distributed to United Church congregations and to alumni. Photographs of Wilfred and Eileen, smilingly counting the cards, appeared on the front pages. In this penultimate week, Gordon Churchill, a Diefenbaker cabinet minister, United graduate, and regent blew into town – as unofficial conciliator. After talking with Harry (but not with me, Stewart, or Dick), he concurred in the plan worked out by Blake and Watson: capitalize on the wave of sympathy. On 15 December the board announced, with no comment at all, that it had withdrawn the two dismissal letters and that Harry was reinstated, effective immediately. In an interview, Lockhart said his own resignation 'stands,' but added, 'as you know the board has not accepted my resignation.' It would take until the following day for his resignation to drop entirely out of sight.

At the end of December, the Lockharts went off to New York for a holiday – after receiving a petition signed by eighty-one of the eighty-six United Church ministers in the Winnipeg area begging him to stay on.

Presenting the petition, Dr Hugh McLeod said: 'Tyrants may raise the cry of freedom, but you have exemplified how, as the wolves howl and the mob roars, the spirit of a man and his wife beside him, may remain at liberty. This you achieve because of the faith in which you stand.'

From January through March the predictable final solution was merely postponed. Amidst sporadic exchanges in the press, one had particular poignancy. In an interview in Toronto, Lockhart said that two police detectives who had investigated the problem of Harry's letter to Packer had told him they believed that Viljo had received the letter and then lost it. In Winnipeg, police chief Robert Taft said he didn't know where Lockhart had got that notion; no one in authority had made that statement. Lockhart then said he accepted the statement that Packer had never seen the letter. Viljo got the last word: 'Dr. Lockhart seems to have missed the point ... that it is irrelevant to the ethics of the case how a private letter came into his possession without authorization.' From the Blake-Watson point of view, it's a good thing they never got the 'judicial investigation' for which they called intermittently.

On 22 March Harry resigned. Of course, he had to. From the moment of his 15 December 'reinstatement' it had been clear to Stewart, Dick, and me that hell would freeze over before Watson, Blake, or Lockhart would see us return to old United. In his resignation letter, Harry said that when Watson had reinstated him, the chairman had appealed to 'all concerned' to unite in rebuilding the college – and that he took this to mean that our resignations would be cancelled. Watson in a press release could say, however, that 'there was no undertaking sought by Crowe and none was given' about our three resignations. Our requirement that Blake relinquish his deanship was Watson's trump card: 'The reinstatement of Professors Reid, McNaught and Stingle would have been greatly resented by the majority of United College faculty members and would create an intolerable situation.'

Had Harry simply been outsmarted? In part, yes. Properly enraged by the unscrupulous use of his letter, by disregard of personal and academic rights, he had spent seven months battling to re-establish those rights. Unconditional reinstatement had become the symbol of vindication. In a characteristic fit of wishful thinking, he reached for it. In the offices of church, college, and newspapers, the end of the Crowe case brought a great sigh of relief. Stability could return: troublemakers had been turfed, Lockhart had been rehabilitated, and the building fund reached its target.

My mind went back to Dick Stingle's unnerving question on Garden Island: 'What if we win?' Well, the long struggle certainly invigorated CAUT and the faculty associations that had unanimously supported the actions of their national body. Even at United a joint faculty-board committee would work out contracts defining tenure and dismissal procedures. At its general meeting in Saskatoon in June, CAUT adopted the report of a committee chaired by Frank Scott which strongly endorsed Fowke-Laskin, Barber's enhancement of the executive's role, and the people who had resigned from United – eventually, about one-third of the faculty. And out of the year's turmoil came the establishment, that spring, of a national CAUT office with a permanent executive secretary. Stewart Reid became the first (after open competition), setting up business in a tiny office in Ottawa with one assistant. To my mind, 'win' meant simply the overwhelming support of Canadian academics for several simple notions: the privacy of personal communication; untrammelled scholarship, sustained by closely guarded tenure; rejection of the corporate model in university governance; and strong professional organization to sustain a composite of these concepts.

In the wind-down of the Crowe affair were many poignant touches. All seven members of United's graduating class in theology signed a letter to the United Church *Observer* blasting the regents, adding that 'the whole United Church at every level – church courts, boards, local congregations – shares in the board's failure.' Virtually all third- and fourth-year honours students decided to transfer to the Fort Garry campus – including Carl Berger and Arthur Sheps, who would become my colleagues in history at the University of Toronto, Donald Swainson, whose thesis I would direct at Toronto, Allan Smith, who is now a historian at the University of British Columbia, and Bruce Lundgren, now teaching at University of Western Ontario – and many of other years. For the student transferees, we gave an 'alternative' graduation party at 739 Macmillan. And we relished Underhill's *obiter dicta* during an address on academic freedom at Saskatoon. He observed that he had always looked upon Winnipeg as 'a city of the world. But I learned in 1958 and 1959 that it was not that kind of city at all ... it has sunk to the intellectual and moral level of Toronto.' I don't think Frank had read Thorstein Veblen's 1918 *Higher Learning in America* – still the best guide to North American universities – but his description of university presidents sounded as if he had: 'garrulous, itinerant, academic Rotarians.'

All of those who resigned found other jobs quickly. Dick Stingle, whose view of possible reconciliation was never robust, had accepted an appointment at the University of Saskatchewan in February. Partly through the influence of Stanley Knowles, the Canadian Brotherhood of Railway Transport and General Workers appointed Harry Crowe its research director in April. On 9 July the *Free Press* carried a brief notice of my appointment to the Toronto history department. The background of that most palatable outcome belongs to our post-Winnipeg years. Like Sarah Binks, Sweet Songstress of Saskatchewan, who referred often to what she had learned on a visit to Regina, I felt that I, too, had learned something from sojourning in a prairie capital.

11

December had been the cruellest month. As the days shortened, we tried to conjure up the future; trepidation set in. Talking with Jack Clough at St Luke's helped a great deal, even if his summary secular conclusion surprised me: 'Ken, you were right; no gentleman reads another person's letters.' Spontaneous warmth came from students and from academics whom we scarcely knew. That warmth, added to the support of our cross-fertilized circles of close friends, eased our worries while deepening the emotional ambivalence as we prepared to leave Winnipeg for good. When we drove down the Pembina highway for the last time, Bev used a lot of Kleenex.

The tone had been set the day my resignation was announced in late November. That evening I answered a quiet knock at the front door. Two first-year students stood there in the snowy darkness. Arthur Sheps and Allan Smith, looking about fifteen, had very little to say and came in only for a few minutes; but they had known what to do. A few days later a one-sentence letter blew in from Carleton University. I had met the young Canadian historian Stan Mealing once at a conference; he ended his missive: 'It seems to me a most praiseworthy thing to have done.' The same mail brought a letter from Dalhousie, from Jim Aitchison, whom I had met at the CAUT council meeting in Toronto: 'So you dared to say Boo! to a principal ... I do admire the courage of you and your colleagues in resigning and I do hope that none of you will suffer materially.' And a few days later, also from Dalhousie, a splendidly characteristic note from George Grant: 'In writing, I wonder whether you are the Ken McNaught I knew many years ago. Whoever you are, this brings expression of great admiration.' Frank Underhill wrote: 'It is very seldom that academic men have the courage to resign and risk their own careers for a cause in which they profess to believe, and I honour you for your action ... I wish some of the history departments that have written in support of Crowe would carry their words into action by offering jobs to you.'

I record these samples to show the support we needed and received while the old guard and the church were calling us institution-wreckers and self-seekers. And then there were offers of practical help. The first three (and I should not have been surprised) came from people who had taught me at Upper Canada College. George Spragge, the Ontario archivist: 'I heard on the radio last night that you were leaving United College ... Perhaps you will prefer to continue teaching ... I shall be glad if you will drop me a line letting me know the salary you would expect.' Remorsefully, I recalled how we used to giggle in his class when he had trouble controlling saliva – the result, I later learned, of a World War I bullet through his cheeks. Alan Stephen, headmaster of the Prep, offered a stop-gap post, as did Jim Biggar in the upper school history department. Lewis Thomas asked if I would be interested in an upcoming appointment at the University of Alberta, as did Gordon Rothney at Memorial in Newfoundland.

January's frigid brilliance suddenly seemed bearable. The first week brought two letters of deliverance. Eric Harrison's 'annual' invitation to Queen's summer session ensured, again, the therapy of Garden Island. The same mail brought from Maurice Careless, in the Toronto history department, news which, I suppose, I had subconsciously believed would come. At the conscious level I knew Toronto was tight as a drum. Maurice and I had corresponded regularly for several years, extending conversations that originated in springtime parties during our Toronto stopover en route to Garden Island. He is a realist and had never even hinted at light on the horizon. So his New Year's missive conformed to my wishful thinking while coming, also, as a wild surprise. In our usual bantering tone, Maurice wrote: 'I'm to sound you out on a highly informal, very secret, first-time-ever inquiry as to whether you'd be interested in joining the History Dept. (could have knocked you over with a tank?). We had a senior committee meeting on staff on Thursday ... DGC [Creighton] reported the administration 'favourably interested' in securing your services ... There's really no question now that DGC will put in for you (one Western body, slightly mauled) and the administration will pass you in the budget if I can report to him that you can be had.' That I would drop two ranks and a thousand dollars in salary seemed not even a 'price' for this salvation.

Gerald Craig's decision to spend a research leave in Montreal had provided the immediate opening for my appointment; George Brown's impending retirement and appointment as general editor of the Dictionary of Canadian Biography, with reduced teaching, confirmed that I would be in the tenure stream, with most of my teaching in American history. I had come to know Craig at the end-of-term parties in Toronto and believed him to be by far the finest scholar of American history in Canada. This did not prevent me from sparring with him, especially on American 'manifest destiny' and its implications for Canada. In 1957 the *Globe and Mail* had published a longish letter in which I argued that we should withdraw from NATO and distance ourselves from the new American empire. Gerry answered it with an Underhillian flourish, observing that we were fortunate to live next to a relatively benevolent empire and referring to me as a 'young Lochinvar out of the west.' Craig's sardonic realism (he believed in objective history) produced a steady stream of penetrating book reviews, articles, and books – as well as a perpetually pessimistic view of departmental and university affairs, and of many of the people who conducted them. Just before leaving for Montreal, he wrote outlining some of the teaching responsibilities in the U.S. and Canadian fields. He sprinkled his welcoming letter with customary astringencies: 'It is comforting to know that a professional colleague is leaving a happy ship for an even happier one.' Noting that I had chosen 'The American Progressive Tradition' as the title for my fourth-year seminar, he observed that it 'should be a suitable vehicle for sound and positive doctrine ... I shall be looking forward to working with you in the Department when I get back. What the students will make of the resulting confusion remains to be seen.' A missive from Freya Hahn, still the do-all departmental secretary, enclosed a short note with the 1959–60 calendar: 'Welcome home!' I guessed the ship couldn't be *really* unhappy.

In a leisurely correspondence, from March through May, Donald Creighton spelled out the details: while I would come as an assistant professor at $7500, just below what John Cairns (modern France) and Jack Saywell (Canadian) earned, our moving expenses would be paid and I could expect early salary improvement. I would lecture in the post–Civil War half of the third-year honours American history course, cover the whole of American history (!) in lectures for the third-year pass course (Canadian and American history), give my fourth-year American seminar, and take on six tutorial groups – four in the honours course, two in the pass. I would not be idle, nor would I so much as whisper about 'the load.' Just before the formal letter of appointment arrived, Jim Conacher wrote: 'Have you heard our big news? DGC has resigned as Head of the Department and Maurice Careless has accepted the post. It will be a much happier department for the change and you come at a good time.' Avuncular advice followed: 'May I say as a friend that when you get here you should try to detach yourself from [the United College case] ... after a year in such an atmosphere you will find there is an adjustment to be made.'

With the Reids and the Crowes moving to Ottawa and out of teaching, and others in the throes of serious readjustment, 'detachment' was unlikely. However, little showers of satisfaction continued to nourish our springtime. Gordon Rothney secured the appointment of Gerry Panting to Memorial's history department. Gerry's MA thesis had been my first bit of graduate supervision and, as a teacher in United's high school, he had put his neck prominently on the block. Also, Harry Beer, whom I had known at Pickering College and who was now headmaster there, appointed Bruce Lundgren to the Pickering staff. Bruce had been a forceful leader of the United students who transferred to the Fort Garry campus.

Arthur Lower's constant admonition, 'publish or perish,' I had always taken seriously. It's brutal truth he pointed out when he wrote that he could not push an appointment for Crowe because Harry had neither finished his thesis nor published academically. I surmised that Creighton and Careless, however warmly disposed, could not have thrown out the lifeline to me without producing a credible CV and reasonable hope that I would produce more of the same. The articles, reviews, and two books to be published in 1959 had been *sine qua non*. Yet, while I saw the academic utility of all this writing, I recognized, too, its protective function. I knew that I would continue to give interpretive lectures. I expected also to speak and write, whenever possible, against Canada's involvement in the American nuclear alliance system and in support of efforts to salvage the CCF – which had been badly mauled in the Diefenbaker earthquake. For a similar approach to academic partisanship in the past, many people had been given a very hard time; it was prudent to nourish one's CV. It was also, of course, what I *wanted* to do. I was pleased by a letter from the editor of the *Dalhousie Review* in the spring of 1959 praising a long review he had asked me to write of R.M. Dawson's first volume of the official biography of Mackenzie King: 'Robert Dawson was a friend of mine and I feel that there is nothing in your review to which his family, friends or Alma

Mater could take exception.' Since I had criticized Dawson sharply for ignoring King's role in supporting the owners and politicans who crushed the tragic coal-steel strikes in Cape Breton in the early 1920s, and compared this lapse with the full treatment offered by Harry Ferns and Bernard Ostry in *The Age of Mackenzie King*, I felt that 'partisanship' could survive as long as it was honest and did not ignore or distort facts.

Somewhere around this time I ran across Lord Bolingbroke's aphorism, 'History is philosophy teaching by example.' I felt at once that this sentence expressed more honestly the inherent utility of history than did the impossibility of 'scientific' and 'objective' value-free, as-it-really-was, reconstruction. As ice-floes in the Red and Assiniboine rivers began their tardy crashing towards Lake Winnipeg, a letter from Mike Oliver (now well established at McGill) further nourished such random reflections. Oliver had agreed to edit a volume of essays whose papers would be similar to those of *Social Planning for Canada* (published by the League for Social Reconstruction in 1935), if not as precise in their socialism. 'Canadians,' he was to write in the preface, 'were being lulled into accepting a glitter of prosperity which covered a reality of purposelessness, mediocrity and inequity and which, moreover, dulled their awareness both of the dangers of a post-Hiroshima world and of its potentialities.' The age of Ike and Uncle Louis was coming to an end; the 1960s would be very different. *Social Purpose for Canada*, the new book's title, was harbinger of a spate of 'left-leaning' social criticism – most of which would lean much further left. Oliver asked me to write the chapter on foreign policy; I agreed, by return.

Social Purpose differed from *Social Planning* in more than its less doctrinaire conceptions of socialism. It was funded to an extent the LSR could not have thought possible. The money came from the Boag Foundation, a trust set up by a wealthy British Columbian, a 'millionaire socialist' of the sort more common in other countries than in Canada. Each author received $1000 for an essay of 10,000 words. Oliver planned several discussion meetings of the contributors, with travel allowances if needed.

This plan worked beautifully for us. Bev and I stopped off in Toronto in early May en route to Montreal. Over several days we absorbed the shock of Toronto house prices. We had decided to live in the centre of the city. The house we chose, on Douglas Drive in north Rosedale, faced Chorley Park with its fine stone mansion – the lieutenant governor's residence until Mitch Hepburn turfed him out. Having survived as a soldiers' hospital, the old pile was demolished in 1960, causing a mass migration of mice to neighbouring houses, including ours. A wonderful location and a quite unrealistic price: $31,000. For the Winnipeg house we got only $11,000 (minus the mortgage payoff). This meant, again, two mortgages and as much outside income as I could earn.

William Christian in his biography of George Grant says that George would not have written his *Social Purpose* essay for nothing 'at that time in his life,' and hints that the socialism he donned for the task was bogus. I think that Christian is unfair on both counts. Grant's employment picture was certainly fluid, but he was as keen as I was to build his CV for much more than monetary reasons. The socialism in his *Social Purpose* chapter, like that in most of the other essays in the book, was non-dogmatic and followed logically from the critique of capitalist technological society he had earlier enunciated in his CBC talks, 'Philosophy in the Mass Age.' And he was excited by collaborating with the people Mike had assembled. For the same reasons, I know I would have contributed without the financial inducement – which was, admittedly, handsome.

Having committed all to fortune* by concluding the house purchase in Toronto (with June occupancy), Bev and I went on to Montreal, where I was to take part in the first of several meetings of Oliver's authors. From the Winnipeg morass to the grassy slopes of Chorley Park and on to the sparkling spring of Westmount proved a tonic indeed. And not just sensual. I felt I was given the chance to help justify the kind of academic tenure we had fought for – to demonstrate (as had the beleaguered warriors of the 1930s) that free inquiry and speculation were not irrelevant to contemporary society.

Most of the contributors came to the meeting, read each other's draft essays, and discussed connective themes. Fascinating, especially with Frank Scott among us, a tower of integrity beaming a light forward from the dirty 1930s to the more complex 1960s. Those whom I met for the first time included John Porter, whose biting social analysis in *The*

Omnia fortunae committo is the device that Grandpa (Colonel W.K.) found, heaven knows where, and alleged was the family motto. He had it engraved on a vast range of gold watches, sterling coffee and tea services, and even a letterhead stamp. I inherited several beautiful sterling pieces including a watch, samovar, and tea service. In the early 1980s, still oppressed by mortgage payments and with the price of gold and silver going through the roof, I was sorely tempted to sell. I'm glad I didn't. But I've always thought that the choice of motto was scandalously secular, even Roman, for a Baptist – however remunerative the wheel of fortune seemed to be.

Vertical Mosaic (1965) was foreshadowed in two of the book's essays; John Weldon, a fine socialist economist and then editor of the *Canadian Journal of Economics*; Gideon Rosenbluth, the leading student of concentration of control in Canadian industry and later a doughty critic of nuclear weapons; Scott Gordon, a Carleton economist who specialized in resource development and investment; Stuart Jamieson of the University of British Columbia and the foremost scholar-activist in labour relations; Keith Callard of McGill, a young student of public administration; Pierre Trudeau, then joint publisher of *Cité Libre*; and Meyer Brownstone, then Saskatchewan's deputy minister of municipal affairs.

Three vignettes of that most lively weekend persist. First, when I introduced George Grant to Scott Gordon, George exclaimed: 'I imagined you a Scot like me, and here I meet an elegant Levantine Jew!' The second episode also involves George. At a small dinner party given by Frank and Marion Scott, Bev, for some reason, thought that one of the guests, George's aunt Louise Parkin, was his mother-in-law – and referred to her as such. George shifted his great bulk, revealing his navel as his shirt sprang open: 'She's not my mother-in-law, God no; my mother-in-law's a drug addict.' Shelagh was not present, although I doubt if that would have made any difference. The third snapshot is from the Olivers' living room, to which Mike, Trudeau, and I had returned for a post-mortem after the final 'session.' Pierre sipped soda water and watched quizzically as our nightcaps evaporated. Our discussion slowly focused on whether or not he should formalize the socialism that clearly informed his essay – an elegant, precise dissertation on the practice and theory of federalism. Somewhat euphoric, I ticked off a half-dozen of the main CCF planks; after each Pierre said simply, 'd'accord.' At the end of this arrogant catechism I said I had a party membership card and would he care to sign it. With a grin he declined: 'One at a time, but not all together.'

Most of the essays in *Social Purpose* took account of the post-1935 experience of democratic 'socialism' at home and abroad. While social planning remained central, the essays stressed public ownership less, and other means of curbing and redirecting the roles of private economic power more. My essay on foreign policy, however, flew more directly against the prevailing winds than had Frank Underhill's 1935 chapter in *Social Planning*. Frank had warned against the blandishments of British imperialism and called for neutrality. The League of Nations had failed because 'it is incompatible with the capitalist imperialism of the great powers ... We should therefore make it clear to London and Geneva that we intend to fertilize no more crops of poppies blooming in Flanders fields ... While we may look forward to a League of socialist commonwealths ... the best contribution we can make in such a direction is to establish a socialist commonwealth within our own borders.' With many Canadians flirting with American isolationism, Frank's arguments appeared less inflammatory in 1935 than they would by 1938–9.

At the beginning of the 1960s my tilting at imperial windmills commanded much less support. I argued that our membership in an American-dominated NATO and acceptance of a purely military response to the Soviet challenge were wrong. We had abandoned our earlier goal of keeping some sort of balance between the two imperial centres of London and Washington. Completely integrated militarily with the United States through NATO, NORAD, and other defence agreements, we had committed ourselves to the terrifying doctrines of nuclear superiority, 'containment,' and support of reactionary regimes around the world. I urged withdrawal from the alliance structure and an active role in the Commonwealth. The emerging multi-racial Commonwealth held promise of dealing with the problems of crumbling empires, underdevelopment, and Third World national aspirations in a manner very different from that of shoring up repressive regimes. Socialists, especially, should endorse massive efforts to minimize differentials of economic well-being, to court international 'security' through aid more than through nuclear terror and puppet dictators. To do otherwise was to enhance the appeal of the communist alternative. I quoted American military analysts who pointed out brutally and accurately that NATO's reliance on nuclear weapons left Canada with no influence whatsoever on alliance policy. We should recognize this fact and free ourselves to use the kind of influence that the revolution in weaponry had made possible: a militarily non-aligned policy designed to reduce disastrous inequities and promote peaceful evolution of the ex-colonial world.

In June we moved into Douglas Drive – staying just long enough to distribute furniture before setting out for Garden Island. Unblemished by wall-to-wall palaver about Harry Crowe and Wilfred Lockhart, the summer of 1959 was a luxurious renewal: mornings at the desk, afternoon lectures at Queen's, and many dinner gatherings with other islanders and friends from Kingston. Garden Island had become the palpable centre of our lives. For the children there were unlimited choices – in the tree-lined meadow and on the water. We bought a second-hand Albacore centre-board sailboat. Chris spent six weeks each summer at Camp Mazinaw, where he became a counsellor and waterfront director. The camp, on a Precambrian lake about 50 miles north of Napanee, was run by Reg Blackstock. Blackie, head of the Prep and athletic director at Pickering College, infused Mazinaw with a poetic amalgam of Indian lore and subtle discipline. My close friend from Pickering, Fred Hagan, gave a no-nonsense vigour to the arts and crafts program. Chris became an accomplished draughtsman during those summers, yet I've been fascinated to watch him shed all traces of Fred's conception and style. Christopher's finely drawn watercolours of every facet of Garden Island life glow with increasingly dramatic colour – a cause of pride and envy for me.

For $15 a season I became an out-of-town member of the Kingston Yacht Club. Allison became my crew as we sailed across the 2 miles to join in the thrice-weekly evening races. During six or seven years we won one race – with a borrowed spinnaker. Yet I am persuaded that anyone who has never planed a centreboard boat in a 30-mile wind is unfulfilled. On the island, Allison made some fast friends, including Kippy Edinborough, Pat Conacher, Tink Whalley, and Sylvia Small-man. Kippy's father, Arnold, and I disagreed on politics, but we were as one on the magic of the island. We spent many evenings casting for bass from my leaky outboard, drifting on the shoals, nudging the shadows of darkening willows. What made us such close friends?

A graduate of Cambridge, Arnold had come to Kingston after the war with his wife, Tish, to teach English at Queen's. Although a popular lecturer, he did not take kindly to academe, particularly to its starvation wages. Instead of finishing a thesis on the 'Revels of Henry VIII,' he became editor of the *Whig Standard*. Rapidly informing himself on Canadian politics, letters, and theatre, he also moved easily among businessmen, whose activities he defended against my sometimes facile criticism. His entrepreneurial enthusiasm, however, ran in tandem with sturdy integrity and a faith enriched by formidable reading in Christian literature. I guess friendship grows from shared notions about individual worth and purpose quite apart from the problems of maintaining a social environment in which such notions will be secure. There was also Arnold's sheer zest. A happy mental snapshot reveals him strolling with his guest, Robertson Davies, down the blazing island lane. Two large figures, each shaded by a huge, ragged straw hat, each wagging a beard at the other – oblivious to everything but their conversation.

Soon after becoming editor of *Saturday Night*, Arnold asked me to write a monthly article on political affairs – national or international. I became a contributing editor and, for nearly ten years, served as in-house radical for the businessmen's magazine. The editorial board met over sumptuous lunches at the Albany Club – the Tory Party at the trough. By coffee time, John Gellner and I had usually called a truce in our battling over NATO and nuclear arms. John wrote well-informed pieces on military-defence matters. A pre-war emigré from Czechoslovakia and airforce veteran, he spoke with a slight stutter and, from under shaggy brows, treated me with mild amusement. Genial, right-wing, and a Cold Warrior, I found in him a good deal to admire – and was slightly intimidated. My work for *Saturday Night* brought in $50 a go, rising to $100 after several years. This, plus fairly frequent reviews and articles for the *Globe and Mail* and the *Star*, kept our heads barely above the financial surf.

For our return to Toronto I had bought a wonderful seven-year-old Cadillac. Many Winnipegers still called such luxurious monsters 'eastern cars,' yet I got it for less than a similarly used Ford would have cost. As I wheeled around the gravel drive in front of Flavelle House, now home to the history department, to begin the longed-for return to 'my' history department, I noticed a rather stout figure watching from beneath the pillared portico. Charles Stacey took careful note of the car, my homburg hat, and, having heard that I'd moved into Rosedale, let fly: 'Ah, Ken, my favourite socialist.' Colonel C.P. Stacey was one of six 'new boys' in the department that year – having just returned from being head of the army's historical section. No lover of Mackenzie King, he had, nevertheless, forthrightly savaged my 1957 CHA paper, so we were on good sparring terms that led to warm friendship. Charles, for my money, became our pre-eminent 'professional historian.' Equipped with a Eugene Forsey–like memory, his research never ended, and he really believed you could write history objectively. Yet his history was full of judgments. Because he was largely uncritical of the existing social-economic system, his writing, while it detailed the military-economic-political workings of the system, always focused on individuals and particular policy choices. Charles was, in fact, as much *parti pris* as I; his notion of 'objectivity,' of telling it as it was, ended up as a defence of the status quo. He would continue to view my socialist 'slant' as subjective, and therefore questionable, history.

In a long review of Stacey's 1970 masterpiece, *Arms, Men and Governments*, I praised his scholarship and also suggested that he had some very firm interpretative starting points: 'If he accepts with a shrug the general structure of our market-place society, however, he has nothing but contempt for those who would sell Canada down the river [to Britain or the U.S.] ... The great achievement of this book is that it reveals real people making decisions within a framework which, however binding in terms of real power, still allowed very considerable room for important decisions to be made by individuals.' As I came to know Charles Stacey and Donald Creighton as colleagues, I noticed with surprise a deep rivalry. The two departmental giants continued to amass academic dignities and awards, yet each felt insufficiently recognized and hinted that the other was unduly so. I never really understood this attitude; but their silly competitiveness made me anxious not to get trapped in any similar pitfall. More important by far to fix your own signposts and let kudos look after itself. Of course, being 'true to one's self' carries its own risk: of self-righteousness. As I reveled in the new teaching and research environment throughout the 1960s and 1970s, I also went noisily public on the nuclear peril, the ominous character of 'the new American empire,' and the directions to be followed by the 'New Party,' the NDP. While fighting happily with many of my colleagues and friends about such matters, I gained from them at least a measure of balance. That so many more of my intimates were sober-second-thought types than wide-eyed radicals no doubt reflected my own conservatism – certainly it warned me against mono-causalism either in politics or in the writing of history.

In a department still small enough for the chairman to hold a reception in his home each autumn, we actually enjoyed what has become so ephemeral: collegiality. Each day at 4, Miss Hahn presided at the gleaming samovar in Sir Joseph Flavelle's basement billiard room where, also, we held our infrequent departmental meetings. Only occasionally was a voice raised sufficiently to disturb George Brown's snooze: Jack Saywell, perhaps, leader of the Young Turks and not above challenging DGC, reflecting that our practices in hiring and curriculum were not beyond reach of fresh thought. Or Willard Piepenburg who, because of his passions for efficiency and his role as academic secretary, was dragooning us into a recognizable order based on showers of notes, files, and records.

A Wisconsin Quaker, 'Piep' was one of the first American imports. He arrived in 1952, the same year as my old friend from graduate school days, John Cairns, who brought with him a distinguished Cornell doctorate in French history. Willard had chosen alternative service during the war, volunteered for a medical experiment, and emerged with a glistening bald pate, pre–Yul Brunner. Above all a teacher, like his senior, Donald McDougall, Piep had mastered the English seventeenth century; each revered what was left of the formalities and standards of university life. They shared two other passions: a well-tutored love of music and an equally well-honed dislike of Donald Creighton – who reciprocated their disregard in each case. Creighton nursed his memory of McDougall's support of Underhill as successor to Flenley as chairman in 1955. He saw Piep as vanguard of a second American invasion of Toronto. Willard did nothing to dispel his fears. In unpunctuated, ebullient sweeps of rhetoric, he cheerfully chided Upper Canadians for failing to recognize the wave of the future – as it washed through the better American universities. His friendly barbs stung; Creighton failed to see any merit, even in Piep's more sensible remarks. Piep mellowed steadily year by year. Losing none of his affection for the progressive Midwest, he took citizenship and, with unrepentant respectability, frequented services at St James Cathedral.

Another American invader was an easy Creighton target. Milton Israel, in the early 1960s, became the department's second Jew – and thus doubly anathema to Creighton. Milton and his wife, Beverley, each radiated a statuesque, exotic glamour. From well-to-do New England families, they exuded self-confidence. Bev did not hide her amusement at the ways of what she called OT – yet she quickly matched, and often outshone, the local ladies in sumptuous hospitality and a kind of natural multiculturalism. Milton, looking like an Epstein depiction of a rabbi, proved himself a fine teacher and expediter – in imperial history, and increasingly in the history of India. He was well equipped to slough off the slights of Toronto's vestigial anti-Semitism. On one occasion when Charles Stacey was gathering a group for the lunch table over which he regularly presided with oracular humour, he called down Creighton's corridor: 'Join us for lunch, Donald?' A pause, then, 'Who's us?' 'Milton and I.' Another hesitation, followed by, 'I think I'll lunch later, thanks.' The Israels and ourselves became fast friends; they, too, regret the passing of a department that used to be – with all its vagaries.

I found many of the points of continuity around the commodious tea table in Flavelle House. Ramsay Cook had joined the department in 1958. He had just finished his doctorate, on J.W. Dafoe, for Creighton, and was the second Toronto PhD to be taken on board – after Morris Zaslow the pervious year. Ramsay and I shared a good student-teacher relationship from Winnipeg, and we also walked the same tightrope in our various dealings with Creighton. Donald remained too aware of my friendship with Underhill, but he approved my increasingly critical commentaries on the new American empire. While proud of Ramsay as his protegé, he was leery of Cook's close friendship with Arthur Lower – with whom Ramsay had done his MA work at Queen's. Both Ramsay and I admired Creighton as a teacher and biographer, but casual conversation often foundered on the shoals of paranoia. Even Bev found herself at risk. On one occasion Jack Saywell gave a departmental party, hoping to mollify Creighton, who was congenitally nervous about rising stars in the Canadian field (and Saywell certainly was one). Chatting with Bev, Creighton said he'd heard we 'saw' the Lowers each summer. 'Don't you think,' he said, 'they're the most pestiferous people you've ever met?' After Creighton moved off, Bob Spencer (modern Europe) thrust a clipping into Bev's hand, saying, 'I think you should read this.' In a review published that day, Lower had written of a new edition of Donald's *Dominion of the North*: 'This book could only have been written for money.' The ice was always thin. Nevertheless, the party went well and, before long, Saywell removed himself to York University.

For my lectures in American and Canadian history, I had a good backlog of notes, but I never let them go yellow. Despite snide remarks from some of my non-academic friends about the soft professorial life and four-month holiday, I suspect that even in hours per week I more than matched most of them. For my fourth-year seminar, American Progressivism, I read extensively, becoming ever more intrigued by the similarities and startling differences to be found in a comparative analysis of American and Canadian history. The stimulus of this senior seminar induced me to make research and writing in American history (with its irresistible Canadian comparisons) my major academic fascination in the following years.

Students balloted for places in the 'special subject' seminars, whose membership was held to about eight. I held mine in a small office under the eaves of Flavelle House. A gable window moved a beam of soporific sunshine around the room. But no one slept in that group. All its members had made their selection because they were fascinated by the revival of the left in Canada and because of the critical political stage being reached by the new American empire. Most of them were New Party activists who thought the other seminars on offer were too traditionally objective. For their political science option they chose

Brough Macpherson, to more than embrace their plunge into the 1960s. And Brough's white Jaguar sat well matched beside my old Cadillac – to the sour amusement of our colleagues. We worked together on several projects that decade. We saw eye to eye on 'the bomb' and foreign policy, and Bev and I did a lot of socializing with the Macphersons. I was damned if I could see any evidence, other than some of his friends, of communist 'card-carrying.' I was more than content to be able to talk frequently with the most brilliant Canadian working in political theory and analysis.

The American seminar crackled. Among its members were Gerald Caplan, Stephen Lewis, Harvey Levenstein, Martin Robin, and Larry Zolf. I have never seen the joy of debate so uninhibited. That year the university model parliament elected a CCF government; all the seminar members had worked in the campaign, Caplan emerging as prime minister and Lewis as minister of external affairs. Rather than sidetrack discussion of our assigned topics, the election debates gave point to many of them. They brought immediacy and lively comparison to the post–Civil War history of American progressivism and socialism. I told Bev, one evening, it had been a red-letter day: I had got in two words. Occasionally Zolf's growling voice seized an opening to rattle off a fine story about people and events in Winnipeg's broiling radical north end – that legendary source of talent for the rest of the country. His imagery was flamboyant and always relevant – but we put a tight time limit on him. Each of these enthusiasts would distinguish himself – in politics, broadcasting, diplomacy, history, or political science. There would, of course, be many more such – but that first congenial plunge into Toronto's academic life would be like a fine elixir. Only one came a cropper academically. Stephen Lewis was so absorbed by the subject matter of the seminar that he paid insufficient attention to some of his other courses – and consequently failed them. This cost him his BA. Because I had given him a well-deserved A and because his father knew me well, David invited me to lunch (before the marks were recorded). At the end of an excellent meal, David came to the point: Could I possibly speak to Willard Piepenburg, who had assigned the failing grade? Of several embarrassing conversations I had with David, this was the touchiest. He took my refusal in good part. I was amused that some of Stephen's later campaign literature assigned him the BA – until the slip was caught. Like many other public figures, the lack of an earned degree proved no impediment.

For the children, Toronto proved not too difficult a move. Allison finished her remaining two years of public school at Whitney and then went to Jarvis Collegiate. Chris went straight to Jarvis. I abandoned the notion of Upper Canada College for Chris when I inquired about fees. Andrew followed suit after completing Rosedale Public School, although he had the misfortune of spending two years at Deer Park School just as the trashing of the curriculum instigated by the Hall-Dennis report was under way. Jarvis, however, proved excellent – emphatically academic, racially mixed, and with a full range of music and athletics. Chris and Andrew are natural athletes, and I drew great satisfaction watching them excel where I never had. And Allison took the Chase Prize in English, which Dad had won many years before. Allison also caught the 'protest bug': in her final year she organized support for a youngster from Montreal who refused to cut his hair when the stiff-headed principal threatened to expel him. Allison and friends picketed the school. Allison's sign read: 'It's Not What's on Your Head, It's What's in It.' Paraded before Principal Jewell, Allison was asked, 'What would your father think of this?' Allison replied, 'Dad painted the sign.' Unfair. She escaped punishment because removing her name from the honours list would have diminished Jarvis's cherished academic record by one.

We moved from Douglas Drive to 121 Crescent Road in the spring of 1961. Paradoxically, I did this to cut down house expenses as well as gain more living space. The Crescent Road house was a handsome old monster with eleven rooms plus a finished basement. But it had been on the market for two years, and the owner was breaking the zoning rules and behind in all his payments. When we bought the house, it housed seventeen people from top to bottom and the owner lived elsewhere. We got it for $25,000 – the best purchase we ever made – a perfect house for twenty-three years.

While I was working into the routine at Flavelle House, Bev kept our home humming with social activity. One Christmas cocktail party in 1959 at Douglas Drive capped all the others. Dick Stingle was visiting from his temporary post at Saskatoon, so we made a point of inviting Northrop Frye as well as a clutch of historians. The party flourished; we learned among other things that the Creightons had not previously met the Fryes. Louella Creighton, just recovered from flu, much enjoyed my martinis while chatting with John Cairns – one of her favourites. Without warning, she rolled off the chesterfield, crushing her glass as she came to rest under the Christmas tree. Conversation paused politely as three of us carried her upstairs and set her down on one of the twin beds in our room – where she fell fast asleep. The party rolled on most successfully until Donald, who had rushed upstairs every ten minutes, beckoned Bev to follow him. He was sure that a blood stain on the coverlet bespoke a hemorrhage. It was, of course, a slight cut from the broken glass. Louella sat up briefly and, announcing that 'it has nothing to do with me,' resumed her slumber.

It became clear that Louella would not be joining the departing guests. Instead, Donald phoned his daughter, Cynthia, to drive over and stay the night with her mother. With his women bedded down, Donald descended. Bev had prepared the usual light supper for late-stayers, and Donald joined the little group around the dining-room table – which included Ramsay Cook (not yet married), Elliott Rose (the department's wonderfully eccentric Reformation man), Dick Stingle, and several others. About midnight we reached dessert – strawberries on ice cream. Dick, unnerved by the tension, spilt his across the table-cloth. Bev, noting a Far Eastern hospitality custom, at once turned her dish over, nicely spreading the red and white motif. Donald, extremely agitated at the passing time, said he really ought to be getting home. Since he did not drive, he kept looking hopefully around the table. Finally, Ramsay said, 'Donald, I'll drive you home.' And so the party wound down. Half an hour later the phone rang. It was Ramsay: 'Ken, if I ever get to be chairman, remind me I can afford a taxi.' At breakfast, bright and early, Louella said she had told Cynthia to have a good look around because they wouldn't be invited again. And a monster bouquet arrived in the afternoon. Dick said he'd had his money's worth.

At the university I had almost to fight against euphoria. I found the teaching exciting, but there was also a feeling that something really worthwhile might be done. Beyond the yeasty activists in the seminar, young colleagues in cognate departments seemed eager to use their knowledge and skills to influence the direction of affairs and the quality of Canadian society. During the 1960s and 1970s several groups coalesced: The University League for Social Reconstruction, the Canadian Committee for Unilateral Nuclear Disarmament, and even the exotic, ephemeral Fair Play for Cuba Committee. Books, meetings, marches, and teach-ins would be the order of the day. The mainstream university remained largely aloof and we put up with a lot of chilliness from colleagues who, not very subtly, charged us with grandstanding and worse. It was the old question: When does conviction slide into the gratification of being listened to, of enjoying responses to what many of your friends think is irresponsible?

I entered the 1960s with an inner confidence which would take some serious buffeting, but which has pretty well stayed with me. A sort of jump start came with a letter from Frank Underhill in September 1959: 'Thanks very much for the copy of your book on Woodsworth. I think this is just about the best concrete thing that I can point to as having come out of my years of teaching at Toronto.' Many other kind letters arrived, including particularly generous ones from Norman Ward and Lorne Pierce, but none would equal Underhill's for the sheer joy it gave me. At the same time, *The Source Book of Canadian History* was doing very well and a second edition was on the horizon. What I had always sensed in Winnipeg, moreover, proved correct: in Toronto you didn't need to work nearly as hard to 'make opportunities.' It really was 'Hog Town.' The editors of academic journals were down the hall or across the campus, publishers and broadcasters were a few blocks away, visiting lecturers from the United States and Britain were thick on the ground, and the university itself was alive with every possible activity in every section.

Despite the size of the place, people of like mind found one another and groups came together for lunch, for special seminars, and, increasingly for reformist proselytizing. Thus, during 1959 and 1960 I joined the advisory board of *Canadian Welfare*, published by the Canadian Welfare Council, and contributed several articles. For the summer of 1960 I was director of a summer study centre at Queen's under the auspices of the Canadian Historical Association. The program provided a study grant for half a dozen history scholars – to free them from summer teaching and allow them to pursue work in progress. Richard Van Alstyne and Arthur Lower had been the previous directors, and the organization was minimal – basically luncheon meetings for the exchange of ideas. For me it was the perfect arrangement: Garden Island and no lecturing.

That spring, Mary Quayle Innis got me to join the Advisory Board of the Student Christian Movement, but I declined Graham Cotter's invitation to become a member of the Anglican Diocesan Council for Social Service. I sensed that I would never become a thorough churchman – not from lack of conviction, but quite simply believing the parable of the talents, and realization of temporal limits. We went most Sundays to the Church of the Holy Trinity, tucked in behind Eaton's – often in company with George and Shelagh Grant and Michael and Hilda Powicke – Michael is a medievalist, and he and his wife are mainstays of the church. When we moved to Crescent Road we moved also to St Simon's Church – our very interesting parish church. On Bloor near Sherbourne, it draws mainly from Rosedale, but has moderate success in relating to St Jamestown. Its great glory is the choir – relentlessly 'the gentlemen and boys.' We pushed Andrew into the choir, where he sacrificed his Sundays for four years. Head chorister, in his last year, he had a beautiful voice and hated every minute of it. Strange how we know what is best for our children. I've not heard Andy sing a note since leaving the choir. But we have much to be thankful for: although he was a postcard chorister, he was not one of those molested by the choirmaster, who later served time. I think Andy has always had a pretty formidable demeanour.

Academic years, apparently sharply defined, are in fact completely fluid. At the Learned Societies meeting in June 1960, Terry Grier, who was on the committee to establish the New Party (which would become the NDP), persuaded me to prepare some thoughts for the conference that would frame a party program. So with the summer study centre, the *Saturday Night* articles – and some time stolen for sailing, fishing, and priming – the academic blender worked extremely well. It even produced one big bonus. We had arranged for Jamie and Colleen Reaney to sublet a cottage for a month. Jamie in a panama hat thinking dark thoughts about the black Donnellys, and Colleen in a mile-wide floppy straw pursuing her fey streams of consciousness, put icing on the summer for us all.

12

A kind of contrapuntal quality gave zest to the 1960s – as, I suppose, it had all along. I had become pretty well pegged as a 'radical,' academic and political, yet I attended the Anglican Church, 'the Tory Party at prayer.' I wrote for the 'businessmen's magazine,' yet belonged briefly to a propaganda group that turned out to be controlled by Trotskyites. My political hero in the first half of the decade was Tommy Douglas, yet I supported the unstable Hazen Argue for leadership of the NDP. In mid-decade I flirted incautiously with the New Left and 'student power' – from which I withdrew with much recantation, ending up in the *Varsity* as 'a spokesman for the conservative section of the faculty.'

In August 1960 Maurice Careless asked me to contribute a chapter to the centennial volume on Canada since 1867. Edited by him and Craig Brown, *The Canadians* was organized one chapter per decade, each written by a 'distinguished historian.' The authors included Donald Creighton, W.L. Morton, George Stanley, and Charles Stacey. My chapter was the 1930s, and Stacey's, the 1940s. I gave a good socialist analysis of the Depression and the deceptions by which King and Lapointe led a 'united' country into war, noting that 'many of the enlistments for the first Canadian Division were the products of relief camps and brought with them a feeling of resignation rather than patriotic enthusiasm.' Stacey modified this view sharply when he wrote: 'The men of the country came forward in their thousands. Patriots, idealists, adventurers ... the dominant fact in the early days was the unity of the country.' The two chapters were beautifully contrapuntal, and there was truth in each.

In November 1960 I wrote a piece for *Saturday Night*, 'Canada's Stake in the US Election.' I argued that either Nixon or Kennedy as president 'will pursue a much more vigorous line than did Eisenhower with respect to delinquent allies, with respect to trade policy, and in missile and submarine production – and neither one is likely to be as earnest in pursuit of realistic disarmament negotiations as most Canadians would wish.' That last assumption was wildly wishful, of course. 'Most Canadians' were brainwashed by the rhetoric of NATO, NORAD, 'the missile gap,' and the 'loss' of Red China. Yet Ottawa had shown doubts about the U.S. thesis of a monolithic communism and was quietly considering recognition of China and rejecting demands to isolate Castro – and so far had no nuclear weapons in place. In my *Saturday Night* articles, with the merest figleaf of objectivity, I presented for nearly a decade the democratic socialist position in Canadian affairs, the need for disentanglement from the new American military-economic empire, and the perils of our failure to comprehend the ultimate sin of the nuclear arms races. As I look back over those articles, I marvel at Arnold Edinborough's guts in publishing them.

One piece in the spring of 1961, 'Canada, Cuba and the US' was particularly forthright on the need for Canada to 'contract out of the Cold War.' I had been following the policy towards Cuba closely since Castro had overthrown the Batista dictatorship. Books such as *Listen, Yankee* by C. Wright Mills, father of the New Left in the United States, and long conversations with Leslie Dewart, a philosopher and theologian at St Michael's College, convinced me that Cuba was a crucial test of Canadian independence. So far, John Diefenbaker and his external affairs minister, Howard Green, had refused to go along with President Kennedy's economic embargo of Cuba despite intense pressure from Washington and scarcely veiled threats of trade retaliation. I argued that Canada should stay the course, thus demonstrating to Third World countries that 'the West' was not unanimous in wishing to beat back legitimate nationalist revolution against colonial and native dictatorships in the name of anti-communism – from Southeast Asia to Africa to Latin America. The Kennedy policy of driving Castro into the Soviet orbit was being opposed by liberals in the United States and Latin America: 'to sponsor a counter-revolution through official policy and cloak and dagger schemes of filibustering is to make certain the increasing reliance of Castro upon non-Western support ... Perhaps the Cuba crisis (like that in Laos) offers Canada herself the opportunity of contracting out of the Cold War and of basing Canadian policy on real independence of judgment.'

I don't know how this went down with Arnold's business readers (just weeks and months before the Bay of Pigs and the Missile Crisis), but he must have been shaken when he got a request for permission to reprint the article from the editors of the *Monthly Review*, America's leading Marxist journal. Soon after the article appeared in the United States in April 1961, Harvey Levenstein, who had gone to the University of Wisconsin at Madison for graduate work, drew it to the attention of the graduate student group who were working with W.A. Williams, then the most prominent revisionist of Cold War history. This contact resulted in a close connection with *Studies on the Left*, the excellent student journal at Madison – and thus with other revisionist historians across the States. I was, and continue to be, impressed by the fact that the most informed critiques of American policies come from Americans themselves, and equally distressed to note what little impact these critiques have had on American policies at home and abroad.

My concern with the Cuba connection deepened as I discussed it with Dewart. He had grown up in Cuba, leaving for Canada when he was eighteen. His feelings about what American corporations had done to the island, especially under the Batista dictatorship (itself a legacy of Roosevelt's 'Good Neighbor Policy') were strong, and he was proposing a book, *Christianity and Revolution*, which dealt largely with Cuban questions – and with the need for Catholics to understand the crisis of the Third World. In the early winter of 1961 Leslie and I joined the Canadian Fair Play for Cuba Committee. This group emulated the American Fair Play for Cuba Committee. We were naive in believing that the Canadian committee was an independent group whose purpose was to keep the issue before the public and to rally support for an independent Canadian policy. Shortly after we joined the committee's executive, we discovered that it was, in fact, the creature of American Trotskyists and Canadian communists. We at once resigned, but not before our membership had been unfavourably noticed by the Toronto *Telegram*. The brief embarrassment did not stop us from publicizing in every possible way the inequities of U.S. Cuban policy and their relationship to policies that were clearly leading to disasters in Southeast Asia and elsewhere.

That same winter and spring also saw the culmination of preparations for the 'New Party,' or New Democratic Party. I had never taken an active part in CCF clubs or councils, nor did I do so at this formative stage of the NDP. Friends like Walter Young, Harry Crowe, Stanley Knowles, and Mike Oliver were diligent on a variety of committees, and Mike would become the party's first president at the huge summer convention in Ottawa. I knew this marked me as a political dilettante, but I had no talent for organizational work. To say that I simply couldn't spare the time would be hypocritical – when one thinks of others such as Frank Scott. I fear that a kind of lazy disinclination reinforced my conviction that, for me, organizational activity would be dysfunctional. However, I did take part in a clutch of workshops and mini-conferences – enough to make me thoroughly objectionable to the people who were labouring to convert the labour-CCF alliance, which could recoup the 1958 electoral disaster, by fashioning a more pragmatic social-democratic party, endowed with union funds. In each of the platform-discussion meetings, I battled not only for retaining a stress on public ownership but, most vehemently, for total renunciation of nuclear weapons, and of alliances dependent on them, particularly NATO and NORAD. Quite apart from whether my position on these issues was realistic or even 'right,' it was hopeless. On the foreign policy question I ran up against Kalman Kaplansky at every turn. Director of international affairs for the Canadian Labour Congress, Kaplansky was an American-style cold warrior – and, of course, he laid down the union position with absolute authority. The CCF representatives such as David Lewis, Stanley Knowles, and Mike Oliver were not inclined to argue – even if they had agreed with me. Old-guard CCFers such as Colin Cameron and Herbert Herridge of British Columbia and Carlyle King of Saskatchewan gave strong support, but once Tommy Douglas had committed himself to the CCF-CLC political union, the game was lost.

At the height of the battle in March 1961 I wrote a piece for the *Canadian Forum*: 'J.S. Woodsworth and the New Party.' I accused the New Party managers of abandoning socialist principles in favour of a domesticated J.K. Galbraith progressivism and of cynicism with respect to nuclear alliances – all for the purpose of electoral victory. Woodsworth, I noted, 'never believed that the only purpose of a political party was to gain office.' Although I did much less than justice to most of the people involved in the New Party project, I don't think I exaggerated the extent of the change in the nature of the left's political procedure. In any event, I upset Ramsay Cook more than a little. In the May issue of the *Forum* he replied with 'The Old Man, the Old Manifesto, the Old Party.' It was almost a reprise of 1950, when Frank Underhill had ticked me off in the *Forum* for failing to understand Cold War realities. 'It is,' wrote Cook, 'when Professor McNaught settles down to examining, or rather declaring, socialist principles, that one becomes aware of his inherent conservatism ... to make a fetish of the past and indulge in excessive ancestor worship can only hamper the growth of a new radicalism.' Cook asked, 'Will a New Party whose existence only serves to keep the present government in office, as the CCF helped to keep W.L.M. King in power, provide a genuine alternative in Canadian political life in the sixties?' I still think it was useful to blow the whistle on those who overvalued office *per se.* Our best governments in the 20th century have been minority governments. David Lewis accomplished a good deal by this route, and Bob Rae was far more effective when he held the balance of power than in office.

A letter from Carlyle King, the English professor from Saskatchewan, cheered me and pointed to the course we would each follow after the NDP was established.

The spirit of Woodsworth will have no connection with what will come out of that convention ... That is why I retired from the Presidency of the Saskatchewan CCF last July, after fifteen years of it. For a couple of years I fought a rearguard action against new-partyism in Saskatchewan, and the Sask. CCF has as yet not joined the new party. Outside of trade union circles in the cities there is no desire for a new party. Most of the CCF constituency organizations don't like it, but under the urgings of TCD [ouglas] they will reluctantly accept it ... I have no relish for denouncing or repudiating people with whom I have worked for a quarter of a century, and I suppose I shall continue to work for their election no matter what new label they attach to themselves ... I foresee the need for a constant stream of constructive socialist criticism directed towards our friends in the 'new party.'

Sanctimonious, no doubt, but it expressed my feelings at the time; and, of course, the situation was absolutely standard in left-of-centre politics.

The founding convention in Ottawa was a political success and produced exactly the compromising ambivalent policy statements I expected. Because I did not attend, Harry Crowe wrote me a nine-page, excellent account: 'It was a magnificent convention, marred by your absence and by few other things.' I know I should have been there, slashing one more time at Kaplansky. I felt guilty when I learned afterwards of the way Forsey had been bashed for fighting against the banning of the word 'national' from every convention document – particularly when Harry ended his long report with the remark: 'Forsey made a ruddy fool of himself at the Convention.' Forsey knew *his* cause was lost, but he went and fired off his cannons anyway. But, like King, I knew the game was up. Then, just as I had decided not to go, Eric Harrison made an offer that was so exotic I couldn't resist. Would I like to teach a course in the summer session offered in Bermuda for teachers there who wished to get a head start on a degree program at Queen's? I jumped at it.

The Bermuda Board of Education arranged for us to rent a large house owned by the superintendent of black schools, a Mr Robinson, who had a PhD from Howard University and was in England for the summer. The house was in a largely black neighbourhood on Spanish Point Road, so we experienced the last phase of desegregation. Ninety percent of the teachers in my class were black and taught in all-black schools. When we went to the parish church, a white usher walked ahead of us to the front pews and turned around, waiting for us. But we had peeled off and taken a pew in the black section. He was furious – and, to our chagrin, our neighbours seemed to resent the move also. Beware ostentatious liberalism!

Allison and Andrew had come with us, but Chris chose to spend the summer at Camp Mazinaw. Our six weeks were idyllic. I lectured from 10 to 12, Mondays to Fridays. Every afternoon we packed a picnic supper, hailed a passing cab, and went to a beach, different each day, and all wonderful. I managed a lot of watercolours, Allison and Andy nearly drowned in the surf several times – and there were long, hot evenings with TV from the U.S. airbase. We wound the summer off with a couple of weeks on Garden Island.

While we were in Bermuda, Bev's mother and father house-sat for us; barely, because painters and plasterers were at work a lot of the time repairing the wear and tear of its rooming-house days, including removal of a pay-phone from the second floor. On our return, we took up residence in a white Edwardian jewel. The house was built for Bev: a monster kitchen, large living room, dining room, and entrance hall – I suspect she could see the easy flow of guests the first day we looked at it, when there was a clothesline strung across the living room and plywood blocked off the fireplace. I think my great pleasure in Crescent Road was heightened by a move the history department made at the same time: from gracious old Flavelle House to the inhuman atrocity of Sidney Smith Hall. The University of Toronto's first contribution to the wild expansion of universities in the 1960s, Sid Smith was a vast box-like structure – cement slabs on the outside, cinder block dividing walls inside, sealed plate-glass windows, a building without soul and no hope of getting one. A sea change overtook the department: with no common room, the tea hour was no more, and Miss Hahn herself departed shortly after the move. And all this coincided with the rush of new appointments – to accommodate the babies of the boom. From 1961 to 1971 we took on a net increase of fifty-three teachers. Most were young, most American.

As we expanded overall, so did the relative stress we placed on graduate teaching. To my great satisfaction, this role enabled me to offer a graduate seminar and to begin supervising doctoral students in 1962. Again, there was continuity. Don Swainson, who had been in classes with me at United and had been forceful in the Lockhart struggle, joined my first graduate seminar. A tall, gangling Icelander, Don had a passion for factual detail and a keen eye for human foibles. He was a near match for Norman Zacour in cynicism and keen appreciation of irony – too keen for some of his future colleagues. We got along well and he chose to do his thesis with me. Those were great days for bright graduate students. As soon as Don had finished his comprehensive exams I wrote to Eric Harrison, and Swainson was appointed a lecturer at Queen's forthwith. Over the next several summers Don and I discussed his thesis chapters on a waterfront bench at Garden Island. By the time his thesis was passed, in 1964, he and his wife, Eleanor (also a Winnipeger, the daughter of Stuart Garson), had themselves become Garden Island tenants and have remained very close island friends. Over the years I have made twenty or thirty bets with Don; I won only one.

During the 1960s and 1970s, I became much involved in graduate teaching and in the primary research it always involves. By 1982 I had supervised eighteen doctoral theses – eight on Canadian topics, ten on American. Ten of these were published – four in the United States and six in Canada. My two graduate seminars – The Canadian Political Tradition and American Reform Movements – challenged me constantly, yet my recollection is clear: our discussions about methods, interpretations, and sources seldom became pedantic. There always seemed to be someone to share my pleasure in puns, irony, unexpected parallels, or subtle differences in the meaning attached to words by Americans and Canadians: democracy or liberalism, for example. Our conversations seemed to weave in and out of the light-hearted and the passionately serious without noticeable breaks. The dominant themes remained pretty consistent: What were the roots and nature of democratic socialism in Canada? Why was the United States the only industrialized nation not to have produced a viable socialist party? What were the varying meanings attached by Americans and Canadians to democracy, liberalism, individualism – and who were the great exponents in each case? What were the comparative experiences of colonialism and imperialism? Why the differing conceptions of equality, order, and liberty?

Out of all these seminars came some close and lasting friendships – which happily ignored some profound differences in opinion. Occasionally we would hold a session at Crescent Road. Bev and I gave regular cocktail parties, often mixing people from the fourth year and graduate seminars – and the more senior who were launched on their theses. In recent years I have, of course, discovered that there were student perceptions of my 'methods' and point of view of which I was largely unaware. Most of these were genial, as when I used my grandfather as an illustration of 'Red Tory' or American progressive. Christopher Armstrong still takes pleasure in reminding me of this – and of other favourite 'illustrations.' But it was more than the enjoyment of ideas, of 'discovery,' that gave verve to the long sequence of senior and graduate seminars – and to many of the tutorial groups attached to the big lecture course in American history. Watching the several hundred students respond, gain confidence, and finally 'fight back' was a reward of pure gold. The reward was cumulative – as many of them became colleagues at Toronto, York, Queen's, and across the country.

Sally Miller came from Chicago in 1962 and was the first to finish a doctorate with me in 1966. Her thesis was published in the United States and is the standard work on Victor Berger and the Socialist Party of America. She became a leading labour-feminist historian. Bill Dick finished at about the same time. A stocky Scot with MAs from Edinburgh and Oregon, Bill's quizzical eyes revealed an independence of mind reminiscent of Stewart Reid. His thesis analysed the curious relationship between labour and political socialism in Sam Gompers's America and was published in 1972. Bill, Sally, and I saw eye to eye in the reasons for the 'failure' of American socialism and the malign influence of Sam Gompers; they were both self-starters and burrowed prodigiously in American primary sources. In a sense, they spoiled me, but they made my job of supervision extremely pleasant. After graduation, Sally returned to a solid career in the United States and Bill, after a stint at Ohio State, returned to a permanent job at Scarborough College at the University of Toronto.

As teaching colleagues, Bill and I attended many conferences together in the United States. We came to know most of the American specialists in the labour-history field, especially at Wayne State in Detroit and Rochester. I found myself on the board of *Labor History* and enjoyed immensely the offers to read papers and review books for it and other American journals. I had, of course, some special advantages. At that time, few people in Canadian universities specialized in U.S. history. Also, U.S. 'revisionist' history and the ideas of the New Left were riding high; the nature of American capitalism and imperialism, and especially their impact on Canada, coincided with the subject matter of my teaching. While Gerry Craig and Bill Nelson did graduate seminars, Craig emphasized the pre–Civil War period and Bill the colonial and revolutionary periods. The result, on not very good historical grounds, was that I supervised most of the U.S. theses in the 1960s and 1970s. A certain tension arose, but fortunately not enough to interfere with good relations in the American area of the department. With no proof, I suspected that some of 'my' graduates were disadvantaged in applying for vacancies that occurred in the department – the appointments going instead to new American PhDs. I think a case in point was Steve Randall, who did an outstanding thesis on U.S. foreign policy that was quickly accepted for American publication. The argument was made that we should not become 'ingrown.' So Steve went off to McGill, where, in short order, he became chair of the department and, some time later, moved on to a distinguished career at Calgary. In the meantime, the balance between Canadians and Americans in our department continued to tilt to the south, causing Robin Mathews sleepless nights – planning his hyperbolic but effective campaign against the Americanization of Canadian universities.

When I added a seminar on the Canadian Political Tradition, I also took on some Canadian doctoral students. One of the first (apart from Swainson and Miller) was David Bercuson. He had come to Toronto from a socialist working-class background in Montreal. Mercurial, a person of passion, his seminar work was outstanding – but he nearly blew it on the day of his general oral examination. Unable to sleep the previous night, he had taken heavy sedation. Next morning, to snap out of it, he took countervailing 'uppers.' When he reached my office for the oral quizzing, he was pretty well incoherent. Fortunately, we knew he was thoroughly prepared and we simply cut the ordeal short. Later in the day Arthur Silver, who was to face his own oral in the afternoon, let me in on the explanation of the morning's fiasco. David went on to write a fine thesis on the Winnipeg General Strike, published as

Confrontation at Winnipeg. By the time he and I collaborated on a short teaching book, *The Winnipeg General Strike*, in 1974, he was beginning to curb his enthusiasm for labour history. Reaching dizzying decanal heights at the University of Calgary, David was soon into a variety of historical enterprises, from political to diplomatic and military subjects. He also became a frequent guest on Peter Gzowski's *Morningside* where, with wonderful vigour, he seemed to defend positions just to the left of David Frum and Preston Manning. I recently wrote to him after one such broadcast. He replied with a long friendly letter, concluding, 'See what you did?'

If David drifted slowly rightward while studying radical unionism, Irving Abella surprised me by refusing to swallow the CCF version of the 'struggle for industrial unionism in Canada' – and discovering that the communists had, in many respects, been a 'good' thing for the Canadian labour movement. Less ebullient, but no less sure of himself than Bercuson, Irving was also a self-starter. Short, chunky, his serious demeanour covered a quizzical sense of humour; I was surprised when he decided on a history of 'The CIO in Canada: A Study in Canadian-American Relations.' Craig Brown joined me in supervising the thesis and we were both impressed by Irving's rapid and thorough covering of all the Canadian and American sources. His book was published as *Nationalism, Communism and Canadian Labour*.

Not only did the book receive uniformly high praise but it raised a lot of democratic-socialist hackles by revealing how CCFers had used sharp methods to maintain a dominant influence in the labour movement. Irving became a principal organizer of the Committee on Labour History, from which sprang the important journal *Labour/le Travailleur*. This journal, under the influence of young neo-Marxist historians such as Greg and Linda Kealey and Bryan Palmer, became a vehicle of 'the new social history.' Abella took a job at Glendon College and, while he continued to work on labour history, his approach remained more 'institutional' than either 'social' or 'Marxist.' At the end of the 1970s he collaborated with Harold Troper (who, like many of the young labour historians, had been in my seminar) in a study of Canada's prewar immigration policy. Publication of their book, *None Is Too Many*, came as a terrible eye-opener – revealing the depth of the country's anti-Semitism in the 1930s and the vicious effect of that prejudice on our exclusion of thousands of Holocaust victims. Mackenzie King, Vincent Massey, and the Ottawa mandarins had to be reassessed in one very important particular.

Abella continued writing and teaching labour history, but his concern with Jewish history led to active involvement with the Canadian Jewish Congress, of which he would serve as president for several years. Bev and I became close friends with Irving and his remarkable, vivacious wife, Rosie. She had been born in a displaced person's camp in Berlin and lost most of her relatives to the Holocaust. She has the warmest personality I've ever encountered, and concealed a profound legal mind behind unbelievable informality as she rose to become one of the best female benchers in the country.

Four women endured my thesis supervision; their variety was wonderfully refreshing. Shortly after Sally Miller had immortalized Victor Berger, I inherited Anne Woolever from Dick Saunders, who was about to retire. Anne was at work on a study of the American Catholic historian Christopher Dawson – about whom I knew nothing. However, historiography is historiography, and I learned quite a bit while giving Anne what help I could in framing her analysis. The thesis turned out well and she went off to teach in Maryland.

Anne Golden gave quick evidence of her organizing talents as she tore into the topic 'American Attitudes to the Soviet Union.' She could scarcely avoid my revisionist predilections, but she brought her own judgment to bear on the admirable range of evidence she researched. The book was not published, I think largely because the field by this time was already jam packed with dissertations directed by Bill Williams, Gabriel Kolko and Walter LeFeber – not to mention the explosion of radical journals such as *Studies on the Left*, *Radical American*, and *I.F. Stone's Weekly*. Unabashed, Anne moved into municipal politics, supporting David Crombie with reform causes in Toronto, and from there to leadership of Toronto's United Way. Most recently she produced a finely researched report and proposals for the badly needed reorganization of the Greater Toronto Area.

Rosemary Speirs was already working as a reporter with Canadian Press when she entered the graduate program. CP had encouraged her interest in organized labour, especially the railway unions, and she had good contacts in the unions, with conciliators such as Carl Goldenberg, and with company spokesmen. I approved her proposal of a thesis on the impact of technological change on Canadian railway labour relations since 1946. The department was not quite ready for the contemporary nature of the topic, and some even questioned its labour economics subject matter. After a first version was rejected, the only substantive reason being inadequate resources, I took up arms. I knew that Rosemary had tapped sources and gained interviews that few other students could have managed. So I sent the thesis to Jack Weldon of McGill. I had met him during the Boag book conferences, and he was the country's leading labour economist. After reading the thesis, he returned it with a few suggested cosmetic changes – saying he would have passed it happily as it stood. So I secured a second exam, making sure that Weldon was external examiner. The thesis sailed through with flying colours. I've always suspected that the distinctly pro-labour slant in Rosemary's analysis (which in no way lessened its worth) had something to do with our trouble – perhaps, too, her easy journalistic style bothered some who were accustomed to more turgid prose. She went on to become one of our best parliamentary reporters.

Like Rosemary, Wayne Roberts was born a journalist, but with a strong strain of the crusader. An active young Trotskyite, he had taken his MA at Berkeley in 1968 – a time and place not calculated to moderate his enthusiasm. At Toronto he spread his doctoral work over nine years – using his thesis research fruitfully in several scholarly articles, in teaching assistantships, and casual journalism. He was caught up with the young labour and feminist scholars and their attempt to appropriate the new social history of E.P. Thompson and others. I expected ideological trouble, but in fact his 'Labour and Reform in Toronto, 1896–1914,' while not without a point of issue, was first rate – my main problem as supervisor was to curb his enthusiasm. Wayne moved more and more into political journalism, working especially with alternative newspapers such as *Now* in Toronto.

Graeme Mount provided a distinct change of pace. Precise in manner, formal to a degree, he was a different challenge: he really believed in objectivity. When he chose as thesis topic 'American Imperialism in Panama,' I expected at least a modified 'revisionism.' Instead, he presented a thorough, scholarly analysis – one that Richard Van Alstyne, as external examiner, approved without question. He took an appointment at Laurentian, where he had as a colleague Angus Gilbert, who had taken my seminar. I was to enjoy several visits to Laurentian while Henry Best was president. There was much congeniality – including a pub evening where I met survivors of the union struggles of the 1930s and 1940s and heard the anti-CCF side that had impressed Abella. Mount has gone on to do solid work on Canada's external relations – especially the Latin American–Caribbean connection.

Bruno Ramirez was blessed with a personality that would put anyone off guard. Slender, dark, with a soft, almost musical voice, Bruno arrived with a surprisingly scattered academic background. An Italian, he grew up in Catania, attended university in Rome, moved to the United States, where he received a BA from a small college in New Jersey, and came to Canada, to earn an MA in history at Guelph. In my seminar he was quiet as a mouse, but when it came time to talk about a thesis I realized he hadn't missed a thing. Moreover, he was ready to carry forward one of the seminar's themes with vigour and originality: the problem of mainstream American unionism's reluctance to enter party politics – and the resultant 'failure' of American socialism. I put him in touch with David Montgomery, Milton Cantor, and other American labour historians I had come to know through *Labour History* and conferences at Wayne State University. The result was an excellent study published as *When Workers Fight* in 1978. At the end of his note of thanks, Bruno penned a truly poignant conclusion: 'I was unable to obtain any financial support for reasons that may only be clear to the connoisseur of the bureaucratic mind. The only benefit I am accruing from this is that it makes my task of acknowledgment a very small one.' At the Université du Québec à Montréal, Ramirez has become the leading student of Italian immigration in Quebec.

Laurel MacDowell surprised me more than most of my doctoral students. Daughter of Larry Sefton, Canadian director of the United Steelworkers, whom I had met at several conferences, Laurel first came to my attention as a member of a second-year tutorial group. An attractive, quiet-mannered woman, she brought to history the same preconceptions about objectivity and democratic socialism which I harboured at the same age – and which I had learned must be closely watched. Her undergraduate grades were second class, and she spent a lot of time in the late 1960s on the burgeoning student movement and working with the Students' Administrative Council. After her BA, however, she did an excellent MA at the London School of Economics in international history and returned with a firm grip on the essentials of scholarship. For her doctoral thesis she chose the wartime struggle for collective bargaining rights, centring her analysis on the vicious gold-miners' strike of 1941–2. It was published as *Remember Kirkland Lake* in 1983. I was worried, at first, because her father had been secretary of the union during the strike, and Laurel's interest in the affair was highly emotional. As it turned out, her inside lines of information in labour union circles and records more than compensated for any *parti-pris* problem. As her work sailed through the thesis exam and the publisher's evaluation, I recalled the charges I had faced from some people when working on the Woodsworth biography: 'Your mind is made up before you start; you cannot be objective.' My views on objectivity and 'purpose,' both in historical writing and in historical action, would not become less difficult or less urgent. Laurel has continued to balance scholarship and commitment in labour and women's history. I remember my last conversation with Gwyneth Grube; she and George had been close to the Seftons. When Gwyneth asked, 'How is little Laurel?' my mind drifted back to the LSR-*Forum* days at Blythwood – in a warm feeling of continuity.

Alvin Finkel came with an MA and firm Marxist views from Manitoba. I think he must have absorbed them from Clare Pentland. At the conclusion of one of Carl Berger's seminars on the LSR, Al summed the league up as 'a lot of chicken shit.' I didn't detect this depth of feeling when Michael Bliss and I supervised his thesis, 'Canadian Business and the "Reform" Process in the 1930s.' Finkel applied the analysis developed by the American historian of progressivism, Gabriel Kolko: essentially, he argued that the Bennett New Deal, like that of FDR, was directed and supervised by businessmen in the interest of preserving capitalism in the midst of the depression crisis. I am not too surprised that I underestimated the virulence of Finkel's Marxism. A little earlier, when Bliss was in my seminar, I was sure that he was a liberal progressive.

Keith Cassidy possessed one of the sharpest minds I encountered in graduate teaching. He wrote a most perceptive thesis on American concepts of leadership and authority which impressed Christopher Lasch, who came up from Rochester as external examiner. After some preliminary short-term posts, Keith took a permanent position at Guelph. His Catholic concern about 'the right to life' has led him to concentrate on the history of that movement – with the same powerful use of his earlier historical thinking. One early project concerning American Cold War policies was an article in which he collaborated with Anne Golden. I have a poignant memory of these two dissimilar people debating some fine points across the table in my office.

Several other thesis students ran into the hiring slowdown at the end of the 1970s. Bill Gleberzon failed to get a teaching post and moved into administration work, although the external examiner, William O'Neill of Rutgers, said his thesis deserved a *cum laude*. Gene Homel, who had come up from California with extreme New Left views, adapted quickly to the new environment and wrote an excellent, sympathetic study of Toronto's Jimmy Simpson and social democracy. After a series of 'contractually limited' appointments on the west coast, however, he disappeared from my sight – which saddened me. Similarly, Glen Seretan, after writing a fine revisionist study of Daniel de Leon, which was published by Harvard, moved through a series of short-term appointments and out of touch.

In some ways, Gleberzon, Seretan, and Homel were the wave of the future. The affluence of the 1960s and 1970s had led to increasing specialization on the part of tenured faculty and the off-loading of much teaching onto teaching assistants and contractually-limited lecturers. As the financial buoyancy tapered off in the 1980s and 1990s and tenure-stream appointments practically vanished, the temptation to have more and more teaching done by non-tenured people increased: budgets could be pared and tenured professors could still offer small-enrolment specialized courses, with plenty of research leaves. Of course, this trend led to a kind of academic sweatshop and the virtual disappearance of collegiality in many departments. The problem has been intensified by the vicious underfunding of the 1990s.

Many of the most engaging members of the seminars were doing their theses on other fields and chose one of my courses as part of their preparation for their general comprehensive examinations. About 1978 I added a second graduate seminar: The Canadian Political Tradition. Clearly a counterpart to the American, the Canadian stressed the positive aspects of our history and its continuity from its European roots – denying especially the contextual notion that Canada was simply the rejection of the American revolution. It was another chance to examine the differences between the two nations, particularly the notions of the role of government, the meaning of liberty and democracy, and the role of order. I found the seminar immediately stimulating, and out of it grew a fair clutch of articles and book reviews – for the learned journals, the *Forum*, *Canadian Dimension*, and the newspapers. A good many of the students were in both seminars. Not many of my colleagues were offering unabashedly 'left-wing' history and, in the heady days of the New Left, Vietnam, and a revived Canadian social-democratic party, there was no paucity of takers. Of course, this is not to say either course was strictly ideological. I took a serious interest, for example, in revising the hero vision of people like Louis Riel and William Lyon Mackenzie, and also looked at some generally accepted wisdom, such as that of Canada as a 'peaceable kingdom,' a non-violent society. The criminality of the nuclear arms race and Canada's involvement in the NATO-NORAD structure and the defence production sharing agreement with the United States, which enabled us to sell weapons and other equipment to the Americans for the devastation of Vietnam, called for examination of our complicity in the militarized Cold War.

To me, both the graduate seminars combined serious hard work with frequent dashes of good humour and competitive wit. One could scarcely conduct in unbroken solemnity discussions that included, at different times, Christopher Armstrong, Viv Nelles, Chad Gaffield, Robert Cuff, David Marshall, Veronica Strong-Boag, and Brian Hogan, plus those who did theses with me, without recognizing the extraordinary rewards offered by a university that had a strong graduate school. The School of Graduate Studies benefited greatly from the intelligence of Ernest Sirluck, who had come from fifteen years at Chicago to take it over in 1962. The fourth-year special course seminars were almost equally stimulating. How could they not be with such dour intelligences as Robert Bothwell, sparkling water-spiders like Michael Ignatieff, and sceptical observers like Margaret MacMillan? It was in those fourth-year groups that I worked out a pretty thorough critique of the notion of inevitability in history – one which seemed to satisfy about half the students each time around, and which has satisfied me ever since. To put it briefly: if *anything* in history is inevitable, then *everything* must be, and there is little point in treating history as other than chronicle.

A large university poses problems of communication. Departmental members tend to meet and talk almost exclusively with one another. I found that I missed the interdisciplinary atmosphere of a small college. I also sensed that a number of people I knew in other departments shared this feeling. So I talked with some of them about starting a kind of faculty seminar – to bring to bear on current political-social problems the thinking of various disciplines. I had a vague hope that we might recreate something akin to the old LSR.

What became first the University League for Social Reconstruction (1962), and very quickly and significantly the University League for Social Reform (1963), sprang from a conversation I had with Abe Rotstein of political economy. Abe was an elegant young man who, like his clone in the department, Mel Watkins, really believed in the departmental amalgamation of politics and economics – a distinctive feature of the university since the days of Harold Innis. Abe intimidated me a bit because of his heavy-lidded eyes and graceful cigarette holder, but he was a thoughtful socialist and a person who would carry things through. We sent out notices for a founding meeting to a long list of people. That Mel was, then, a free-marketeer was instrumental in our modifying the name of our group; that the free-marketer John Crispo was cheek by jowl with the Marxist Brough MacPherson; or that a few years later, when Abe was editing the *Canadian Forum*, I resigned from the board in protest against his 'bleeding heart' approach to Quebec separatism all suggests that the ULSR was broad based and specifically non-ideological. Nevertheless, I arranged to have Frank Scott and Charles Taylor come down from Montreal to address our first meeting. Continuity with the LSR was not to be, yet the lifespans were about the same (ten years), and the ULSR published in books and articles at least as much as had the LSR. I was mildly disappointed, but the genuine vitality of our monthly meetings demonstrated the worth of purposive discussions of public affairs among academics of different disciplines, and of communicating much of that discussion to people beyond the university. I met and became friends with many people who, without the fragile framework of the ULSR, would have remained names only.

Each September, until 1972, the ULSR met, elected an executive, decided the year's program, and lined up one paper to be read at each meeting. The program organizer(s) also became editor(s) of the volume that printed a selection of each year's papers. Few subjects were untouched, and the ULSR books received remarkably wide attention in the media. Many of the chapters, with slight changes, appeared in journals and other theme books. I think, however, that the best aspect of the ULSR was the intellectual stimulus of the regular meetings and the bringing together of people who would not otherwise have exchanged views and formed friendships. Bev and I played host to two of the book launchings: they were among the liveliest of the great many parties at 121 Crescent. My favourite recollection was a phone call from our neighbour during one of these occasions. Greg Clark kept close watch on 'the sounds and doings of the day' from his study window. 'I have been watching,' he said, 'a lot of thirsty minds going into your place, professor. I just want to tell you that if you run short I have a bottle of Scotch I'd be happy to contribute.' Sadly, he declined my invitation to join the uproar.

13

After teaching for sixteen years, I had not had a sabbatical. Toronto generously offered me one after teaching there for only four years – in 1963. I had a project ready, one that grew directly out of my graduate seminars. I proposed to spend a year in London searching out correspondence between British and American socialists and progressives. I had in mind documenting transatlantic lines of influence in the thinking and politics of the left of centre. When collated with similar research in the United States and Canada, I hoped to shed some light on the curious phenomenon that the United States was the only industrialized country unable to sustain a viable democratic-socialist party. The work of that year was to lead me into extensive comparative history. While no single volume would result, paths of interpretation became clear and led to many articles and papers, and, I hope, steadily enriched seminars.

In any event, the academic side of the year was completely absorbing. I read R.C.K. Ensor's papers in the frigid basement of Christ Church, Oxford; several collections at the London School of Economics, including those of Harold Laski and Graham Wallace; and Ramsay MacDonald's, which were to my great surprise tucked away in a Victorian monstrosity in Blackheath. The house belonged to David Marquard, who was working on a biography of MacDonald. Because I was interested only in MacDonald's American correspondence, he made no objection to my looking at them. Shirley Williams, who was then looking after the Fabian Society library, was extremely helpful; we were able to repay her hospitality when she visited Toronto later while she was a Labour MP. While I was working at LSE (under 25 watt bulbs, which soon caused me to get a pair of reading glasses – free from the

National Health), I met several Canadian graduate students and became good friends with Bob McKenzie, who was lecturing there. Bob took a special interest in Canadian students and was honorary president of the LSE-NDP Club. He arranged for me to speak to the club, which met above the Bloomsbury Wine Lodge at the intersection of Charing Cross and Shaftesbury. I think it was the largest NDP club meeting I ever spoke to – and certainly one of the best evenings.

I encountered only one instance of overt snobbery during the year. It happened that I gave an 'external' lecture at Oxford on the same day that the American historian John Morton Blum was speaking close by. A joint sherry party was held for us after the lectures. Max (later Lord) Beloff patronized us both outrageously, but angered me because Blum was a much more distinguished historian – and a vintage representative of the American Ivy League. During a pause in Beloff's monologue, Blum's eyes reached the ceiling, and I innocently asked Beloff what he thought of the most recent volume in the official biography of Mackenzie King. Beloff did not know it had been published. Without a word, he left us to ourselves. We two colonials got along just fine.

I gave quite a few occasional lectures. The one I most enjoyed was at the site of the founding of the Committee for Unilateral Nuclear Disarmament. Canon Collins, then leader of the CUND, was there and seemed to appreciate any analysis of Canada's hypocrisy in the matter of nuclear weapons. I next saw Collins when he addressed the throng that had marched from Blackheath to Trafalgar Square during the Easter weekend in 1964. I stood at one of the entrances to the square as the long column filed by. Allison, who, unlike me, had done the whole march, waved as she went by under the banner of the Scottish Young Communists – where she had been placed willy-nilly.

It was a golden year. We had left Garden Island at the end of August, gone to Montreal by train, stayed overnight with the Olivers, and boarded the Cunard line's *Franconia* the following morning. What a wonderful way to travel. We didn't arrive in England cramped, burned out for lack of sleep, and requiring two days' time-adjustment. Rather, we arrived after seven magical days – down the St Lawrence and across to Southampton. There were long mornings on the top deck, stretched out in a deck chair under three blankets with a book, and interrupted only by a steward with 'elevenses' of hot Bovril. There were ping-pong games with Andrew on a lower deck at the stern, where we could watch our wake breaking up 20-foot rollers. There were bright nights when Bev and I could lean on the promenade deck rail, listening to the hiss of salt-water beneath us. Only Allison had doubts, suffering four days of sea-sickness. She tried to make me promise that we would return by air; I couldn't, because airfare was then much more expensive than surface fare and we were on a very tight budget. She was particularly peeved because, as my experienced crew in the Albacore sailboat, she had expected to be enjoying the ship's motion.

At Southampton we picked up a little Austin four-door, with a roof rack to hold most of our seventeen pieces of luggage. Because our flat in London wouldn't be ready for another week, we made a leisurely drive up to Edinburgh. We had booked for the Tattoo and, on our evening, the temperature hovered around 50 degrees amid an intermittent drizzle. Our B and B landlady lent Bev a sheepskin jacket and gave each of us a blanket. It was worth it! Amazing how Scottish one can feel. Indeed, the feeling of belonging never left us from the time we first sighted Land's End from the deck of the *Franconia*.

Back in London, we made for 14 Prince Albert Road, where we found our excellent three-bedroom flat on the top floor of a block on the north side of Regent Park. The block of five or so buildings had been acquired by the Nuffield Foundation to accommodate visiting Commonwealth Scholars. From our fourth-floor mansard windows we could see St Paul's dome and a wide range of the park, including the Regent's canal and the zoo. We could afford this splendid location because of the heavy Nuffield subsidy. Very different schooling arrangements were made for each of the children. Christopher, at seventeen, went off to the Canadian school at Neuchâtel in Switzerland – his generous godparents, Gerry and Elizabeth Prodrick, footing the tuition fees. There he completed his Ontario grade 13, became bilingual, and thoroughly enjoyed himself. Allison, then fifteen, profited equally from attending South Hampstead High School for Girls – one of the 'day trust' schools that were 'private' in the Canadian sense, but heavily subsidized, with fees of about $200. Alan Hill, whom I had met in Toronto through Bernard Trotter, then with the CBC, was a governor of the school and smoothed the way for Allison's late enrolment. Like Chris, Allison became bilingual by leaving Canada – a sorry irony, and only one of the advantages of a very fine school. Andrew, then six, to his considerable regret, found himself in Primrose Hill London County Council School, a short walk from the Nuffield Flats. We did our best to ease the bored pain he experienced in this most uninspiring institution. He and Allison came with us on our many weekend and holiday junkets covering most of England.

I think the most rewarding were the two long weekends at Haworth, site of the Brontë manse. On one of these, our landlady packed us a lunch and, with her daughter as guide, we walked several miles across the moors in a dense fog to Top Withins – the probable inspiration for *Wuthering Heights*. Here we had lunch while I did a watercolour – with Andrew seen dimly through the rough mist. During the long Easter break at Allison's school, she came with Bev and me across to Dublin. There we rented a tiny car and toured the west of Ireland. During five 'saft' days we wandered nearly empty roads from Cork to the Ring of Kerry, the Cliffs of Moher, and back to Dublin. The Irish Sea lived up to its reputation.

Alan and Enid Hill became close friends. Alan was director of Heinemann's Educational Books and would later publish a hardcover version of my *Penguin History of Canada*. During the year he invited us to parties at Heinemann's and at their house in Hampstead Garden (which backed on that of Harold Wilson). I remember long chats with Kinua Achebe, the Nigerian novelist 'discovered' by Alan, and, particularly, with Richard Titmuss – who was busy demonstrating how the income distribution in the United Kingdom was worsening – despite the welfare state. But the Hills' most generous act was offering us the use of 'New House' – a fine white-stucco house built on the side of a hill overlooking Rosthwaite in Borrowdale, on the Derwent near Keswick. Alan acquired it partly as a family retreat, partly for entertaining Heinemann business connections. A picture window overlooked the Derwent valley, and a huge fireplace took the chill off not infrequent rainy spells. Alan and Enid hosted us there on our first visit in 1964. Thereafter, they simply said to drive up whenever we could – which we did often on our later stays in London down through 1989. Long walks on the fells, dinners in local pub-hotels (in one of which our table was next to Joyce Grenfell, who put off ordering dessert until ours had been served and she had inspected it), followed by fireside evenings. On our later London 'junkets,' Alan and Enid always took us to dinner at the Garrick Club, where Alan took pleasure in showing us the library, and a letter of resignation written to the club secretary by Charles Dickens.

During the winter in London we haunted the galleries and the West End theatres. Bev took no break in her entertaining: visitors such as Ernest Sirluck, Bora Laskin, Jim Conacher, Sam Freedman, Harry Crowe, and a very young Gerald Caplan, who stored a raft of books with us for several months. Life in the Nuffield flats was very social, including elaborate 'national nights' once a month: Canada night, Australia night, and so on. Our Canada night extravaganza was a great success; I particularly enjoyed serving Corby's Special Old, surreptitiously, to two Moslems whose wives were across the room at the time. We had acquired many contributions, such as a gallon of maple syrup from a friend-of-a-friend in Belleville: the dessert of ice cream swimming in syrup wowed everyone.

An unexpected side-trip came in January, as a result of a letter I had received from Stewart Reid in November. Stewart had, over the preceding four years and on a tiny budget, established an effective central office for the Canadian Association of University Teachers. He had one secretary and, on his cross-country visits to universities, usually stayed with friends rather than incurring hotel expenses. His cancer, had developed steadily; for his last two years he had to use a cane and suffer the other indignities of a metastasizing bone cancer, but none of this slowed him down. CAUT is permanently in his debt. His November letter was one of the last he wrote. Typically, its purpose was to save money for CAUT. Rather than send someone from Canada to represent CAUT at the annual meeting of the International Association of University Professors in Belgium, he asked me to be the representative – thus saving a transatlantic fare. To that meeting in Ghent in January 1964, Bev, Allison and Andrew accompanied me – *not* at CAUT expense! It was quite a strain for me because the sessions were conducted in French – most of which I understood, but I managed only one intervention, which was received with kindly tolerance. Andrew was thoroughly bored, save for our visit to the Castle of the Counts of Flanders. This lowering monster contains an extensive collection of medieval torture instruments; for once, Andrew was the most reluctant to leave.

By January I had to think hard about finances. Our income for the sabbatical was half salary plus a Canada Council grant – and we were determined to take six summer weeks on the Continent. The answer had to be some supplementary income. During 1962 I had, with Ramsay Cook, written a grade 13 textbook – under the eagle editorial eyes of John Ricker and Jack Saywell. I did the U.S. half, and Ramsay did the Canadian. It was published in 1963 by Clarke Irwin as *Canada and the United States*. Allison and Chris told me it was referred to as the 'McNaught Cookbook.' Ramsay and I agreed that we learned a lot from the experienced critiques of Saywell and Ricker. A superb scholar, Saywell has never spared anyone's feelings; Ricker, a seasoned teacher and about to become head of the Toronto Faculty of Education, couched his strictures in gentler terms – but with equal effect. Still, we authors decided we would never write another textbook. Although the book was very successful, the first royalty cheque would not arrive in time to help our summer plans.

I took two steps to solve the problem. Two friends from Garden Island agreed to buy my Albacore, producing $750. Then I followed up a lead suggested by Bob Kilpatrick, schoolbook manager of Longman's Canada (who had published the *Source-Book of Canadian History*). Bob had learned from Dieter Pevsner of Penguin Books in London that a Canadian historian they had commissioned to write a general history of Canada had failed to deliver. I got in touch with Pevsner, an extremely agreeable young man and son of the well-known art historian. He came up to the flat, where we had a long conversation. I agreed to draw up a ten-page chapter outline. The upshot was a contract with a $1000 advance. Bev and I agreed we could add the $1750 to our slender income and 'do Europe' on $5 a day per person – excluding the car rental. In fact, that is just about what we did.

Christopher, now eighteen, decided to hitch-hike through Greece and part of Turkey with two Neuchâtel friends. We gave him train fare to Athens plus $125 and arranged to meet him at Brindisi at the heel of Italy at the beginning of August. He ran out of money before then and got along by selling some blood, and some watercolours to tourists – whom he addressed in French as an added come on. He had become an accomplished artist, and remains so today. By the time we met up in Brindisi, we didn't recognize him at first, so thin and brown had the rigours of the journey left him.

Bev and I, with Allison and Andy, set off early in July in a rented English Ford – a mistake because, with the right-hand drive, I had to rely on Bev to tell me of on-coming traffic whenever I had to pass someone. We hit Paris at 5 p.m. and headed for our little hotel, The Washington, near rue Georges V; this involved me in the rush-hour traffic circling the Arc de Triomphe – many lanes abreast and without posted lane guides. Finally reaching the hotel, I parked the car and, for the next four days, we saw Paris on foot – which is the best way in any case. For me, the beauty and excitement of Paris were dulled by out-of-reach prices and a striking aloofness on the part of its citizens. Bev didn't quite agree, though we both felt that London was where we felt most 'at home.'

Stupidly, we chose 14 July, Bastille Day, to strike south to inspect the

Loire and its chateaux. Thousands of Parisians did exactly the same. So, about 8 p.m., we reached Tours, having failed to get accommodation anywhere along the way. The tourist office in Tours phoned ahead for us and made a reservation in a tiny village 14 miles further south. Our little *auberge* was really a farm house with two guest rooms in the middle of the village. We reached our quarters by way of a huge kitchen permeated by wonderful smells from a monster black stove. The mistress was busy plucking a chicken, so we made our way through and up to our single large room, which was divided by a curtain and served by a cold-water sink. The dinner was excellent – begun by a magnificent soup from the pot-au-feu we had savoured in the kitchen. From there on, our journey down the Loire, across southern France, back through Switzerland, and south again through Milan, Florence, and Rome went without a hitch. We discovered the trick for making a cheap trip thoroughly agreeable. Lunches were always picnics of local bread, wine, cheese, and fruit. I selected our third-class hotels or pensions from the *Michelin* guide – always on a street that boasted first-class hotels. While Coke for Andy cost more than *vin ordinaire* for us at dinners, he made up by seldom wanting more than the inevitable huge antipasto and fruit. My method of hotel selection worked especially well in Rome, where we found ourselves on a piazza directly across from the Pantheon. At the American Express in Rome, we found a letter from Chris: 'If you want to see me again, send $15.' We did this through Kurt Swinton's minion at the Encyclopedia Britannica's office in Athens. On the ferry to Brindisi, Chris slept in a lifeboat, to which a couple of American girls brought him some goodies from their dining-room table.

After our Brindisi rendezvous, we enjoyed a leisurely drive up the Adriatic coast, with a half-way stop at a spectacular beach and a half-price stay at an incompleted luxury hotel. In Venice we celebrated Allison's sixteenth birthday with a fine dinner and an evening gondola tour of the canals. Then we drove along the Italian riviera and stopped for a week high above the sea: each day on the beach, followed by a fine dinner provided by Senora Grande by a window overlooking the town. One night Chris sat out on a balcony to do a watercolour of Alassio's curve of light far below. As sometimes happens with a spur-of-the-moment experiment, the result was marvellous; I've never had the nerve to try one at night. The closest have been several spectacular Garden Island sunsets – one of which didn't look like a postcard.

From Alassio we drove to the Côte d'Azur, on to Aix-en-Provence, and then up to Normandy, to admire the Bayeux Tapestry and to catch the ferry from Dieppe. Chris wanted to go in the icy water, across the vicious round boulders that cover that terrible beach. On another fine voyage the *Franconia* took us back to Canada – one of the last trips on which an anglophone could still feel a whisper of patriotism sailing under the Quebec Bridge and past Wolfe's Cove; not to mention the docks where, until fifty years ago, Garden Island's monster timber rafts were disassembled for shipment to Liverpool.

The second half of the 1960s defy even a casual attempt a pattern making – although one theme I can see clearly: an unmistakable sense of personal involvement in the 'great issues' of the time. The nuclear weapons races – the Cold War – lay at the heart of the matter. I believed that the development and contemplated use of nuclear weapons was one of those absolutes that appear but seldom in human affairs. To base policy on the threat of a nuclear war that would end civilization was an absolute evil, one that had to be opposed by all the feeble means at one's disposal. I still believe this and find it hard to think that we have come to live with the bomb in near complacency. The doctrines of deterrence (which never worked even with 'conventional' weapons) became insane when extended to MAD – mutually assured destruction.

In *Saturday Night*, the *Forum*, and in speeches to union meetings, the Student Union for Peace Action, and the Faculty Committee on Vietnam (of which I was president), I preached Canadian disengagement from all aspects of the Cold War: the 1959 defence production sharing agreement with the United States, through which B-52 bombsites and other military equipment went south for use against the Vietnamese people, as well as our membership in NORAD, which made a mockery of our pretence of eschewing nuclear weapons – in short, for complete Canadian withdrawal from the U.S. nuclear alliance system on the grounds that actions speak louder than words. We should be non-aligned in the Cold War, not only because it seemed clear that Russian imperialism was no more its cause than American imperialism but because real non-alignment would strengthen our support of UN efforts for nuclear disarmament.

Several ironies have etched themselves in my memory, as well as some sharp vagaries of judgment. One example comes from a *Saturday Night* article of August 1963, just before we left on our sabbatical in England. Here I argued that John Kennedy was 'stepping into Lincoln's shoes.' Moving from his overly cautious whiggery, he was ready to support serious civil rights legislation: 'He has allowed events to impose upon him their own revolutionary meaning. The dangers to him, politically and personally, are probably as great as those which lurked around Lincoln ... Upon the passage of the civil rights legislation rests the future peace of the United States and upon his commitment to it rests the president's own future.' Bev and I attended the Kennedy memorial service in Westminster Abbey in November. By accident, we were seated across the aisle from Sir Alex Douglas Home and Harold Wilson. I was fascinated by the barely perceptible movement of Home's reptilian lips as the 'Battle Hymn of the Republic' rolled through the abbey.

As the United States stumbled into the quagmire of Vietnam and the legacy of Kennedy – at least in foreign policy – turned out to be no better than the new American empire of John Foster Dulles, the prospect for the survival of a truly independent Canadian nation became cloudier than at any time since the presidencies of Thomas Jefferson, James Madison, or Teddy Roosevelt. Canadians began to sense this threat, and I did my best to nourish the national feeling of the 1960s. When the University of Toronto proposed to offer an honorary degree to Adlai Stevenson, the Faculty Committee on Vietnam, and others, opposed it – to no avail. As the convocation procession made its way across the front campus, it ran a gamut of faculty and student protest signs. Mine read: 'He lied abroad for his country.' I held it high as Ernest Sirluck passed in front of me, in the procession just behind Stevenson. In a letter that spring telling me of my promotion to full professor 'in recognition of the work you have already done,' Claude Bissell added a handwritten note: 'Extracurricular work not included.'

Opposition to the mindless escalation of bombing and defoliation of Vietnam, as Lyndon Johnson got his green light in the spuriously based Gulf of Tonkin Resolution, was inexorably linked to a tide of economic nationalism in Canada – for which Mel Watkins and Walter Gordon became leading spokesmen. I recall charges of hypocrisy, and more, for public forays against the Vietnam War (and Canada's complicity); for supporting protesters at the U.S. consulate; for helping organize picketing of the Dow Chemical recruiting office on campus; for working with students who organized a massive 'teach-in' at Varsity Arena in 1965; and for bending the law and my conscience in assisting young American war resisters (draft-dodgers and deserters) gain asylum in Canada. University Avenue outside the American Consulate was frequently clogged with protesters and vigil keepers. 'Hey, Hey, LBJ, How Many Kids Did You Kill Today?' rang in the air, and many nights saw dozens of students in sleeping bags 'making their statement.' I often took coffee along the lines, steering clear of the police horses on their regular patrols.

An astonishing melange of people organized the biggest single event of the Vietnam protest movement in Toronto: a teach-in at Varsity Arena in 1965 which drew more than 6000 for its major event. Students and faculty worked well together to make this much more than a 'happening' – in the jargon of the day. Weeks of preparation culminated in a weekend of seminars and a main rally at the arena. To deal with the Vietnam War and related questions of imperialism and student revolution, speakers had been recruited from far and wide. To attract as many people as possible, an effort was made to have all points of view presented – but the very nature of the event made genuine 'objectivity' unlikely. Charles Hanly, a soft-spoken philosopher and budding psychoanalyst, was principal organizer, and the twenty-seven-year-old author Matt Cohen was co-chairman.

Among the faculty who worked hardest on the project were Don Evans, an earnest United Church philosopher; Peter Hughes, an engaging young English professor; Peter Russell, a judicious yet committed political scientist; Mel Watkins, a bright young economist whose fine sense of humour disguised a deepening nationalism; Chandler Davis, a mathematician and American emigré who had spent some time in an American jail, having pled the Fifth Amendment in refusing to answer questions about his political affiliation. When he was offered a job at Toronto, Chandler had trouble at the border. His admission had finally been secured by pressure from Stewart Reid of CAUT and Andrew Brewin, the NDP's parliamentary spokesman on external affairs. I don't know whether Chandler was ever a member of the Communist Party, although I rather think he was. Most important, the question was of no importance in Canada, despite the efforts our right-wing yahoos to make it so. It was Chandler's anti-war work that got him into trouble in the United States. In Canada he continued this work fiercely and maintained contacts with the revolutionary left from Vietnam to Hungary. I found Chandler's feverish activity a bit wearing, yet he always assumed I was ready to rally round every protest from Vietnam to civil liberties. Occasionally I let him down, as when he called one night to say we must rally the troops to get some Black Panthers through the border. They were on their way to some black power conference in Toronto and were being detained because they would not relinquish their handguns. Chandler argued that the Panthers were under constant threat from the FBI, the CIA, etc., and I replied they would have to take their chances in Canada, like the rest of us. But I cherish Chandler's friendship: a vintage American radical to add to my lengthening list of such wonderful people.

Chandler's wife, Natalie, my colleague in the history department, matched his radical zeal. A social historian, she was a devotee of the Annales School, concentrating on French radical movements 'from the bottom up.' Even more than Chandler, she remained essentially American and would pursue a distinguished career in the States. On one occasion I was slightly embarrassed by the fulsome support she gave me when we were both members of the departmental policy committee. Archie Thornton, the chairman, reported that Simcoe Hall (the administration) had asked for a report on the citizenship of members of the department. This was at the peak of the furore raised primarily by Robin Mathews over the Americanization of Canadian universities resulting from the mushrooming intake of American faculty. Archie asked what we should do. I led off, strongly opposing the request, on the ground that citizenship quotas were anathema. Natalie followed, saying that the whole thing had been cooked up by those people 'across the park in ... State House.'

In making the teach-in so successful, students played an essential role, using their experience in such organizations as the Students' Administrative Council and the Student Union for Peace Action (SUPA): Michael Ignatieff's brooding figure, the irrepressible enthusiasm of Rosalie Silberman, the quiet determination of Irving Abella, the evangelical zeal of Ian Gentles, the sophisticated involvement of Howard Adelman, and many others. A lot of them I knew either through SUPA or tutorials and seminars. Ignatieff was in a senior tutorial; his uncle had taught me at Upper Canada College, and I came to know his father, George, quite well later in the anti-nuclear movement. I was directing Abella's thesis; he and Rosie Silberman were soon to be married. Ian Gentles was in my graduate seminar; a leader in SUPA, he would marry my cousin's daughter and, like Abella, became a mainstay of Glendon's history department. I mentioned these relationships because I think they, plus many others less close, help explain a special feeling of commitment I had to the 'radical' students – those who would involve themselves in their community and their nation. I think my sympathy with these youngsters accounts, in large part, for my failure to see the peril when many of them went for 'student power' in the later 1960s – when the arguments against imperialism were used to attack the 'liberal' university as an agent of that imperialism and to demand control of its government.

For the teach-in, Bev was put in charge of billeting all the guest speakers and ensuring that there were hosts to look after them. They were a mixed lot. Representatives from North Vietnam and Cambodia; Robert Scalapino and Zbigniew Brzezinski from Berkeley, representing the official U.S. position; Staughton Lynd, the American Quaker and labour historian, whose position at Yale had just been terminated because of his anti-war activities. I was able to offer Lynd a temporary position at Toronto, but he declined in favour of working for the United Steelworkers in Indiana. Fenner, Lord Brockway, a leader in the British Committee for Nuclear Disarmament, stayed with my colleague Jim Estes, who, at that time, was still accustoming himself to becoming a Canadian. He was amused when Brockway said, 'Just call me Fenner.' The French Catholic Marxist, Roger Garaudy, stayed with Les Dewart, and they had a fine time discussing the relation of Christianity to revolution.

After the final session we had a huge party at Crescent Road. Greg Clark must have been bug-eyed as he watched Cheddi Jagan, the Marxist leader of the opposition in Guyana, arrive perched on the back of a white MG, escorted by Allison and her current boyfriend. George and Sheila Grant arrived as the party was going strong. George had given one of the best of the teach-in papers, and I think he sensed this; Mel Watkins, who had never met George, told me he was quite swept away by it. When Sheila spied Brockway, she flung her arms around him, saying, 'The last time we met was in jail.' I recall Abe Rotstein, elegant cigarette holder at an FDR tilt, watching the scene with quiet pleasure.

The teach-in and its attendant publicity did much to stir up real concern – particularly about Canada's complicity in the ever-escalating war. In 1966 we established the Faculty Committee on Vietnam. The executive committee included Elliott Rose, the brilliant medievalist; Anton Kuerti, an emigré well on his way to becoming Canada's most accomplished pianist; Chandler Davis; David Gauthier, a completely committed philosopher; Peter Hughes; and Jack Robson, a sharp young English professor who would later edit the complete works of John Stuart Mill. Our committee helped organize several smaller teach-ins and a number of protest marches. We were also in contact with the Montreal University Committee and the Vancouver Committee. A lot of us were in close touch with the young American war protesters, whose number increased daily. Exact figures, by the very nature of the operation, are impossible to arrive at, but the usual estimate is about 50,000. I consulted with dozens of them and helped organize contributions to a little publication, *Amex*, put out by the Toronto Anti-Draft Campaign. *Amex* contained information for new arrivals on where to go for accommodation and advice, and also some fascinating pieces by early arrivers on what differences to expect in Canada. Mark Satin, whose powers of observation matched those of Douglas Fetherling, was a principal organizer of services for the Toronto exiles. He occasionally used the spare bedroom in my cousin Carol Jack's apartment, and I recall the evening in 1968 when Bev and I assembled with several others at Carol's to hear the special broadcast made by President Johnson. When LBJ announced he would not run for re-election – obviously because of the civil discord occasioned by his policy – Mark made the sadly premature comment: 'I guess our work is done.'

As the stream of emigrés increased, we redoubled our efforts in several directions – each aimed at changing Ottawa's policies. We raised money for the Canadian Unitarian Service Committee's medical aid for Vietnam. Another major thrust was to publicize the way in which the 1959 Defence Production Sharing Agreement tied Canada closely to the American military assault on Vietnam. Several of us researched defence department documents, and Gideon Rosenbluth, a brilliant economist and member of the Vancouver committee, provided supporting material. In newspaper ads, an open letter to the prime minister, and a stream of letters to the editor, we listed the military equipment that Canada sold to the United States each year. Nearly all of it was clearly for use in Vietnam – from guidance systems to engines and explosives of all kinds. By 1967 the dollar value of the American purchases reached $300 million annually – from a country that professed non-engagement in that war.

Committees in Montreal, Toronto, and Vancouver arranged protest demonstrations outside some of the war production plants and American consulates. In March 1967 the Prime Minister's Office issued a formal reply to 'representations about the Vietnam situation from university professors.' Montreal papers published substantial portions of Pearson's lengthy statement. Amidst the verbiage, he made perfectly clear the reasons for Canadian 'complicity' in the Vietnam War. Canada's goal, he maintained, was to help end the war. However, 'constructive action, in turn, depends on a realistic assessment of the nature of the situation which it is designed to change and of the likely consequences of any given activity, whether public or private, in relation to the problems ... Any answer to this question becomes doubly difficult in the context of problems where the direct involvement and the direct responsibility for action rest essentially with others.' I winced at these words, having been arguing for weeks in *Saturday Night* that actions speak louder than words and that our military involvement completely undercut the soothing phrases of Pearson's 'quiet diplomacy.' I had pointed out that Sweden placed an embargo on arms to the United States, recognized the North Vietnamese government, and allowed the National Liberation Front to operate an information office. In some quarters this involvement marked one as a communist, but the number of professors who signed our growing flow of letters and petitions grew remarkably.

Pearson's letter continued: 'When it comes to making channels, or "good offices," available to the parties to enable them to make contact with each other, I think that too many public declarations and disclosures run the risk of complicating matters for those concerned.' The sentence might have been lifted from Mackenzie King's 1930s advice to leave European affairs to Europeans. 'I have repeatedly stressed that I would like to see the bombing [of Northern Vietnam] stopped, northern infiltration into the south stopped, and unconditional peace talks begin.' The prime minister went on to point out that the Defence Production Sharing Agreements were of great benefit to Canadian industry, industrial research, and development generally, 'which in turn are fundamental to the maintenance of an advanced technology in Canada ... For a broad range of reasons, therefore, it is clear that the imposition of an embargo on the export of military equipment to the USA, and concomitant termination of the Production Sharing Agreements, would have far-reaching consequences which no Canadian government would contemplate with equanimity ... nor am I convinced that by taking such a step, one would be contributing in any practical way to achieving a political solution to the Vietnam problem.' Clearly, Canada was not prepared to back up his opposition to the devastation of Vietnam with any action which would have an economic cost or which would imperil what Pearson called 'the collective defence relationship of Canada and the USA.' We were in the American imperial system and might do nothing more than wag a finger.

Some limits, however, could be put on complicity if enough pressure were brought to bear – and if the specific policy had no economic implications. One reason that almost as many war resisters came to

Canada as to Sweden was the cooperative work, of the Anti-Draft Programs in Toronto and Vancouver. I had quite a bit to do with this work, but the really hard work of coordinating efforts and accumulating accurate information (which finally won the day) was done by my wonderfully committed history department colleague Elliott Rose, Mordecai Briemberg, the American emigré sociologist at Simon Fraser University, and my friend Andrew Brewin, who was NDP spokesman on external affairs in Ottawa. Apart from organizing assistance to those who managed to cross the border, our goal was to eliminate the widespread obstruction experienced by would-be emigrés at Canadian consulates in the United States and at most border crossing points. Many immigration officers, using inappropriate interpretations of such clauses as 'fugitives from justice,' and ignoring instructions not to inquire about draft status, were refusing admission on grounds that the applicant was avoiding his legal obligations in the United States. A good deal of the problem was that Canadian veterans had been given preference in immigration department appointments, and they all too often found ways to reject draft-age applicants.

With the help of Andy Brewin, the various Canadian anti-draft committees gave advice to those who managed to get across the border. But a great many were refused admission. In Vancouver, Mordecai Briemberg's committee compiled an impressive case list, and I used this as the basis of an article that the Toronto *Star Weekly* printed late in 1967. The *Star* gave it a big splash. I received a heated letter from Tom Kent, who was then deputy minister of immigration. He claimed that my charges were not well substantiated, and that new regulations and specific instructions to follow them were now in place. Whatever the reason, the situation improved markedly. Kent is a most civilized and liberal person. Our relations in Winnipeg while he was editor of the *Free Press*, and before the Crowe case, were cordial. After the war resisters' dustup, we had no communication for many years, although I admired his work as royal commissioner on the press in 1980–1. Our paths crossed again in 1990 when I invited him to contribute a piece to the book Jack Granatstein and I were putting together, *English Canada Speaks Out*. Tom wrote an interesting, if somewhat exotic, proposal for constitutional change; sometime later we had a very agreeable lunch together in Toronto. The happy smallness of the Canadian population facilitates a kind of basic civility – one I hope is not imperilled by demographic turbulence. Certainly it was not endangered by the 50,000 or so young Americans who came here during the Vietnam years.

In talking about our sabbatical and our involvement with the fallout from imperial policies, I have left untouched the extraordinary convolutions of academic affairs and my, as usual, tangential solutions to them. No, they were always tangential, but I long ago recognized my tendency to be a gadfly rather than a long-haul organizer. Thus I continued writing for *Saturday Night*, taking part in CBC opinion programs, and offering excellent advice to political leaders of all stripes in letters to the editor, op-ed pieces, and conference papers. Perhaps I found this role too congenial, yet I derived much satisfaction from it – and even from the not infrequent and sometimes malevolent charges of irresponsibility.

14

My position in the Department of History depended on a number of variables: length of my connection with the department and with the chair; the number of courses, students, and theses I dealt with; and my relations with my colleagues. My long connection with the department was of no particular advantage; at least half a dozen others equalled it, and, in any case, as the numbers exploded in the 1960s and 1970s this was a minor factor. 'Old guards' are never popular. A number of the new American appointments considered that our course structure and teaching method were out of sync. As one or two put it, they didn't stand up to the Big League. In the long run it is not surprising that the Americans should have had a heavy impact: less emphasis would be placed on the senior tutorials, and a great deal more on specialization – which was all too often equated with professionalism. The expression 'term' gave way to 'semester,' and the method of recording marks incorporated the American grade-point system.

Despite some sharp divisions of opinion – especially over opening up choice and specialization in the curriculum – the department remained remarkably collegial, even though it peaked in size by the late 1970s at about eighty members, including the Scarborough and Erindale campuses. That is not to say that 'parties' did not emerge over particular issues, nor that personal rivalries did not arise, but there was a continuing consensus on the relative values of research, teaching, and administration. Departmental and committee meetings were usually civil, and the chair could preside quite safely at Christmas parties. Much of this would change in the 1980s. Class sizes rose, appointments were frozen, and attrition set in. Together with the unremitting stress on professionalism and specialization, these conditions led to decreasing concern with students, competition for research leaves, and absorption with advancement within one's field. The old notion that one must be prepared to teach in any course (within reason) that needed you had long gone. The community that existed, with all its tensions, when I returned from Winnipeg was no longer. The process of departmental disintegration was probably more drawn out than I have suggested; as early as April 1964 John Cairns wrote to me in London: 'Certainly as a department it does not exist.' We have been telling ourselves this ever since.

Despite the growing number of Americans in the department, my contacts with American academics were wider than those of most of my colleagues, except John Cairns and Bill Eccles. I regularly attended the meetings of the American Labor Historians, served for several years on the Board of *Labor History*, and worked in several archives, including the great labour collections at Wayne State University in Detroit. I became friends with quite a few of the New Left revisionist and labour historians, including several mainstream people and some who may best be described as idiosyncratic. Most of these, at one time or another, I invited to give lectures at Toronto. Bev always managed a smashing dinner evening on such occasions, and once again we discovered what fine people Americans are – taken a few at a time.

W.A. Williams of Wisconsin was the best-known and most flamboyant of the revisionists. His books portrayed an imperial America masquerading behind John Hay's 'doctrine' of the Open Door: America stood for free trade everywhere, except for American protection. Williams was immensely popular with students who aligned themselves with the New Left – that amorphous attack on the American establishment which incorporated everything from draft-card burning, mind-altering drugs, and civil rights to student power in the universities. Like C. Wright Mills, the intellectual father of the New Left, Williams was, in fact, pretty bourgeois. An Episcopalian with a large family, he was a person of brilliant insights and a charismatic teacher. His hostile analysis of American imperialism, however, was not sustained by the disciplined scholarship that underpinned Richard Van Alstyne's work – which arrived at similar if more muted conclusions. In 1964–5 Williams toyed with the notion of moving to Toronto; he was weary of his absurdly large roster of graduate theses at Madison, and he liked the Toronto atmosphere. We offered him a one-year history professorship – to see how things worked out. He eventually said no, for several reasons. His wife didn't relish the prospect, but, more important, he was simply too American and lacked career reasons for making such a move. I think he was a vintage American radical: he held all government suspect and ended up at the University of Oregon, where he propounded a restructuring of the United States into small units which, to my mind, came close to a philosophy of anarchy. I liked him very much, although Bev tells me that on one evening he appeared by her side in the kitchen to tell her she was an attractive woman.

A letter from my old friend Margaret Prang (now at UBC) at the end of December 1964 was the real eye-opener to the state of American historical debate. Margaret chaired the program committee of the Canadian Historical Association for the 1965 meetings and invited me to do one of the two papers for an experimental session in American history. She knew I had been working on the relationship between the British and the American left, and I proposed a paper on the theme 'American Progressives and the Great Society.' The session would be chaired by Martin Ridge, editor of the *American Journal of History.* I worked extremely hard on the paper, which like anything I got really interested in was highly interpretive, although laced with supporting evidence from British and American archives. The thrust of the argument was that American progressives, unlike their British counterparts, shied away from socialism and the party method of attacking the evils of capitalism for a number of reasons: they failed to attack head on the constitutional obstacles erected by the checks and balances in the congressional system; and they were seduced by the argument that honesty, efficiency, and leadership would provide the necessary reform for the injustices of American capitalism. American socialists also faced a concerted and successful campaign to portray them as un-American. The same kind of smear was attempted in Canada, but with much less success: socialism had come to Canada largely in the baggage of British immigrants, and attempts to label it 'foreign' had failed. At a time when the British Fabians and socialists were able to make a firm alliance with unions and establish the Labour Party in 1906, American socialists found themselves increasingly labelled 'alien,' 'un-American,' and unable to answer the charges that their socialism was often German in origin. Indeed, the party broke on this issue and never recovered from the patriotic witch hunting of World War I. It occurred to me that, from the point of view of the left (as well as other points of view), Canada derived considerable benefit from her slow colonial evolution.

Not the least of these benefits was a sense of certainty. Our evolving sense of identity remained for long attached to pride in our roots, which had not been severed by the American Revolution. Our imperial-colonial connections, far from inhibiting or isolating us, opened doors to the rest of the world. Moreover, insofar as British aristocratic and conservative influences touched us (and the influence was considerable), they modified sharply the suspicion of government and the individualistic reliance on the marketplace which has so often crippled the American sense of community. Developing this argument, I took on some of the flashiest of American historians and political scientists – people like Louis Hartz, Richard Hofstadter, Daniel Bell, and Seymour Martin Lipset. Under the flag of 'consensus history,' these men and their followers proclaimed what I termed an 'inevitablist' interpretation of American history.

In his book *The Liberal Tradition in America*, Hartz argued that, when America left Europe, its public philosophy was that of Lockean liberalism. Because of the decisiveness of the breach, that philosophy had congealed in America, leaving no room for any other. Hartz drew a clear distinction among political, economic, and social liberalism, but he made it clear that he meant 'free-market' liberalism, along with its political ramifications. Thus, as Hartz's supporter Daniel Bell wrote, socialism could be 'in' but not 'of' America. To this absurd formulation, Richard Hofstadter, the most perceptive of the consensus grouping, added that the political-constitutional experience of the United States meant that 'third parties' could never survive. I argued that the whole consensus analysis put forward an inevitablist historical interpretation. I got quite heated about it all. I maintained that 'inevitable' is a word that should be unknown to history. It implies a secularized Calvinism, a predestination of all events, and thus robs history of significance. It invariably buttresses the status quo. The consensus historians were, not surprisingly, conservative historians.

In addition to criticizing their underlying philosophical assumptions, I added a more direct assault on the Hartz proposition that America's public ideology could only be liberal. This was so, he said, because it lacked a feudal-aristocratic experience. Hartz, throughout his book, used 'liberalism' and 'democracy' interchangeably. I countered that, quite apart from the inevitability nonsense, this thinking was not only confused but ignored the strength of democracy as opposed to liberalism in American history. The right of dissent and the right to be different (let alone to be eccentric) are essential to liberalism, but they have very shallow roots in U.S. democracy – which de

Tocqeville characterized as the 'tyranny of the majority.' Because Britain and European countries entered the age of democracy *with* an aristocracy, they retained both the unpleasant notion of class by inheritance as well as that of real individualism and the right of dissent. After all, who won the Magna Carta? The British aristocratic tradition led to a positive view of government and community; the American, to suspicion of all government, and especially to a 'patriotism' identified with conformity to majority opinion.

The thrust of my argument was that socialism failed politically in the United States because the right of dissent was so fragile and because patriotism and conformity were so closely identified that most left-wing progressives caved in during and after the war, thereby allowing the socialist party to die. While American progressives abandoned socialism under the heavy pressure of conformity, their counterparts in Britain breathed life into the Fabians and led in establishing and nourishing the Labour Party. These very different patterns, I maintained, resulted not from inevitable forces, but from complex, cumulative traditions and experiences and, particularly, from the series of individual decisions that produced them.

The question, 'Why no socialism in the United States?' was a hot topic in the 1960s and 1970s, part of an explosion in writing on progressivism. I found it a particularly interesting counterpart to the slow but steadier growth of political socialism in Canada and, thus, to wider comparisons between Canada and the United States – my central interest in the latter part of my university career. At the end of the CHA session at which I read my paper, Ridge asked for a copy because he wanted to print it in his journal. The article appeared in the December 1966 issue and was reprinted in two American anthologies. I received a batch of letters from American historians, most of whom I had never met. I invited many of them to give guest lectures at Toronto. We always had them to the house for dinner. Louis Hartz, ebullient and rude, I remember as one long argument. I took him on in print in 1974 in a long book of essays on American socialism [*Failure of a Dream*, edited by J.H.M. Laslett and S.M. Lipset] Richard Hofstadter, urbane and soft-spoken, could not accept my argument that socialism had died in the United States not because of inexorable forces, but because fine people like himself found particular reasons for not stepping out of the two-party system. He assured me that his own political philosophy was socialist.

This admission reminded me of an earlier occasion when I lunched with John Kenneth Galbraith after chairing a meeting of the Woodsworth Foundation at which he spoke about his recently published *Affluent Society.* He told me he was a socialist and that, if he lived in Canada, he would vote CCF. When I asked why he wasn't working for the Socialist Party of America (he was on the Kennedy election circuit at the time), he replied that it was not necessary: 'I have just returned from speaking in Flint, and in Michigan the Democratic Party is a faction of the United Auto Workers.' I replied that this was a small aspect of American politics, even if it were true. I then asked him how he could back a candidate who supported brinkmanship over the Chinese offshore islands of Quemoy and Matsu – as Kennedy had the day before in a speech in Seattle. 'Don't worry about that,' he replied, 'just wait till Berle and Schlesinger and I get back to Washington.' Well, the only thing that happened was that, on their return, they continued to lead the growing battalion of 'Cold War liberals.' While Galbraith walked a tightrope, the Bay of Pigs lay close ahead.

Schlesinger, in particular, was an obnoxious fellow. A couple of years later, a students' organization invited him to give a lecture – for $1500. He agreed, but because he didn't fly, he insisted on being met at Buffalo and then driven back after the lecture. Bora Laskin's son was on the student executive, and this group was invited to the Laskins' home for drinks and a chat after the lecture. Bora invited Bev and me as well. When we arrived, Schlesinger had already come and gone – having refused a drink because Bora had no bourbon whiskey. And the speech had been, at most, perfunctory.

Another American connection developed at the University of Rochester. There I came to know Eugene Genovese and Herbert Gutman, through my writing on labour history, and Christopher Lasch, through our shared interest in the nature of American progressivism. Of the three, I found Lasch the most congenial: another of those sophisticated Americans who kept puzzling me by their acceptance of the two-party system. When I asked him how he could stay in a department with Gutman and Genovese, he laughed and said he was planning a move – which never came. Genovese was a tough, very professional Stalinist who produced some excellent works on slavery, and Gutman contrasted in all respects with the other two. Big and gruff, one never saw him save through a noxious fog of pipe smoke, nor did he ever offer a tentative opinion. Unlike the urbane Lasch and the intellectually disciplined Genovese, Gutman had become a guru of the young New Left social historians. His aim, I think, was to become America's

E.P. Thompson, whose work, *The Making of the English Working Class*, was the bible for aspiring New Left labour historians. Aiming at 'recovering' the actual lives of working people, as opposed to the history of their organizations, these scholars produced some useful studies. In general, however, they tended to let theory get in the way of their facts, and, since the theory was usually a sort of fuzzy Marxism, it seldom suited the facts of American history.

In 1971 I attended an international labour history conference at Rutgers University in New Jersey. The major speakers were Thompson and Eric Hobsbawm, the leading Marxist historians from Britain, and Gutman. Hobsbawm and Thompson each read carefully constructed papers – Thompson resplendent in an expensively casual suede jacket. When Gutman stepped up to the podium, he wore the New Left uniform: ragged sweater and cords. From his briefcase he pulled out what looked like 400 pages of notes and slapped them on the table beside the lectern. He would, he said, not read a formal paper but, rather, treat us to some excerpts from his 'ongoing work.' He spent more time riffling through mountains of notes than presenting actual substance or a coherent thesis. It was, I suppose, what the New Left would call a happening – of the sort that produced the populist mishmash of the Port Huron statement of the Students for a Democratic Society. Both Gutman and the SDS seemed to be trying to resurrect the anarchic stream in American radicalism.

As with the student movements' attempt to take over the universities and run them as structureless happenings, the New Left's assault upon the old socialist left would crumble on its own internal contradictions. Even in the most open of democracies, things don't just happen; there must be structure, rules, and leadership. Without these, violence and irresponsibility will produce either anarchy or authoritarianism. Indeed, a major theme in American populist radicalism is that of the strong man seizing power, unseating the robber barons, and enacting a complete populist program. I had always found this argument mindless. As it blossomed in the New Left, the student power movement, and Black Power, and blended with the steadily escalating anti-war protests, its potential for anarchy grew. I became increasingly cautious about knee-jerk support of any and every 'protest.' It seemed very important to distinguish between the anarchic New Left and the old socialist left. Several situations in the late 1960s and early 1970s sharpened my perception of the danger of losing liberal-constitutional values in one grand, amorphous assault upon 'the establishment.'

One vignette to cherish: in 1970, Genovese invited me to do a seminar on American progressivism and socialism. I arrived at Rochester for the first meeting on a glorious September afternoon. The campus was flooded with a golden light as I strolled past the Prush-Rhys Library to the history office. Contradicting the euphoric ambiance, a figure sat in deep gloom on the library steps. I recognized Greg Kealey, who had been a leader of the more extreme wing of the student movement in Toronto: guerrilla theatre and 'parity' student membership on all governing bodies. Despite my abhorrence of his activities, I greeted him and asked what he was up to. He told me he had registered for a PhD and had just come from an interview with Genovese: 'Ken, do you know what Gene said when I asked him how many students were on the history department's governing committee? He just said "on the *what*?"' New Left had certainly met old left.

A few weeks later, my seminar meeting fell on the day following Trudeau's confronting the Front de libération du Québec (FLQ) with the War Measures Act. The students were eager to talk about that rather than Teddy Roosevelt as a progressive. They were flabbergasted when I defended Trudeau's position: 'In this country, laws are made and changed by the elected representatives of all Canadians, not by a handful of self-styled dictators. Those who gain power through terror rule by terror.' I think only two of the eleven students were sympathetic. I pointed out that our two most prominent politically active socialist intellectuals, Frank Scott and Eugene Forsey, supported Trudeau's action – and that they were also our most distinguished defenders of civil liberties. I couldn't resist the jibe that people like Scott and Forsey, who were crucially important in keeping political socialism alive in Canada, were counterparts of Americans such as Hofstadter, Galbraith, and company who simply stood aside as American socialism petered out. The American slide into violence as a structureless left was, I argued, in large measure a result of this treason of the intellectuals.

During these years, I visited Wayne State University in Detroit several times to work in the fine Walter Reuther labour history archive. Philip Mason, director of the archive, provided me with every possible assistance; in addition, he was the soul of hospitality. On one occasion I was having lunch with him and half a dozen members of the history department. It happened to be the day after the assassination of Robert Kennedy. Walking across the campus I could feel the tension that seemed to keep black and white students at arm's length. The long hot summer that would lay waste the centre of Detroit had begun. Congress was considering a gun-control law, and conversation turned to that question. Not very delicately, I asked how many at the table owned guns and how many would support stricter gun controls. Each owned one or more weapons, and none agreed with tighter controls. My last visit to Wayne State, to read a conference paper, was in the early 1980s. Mason urged me to take a cab from my hotel to the campus, rather than risk walking the two and a half blocks.

Canada also experienced social turbulence in the late 1960s and early 1970s, with student sit-ins and the picketing of defence industry plants (especially Litton Industries) and American consulates. But the movement for Quebec independence, and especially the FLQ, created a potentially more profound threat to the rule of law in Canada than did anti-war and civil rights activism in the United States. In some respects, especially with the intertwining of the anti-war movement and the civil rights crusade, Canadian left-wing groups indulged in a kind of branch-plant radicalism; and this, to some extent, threatened to Americanize the Canadian left.

I worried that the political left in Canada, like the Mackenzie radicals of 1837 whose triumph would have led directly to our absorption in the United States, did not grasp the destructive anarchy inherent in the American New Left or in the similar idiocy of the FLQ – with its wild mix of Franz Fanon, Herbert Marcuse, Che Guevara, and Pierre Vallières. Over the past few years the radical separatists had discovered how easy it was to destabilize large urban communities with letter-box bombs, raids on banks and armories, and mass parades in Montreal.

My worries about the course of the Canadian left deepened as I developed a graduate course on the Canadian Political Tradition. All my earlier courses about the 'death of socialism' in the United States sharpened into more immediate worries as many friends showed sympathy for radical separatism in Quebec. I began to articulate my feelings about the 'Canadian Question' when Mike Oliver asked me to do a major essay for the Royal Commission on Bilingualism and Biculturalism. Mike had been appointed research director of the Bi and Bi Commission. Together with André Laurendeau and Davidson Dunton, they had lined up a series of studies on the background of what their preliminary report had already called the 'greatest crisis' in our history. One of the problems the commission had was how to deal with the constantly reiterated *nationaliste* claim that English Canada had not defined itself, and thus could not understand the claims of the *other* of the 'two founding nations.' Oliver asked me to do an eighty-page paper on the culture of English Canada, with special reference to the impact of regional and ethnic differences. I think the work I did on the paper clarified my own

[The ms ends here.]

Postscript – Kenneth W. McNaught: Untypical Professor

RAMSAY COOK

Today we have come together to celebrate and commemorate the life of Kenneth McNaught, untypical professor. Nearly forty-seven years ago, in the September following the great Winnipeg flood of 1950, I first met Professor McNaught. During the following decades I came to recognize him as a person of quite remarkable virtues and talents: teacher, historian, husband, father, acerbic commentator, accomplished water-colourist, carpenter, wicked martini mixer, sailor, teller of shaggy dog stories, wit, and much more. But for me and many others here, including some from those early Winnipeg years, he was always teacher, supporter, colleague, and, above all, friend and example. Today I can speak about only a small part of the life of this exemplary Canadian intellectual and citizen.

Though a historian by training and a university teacher by profession, Kenneth McNaught was untypical in both of those pursuits. His distinctiveness was his considered conviction that the writing of history – and current comment for that matter – and the teaching of students was essentially a moral vocation. In his research and reading, in his writing and lecturing, his goal was always to establish the truth, to set out in logical and documented fashion what he believed was right and what was wrong in human history and contemporary affairs. The past, weighed and judged, helped to explain and might even help to change the present.

That moral approach to the past and the present naturally drew him to study the life of James Shaver Woodsworth, whom Professor McNaught called *A Prophet in Politics*. When he chose that title, he fully understood that a prophet, in the proper biblical sense, was no mere soothsayer reading the tea-leaves of the past in order to concoct a future. A prophet is a leader whose moral and intellectual clarity allows him or her to see to the very heart of things. Kenneth McNaught's biography explained that J.S. Woodsworth was a prophet in that sense. But in the course of that study he did something else, too. Like all biographers, Ken revealed a lot about himself in his life of Woodsworth. I don't mean that he mistook himself for his subject, for imitation was certainly not Ken's way. What I mean is that he said some things about Woodsworth that revealed his own primary political values – or so I thought as I was rereading *A Prophet in Politics* recently. Here are some examples. At the very beginning of the book Ken remarks that Woodsworth's message to Canadians was that 'one does not "resolve" anything by simple compromise.' Those of us who knew Ken well realized that he was always sure of his essential principles, that he was always ready to defend them and, in the face of a compelling argument, even alter their application, though never their essence. Compromise just to be agreeable – often seen as *the* great Canadian political virtue – was not Ken's style, even when he was left standing nearly alone. So he could defend Woodsworth's opposition to war in 1939, advocate Canadian neutrality during the Cold War, demand fair treatment for Cuba during the early years of the Castro revolution, and criticize his own political party, the CCF/NDP, when he thought it in danger of slipping from the high ground of moral principle into the slough of political expediency. He enjoyed testing *his* belief that 'the libertarian traditions of the British parliamentary system [are] the surest guarantee of a creative Canadian society.'

But the firmness of his moral stance never led to self-righteousness or blind obstinacy. And that was because, like his Woodsworth, Ken was devoted to a 'sceptical individualism,' which meant that he resisted conforming to any unexamined dogma – his own as much as anyone else's. If his socialism cried out for peace and justice, his conservatism for parliamentary monarchy, then his liberalism demanded freedom to question – for himself, and most emphatically for his students. There was no contradiction between sceptical individualism and the rejection of simple compromise. Each stance rested on a search for the right, the morally right answer. For Ken, that search was what intellectual and academic life was about.

Forty-seven years ago we first met in a cramped seminar room in a building near Portage and Spence improbably called 'the Beer hall.' Every week we gathered for a tutorial in the history of the United States – a subject which, like most history subjects, interested me very little at the time. At first the young professor seemed austere, even humourless. He was tall, spare, with a broad forehead and a flat, almost nasal voice. For me, not a promising beginning. But very soon I discovered something else: a sardonic wit, a mind that questioned and pressed his students to question, a mind that proposed answers that were often not in the books we read. Here was a mind and an imagination that made studying history worthwhile, even exciting, not because it surprised or entertained, not because of its anecdotes or colourful characters, but because it could be analyzed, interpreted, disputed. The past, like all intellectual life, was about real questions, human questions, moral questions. History was an intellectual and moral discipline. Kenneth McNaught believed that and, in his teaching, imparted that belief even to his least promising students. That, along with his friendship, is what I and many others owe to Kenneth McNaught.

Soon his students also learned that this professor of serious purpose was no austere pedagogue. In winter he often wore a Homburg, a questionable practice in Winnipeg at any season. And he came back from the East one autumn with a somewhat run-down Cadillac. Obviously from Toronto, we said. Then we met his wife, Beverley, who welcomed us into their home with that extraordinary hospitality that rapidly made guests into friends. Now we realized that with Beverley's love, the warmth of a family of Christopher, Allison, and Andrew – and his sister, Leslie – Ken knew how to live: serious, but never solemn. He could dance elegantly in black tie and tails; enter enthusiastically into New Year's Eve charades; provoke, argue, laugh: a humanist of high spirits, taste, and civility. But he never lost sight of the rooted conviction that at the centre of his moral and intellectual life was the need not only to understand but also to decide, and in deciding to remind his students and friends that, in the end, one must choose between complacency and commitment, between wrong and right. Kenneth McNaught knew where *he* stood.

Towards the end of a memorial lecture entitled 'J.S. Woodsworth: Untypical Canadian,' Ken's teacher F.H. Underhill quoted from a book once well known to Protestants like Woodsworth, Underhill, and McNaught. The quote is well suited to our friend Kenneth: 'After this it was noised abroad that Mr Valiant-for-Truth was taken with a summons ... When he understood it he called for his Friends and told them of it ... My Sword I give to him that shall succeed me in my Pilgrimage, and my Courage and Skill to him that can get it ... So he passeth over and all the trumpets sounded for him on the other side.'

Index